Kyla
Jones

CRAZY
IN AMERICA

CRAZY IN AMERICA

The Hidden Tragedy of Our Criminalized Mentally Ill

Mary Beth Pfeiffer

CARROLL & GRAF PUBLISHERS
NEW YORK

CRAZY IN AMERICA
The Hidden Tragedy of Our Criminalized Mentally Ill

Carroll & Graf Publishers
An Imprint of Avalon Publishing Group, Inc.
245 West 17th Street, 11th Floor
New York, NY 10011-5300

AVALON
publishing group incorporated

Library of Congress Cataloging-in-Publication Data is available.

ISBN-13: 978-0-78671-745-3
ISBN-10: 0-7867-1745-9

Interior design by Maria Fernandez
Printed in the United States of America
Distributed by Publishers Group West

To my parents, Helen and Charles Pfeiffer,
loving people who led by example

Contents

A National Scandal

THIS BOOK BEGAN SIX YEARS AGO with a footnote. It was in a paper prepared by a Legal Aid Society attorney on conditions in New York State prisons. The footnote said that in 1998, four out of fourteen suicides occurred in what the prison system called "special housing units." That was 29 percent of all suicides among just 3 percent of the population, it said. In 1999, the figure was 25 percent of suicides among 4 percent of the population.

Those figures turned out to be conservative. They were my first indication that there was something seriously wrong within these "special" units of our state prisons. A year later, I published the first of a series of articles in the *Poughkeepsie Journal* on what life was like for people with mental illness in the New York State prison system. "Suicides high in prison 'Box'" was the headline, and it included a photograph of the exterior of a low block building with a silver roof, clean and innocuous enough, on the grounds of the Fishkill Correctional Facility in Dutchess County, New York, seventy-five miles north of Manhattan.

Within the walls of that building—inmates called it "the Box"—a quite remarkable phenomenon was playing out. Here, in twenty-first-century America, a prison system had recreated what America thought it had left behind: warehouses for the insane.

Try if you will to conjure up the sights, sounds, and smells of a Victorian-era asylum. Add the brutally cool security of a supermax prison. Put people there for months and years at a time—people whose rights under law are severely curtailed along with their freedom—and you have America's special housing units. They go by different names in different places—disciplinary detention, administrative segregation, the Box, the hole—but in too many states they are remarkably, and sadly, similar.

They are dumping grounds for a difficult and growing population of mentally ill inmates.

They are the end of the line for the schizophrenics, bipolars, and borderlines among us without the resources or wherewithal to care for themselves and stay out of trouble.

They are symptoms of a society that has failed to provide for some of its most vulnerable citizens and has allowed them to be treated as criminals. There has always been a small proportion of people in jails and prisons who think in disjointed ways, act bizarrely, or are outright psychotic. The proportion of such people in the prison population is no longer small, nor is their number.

This book tells the stories of six people with mental illness and their tragic encounters with the criminal justice system. One committed suicide in a Texas jail, another in a New York prison, a third in a California juvenile facility. Two were killed by poorly trained police officers who panicked in the face of psychosis. The sixth, the only one who is still alive, used her fingers, in separate acts, to gouge out both her eyes while she was incarcerated. That she had been hospitalized twenty-five times for schizophrenia and had been psychotic at the time of her "crime" did not influence where she ended up: within the four walls of a prison solitary confinement unit. The road taken by each of these six people was different, the profile of each of their lives unique. The constant is that they had families who loved them, aspirations for the future, and personal histories that went beyond their gruesome experiences in prison or at the hands of police as reported in the morning paper. That is what this book is about: These six people from five states are our sisters, brothers, sons, and daughters who were unfortunate enough to be afflicted with mental illness in an era in which handcuffs and bars have replaced treatment.

Like the photo of the Fishkill prison special housing unit, from outward appearances, jails and prisons are tidy, sterile-looking places where razor-wire fences and guard towers signal a certain kind of order. The image is no mistake. The bureaucrats, county supervisors, political appointees, and governors who run America's lockups work hard at it. The public face of prisons is a careful construct, a reflection of what the public is told and what it is not told about what goes on inside.

When people commit suicide in prison, rarely is the information released to the public. When reporters ask for it, they are given minimal details and told to wait for official reports which, when they are released, are often heavily censored—ostensibly to protect inmate privacy. When reporters ask to tour prisons they are often told they have no right of access or that they can see the visitors' room or the shop where inmates make furniture but not the solitary confinement unit. Unlike hospitals, which are inspected by the board of health, and schools, which report to departments of education, and airports, which are regulated by the federal government, prison systems answer only to themselves. What happens in the system all too often stays there. "Correctional facilities . . . are walled off from external monitoring and public scrutiny to a degree inconsistent with the responsibility of public institutions," reported the Commission on Safety and Abuse in America's Prisons in 2006 after national hearings.

There is a reason that transparency is not a hallmark of prisons, and there is a price to be paid for it.

After reporting on New York State's prisons for five years, I applied for a fellowship from the Open Society Institute in order to explore the national landscape for the incarcerated mentally ill. I was asked, at the time, why I had stayed with this subject, why I'd come back again and again with more stories, published in the *Poughkeepsie Journal*, of mentally ill people who had hung themselves or starved themselves, been killed in altercations with prison guards, or been locked in the Box for years. "It is a scandal," I said. "If people knew what was going on in our prisons, they would be shocked." I certainly was and continue to be.

My reporting often focused on solitary confinement because it was a sort of ground zero. Here, in these tomblike cells, the problem of America's mentally ill could be seen in its most unvarnished, extreme form. Some of the people in these units had broken the law when they were too sick to know the difference. Others had climbed a ladder of petty, illness-driven crimes into prison, racking up so many disorderly conduct charges that they drew hard time for simple drug possession. All had lived in a society in which their mental illness was managed by a system described in a 2002 presidential report as "in shambles." They could not be controlled in the general prison population and hence had ended up in solitary confinement, a place where people screamed day and night, spread feces on walls, threw bodily fluids at officers, and mutilated themselves in ingenious ways.

America fell back on solitary confinement in the 1990s as a way to control too many idle inmates. More than thirty states built units to house what was often called "the worst of the worst." It was that kind of time—when convicts were one-dimensional evildoers (not my phrase, but apt) who got just what they deserved. The country was on its way then to a four-fold increase in its prison population in a twenty-year period. It was an astronomical and ill-advised increase in capacity that, moreover, continued for more than a decade after crime rates began to fall.

Politicians found that instilling fear was an easy sell that got them votes. Prison sentences were lengthened. New offenses against the social order, such as selling drugs near a school, were legislated, which served only to heap on more punishment. Parole as an incentive for inmates to behave was rolled back. Rehabilitation programs were cut.

America now has 2.2 million people in its jails and prisons. Of these, an estimated 330,000 are mentally ill, and evidence is building that this is a conservative figure. Police and mentally ill people tangle every day in unfortunate and sometimes tragic ways. This nation has gone from one bad system to another—from housing people with mental illness in large, impersonal, often abusive institutions called mental hospitals to housing people with mental illness in large, impersonal, often abusive institutions called prisons. The difference is that people who are mentally ill have even fewer rights in prison and often emerge sicker and more damaged than when they went in. The least fortunate die there, some by their own hand. In the hospitals of yesterday, people with mental illness were patients; in the prisons of today, they are inmates. This is a key distinction.

I have titled this book *Crazy in America*. I do not like the word *crazy* when it is attached to people with mental illness. It appears sparingly in these pages and only in a particular context. What is crazy is how we treat people with mental illness in America—it is crazy that the criminal justice system has assumed care of hundreds of thousands of mentally ill people; crazy that they are kept for months and years in solitary confinement when the average stay in Canada is a week, and England has a minute fraction of the number of people we have in such units; crazy that in a prosperous country such as ours there are so few resources to help the most vulnerable among us.

The people in this book paid dearly for their illness because of a society that failed them. The fervent wish of their families, expressed to me over and over, was that these stories might open minds and hearts to the need for change, might influence debate, might help to prevent more such stories in the future. It is mine, too.

Mary Beth Pfeiffer
Stone Ridge, New York

Acknowledgments

This is a book, first, about the bonds between people and how mental illness tests and sometimes breaks them. It is a book about lives and love. It could not have been written without the families of the people I write about, and in particular, their mothers, aunts, and sisters. Women propelled this book forward; they are the keepers of family history and mementos, the guardians of memory. I am enormously grateful to them for sharing the lives of their loved ones with me. Special thanks to Pat Jewell and Elizabeth Vou Vakis, Tricia and Dena Ashley, Ceida and Morgan Houseman, Barbara Nadir and Susan McGowan, Joan Roger and Cora Morton, and Renee Nuñez and Sabrina Perez. My deepest gratitude to Shayne Eggen as well, who survived the indignities of mental illness and imprisonment and shared them with me. The generosity of these wonderful women humbles me. Thanks also to David Houseman and David Ashley for supporting and contributing to this project.

The path to this book began in 2000 at the *Poughkeepsie Journal* in Poughkeepsie, New York, a newspaper that gave me the time and support to pursue investigative journalism of a kind too infrequently practiced by small newspapers. The people who supported these efforts include Meg Downey, Rich Kleban, Dick Wager, Stu Shinske, Derek Osenenko, Kathy Norton, and Barry Rothfeld, who first appointed me exclusively to investigative reporting. We need more such people in American journalism.

This book also would not have happened without the support of the Open Society Institute, which named me a Soros Justice Media Fellow in 2004. Special thanks to Kate Black and Quynh Thai at OSI and of course to George Soros, for underwriting an organization of ideals, commitment, and purpose. During my fellowship, I researched and wrote about the incarceration of people with mental illness across the nation and realized how terribly typical the problems that I had seen in New York were. I wrote an article for the *New York Times Magazine* that became the genesis for this book; thanks to my editor Vera Titunik for all her many suggestions and her support.

Sincere thanks, also, to John Hyde and the Fund for Investigative Journalism, which provided a grant in support of this project. Thanks to Susan Burgess and Lucy Dalglish at the Reporters Committee for Freedom of the Press, which provided an attorney who argued to allow me to tour several New York state prisons along with the judge and parties in a federal lawsuit. (Our motion was denied but it was a thrilling and worthwhile hour of testimony on behalf of an unfettered press.) Thanks to Dave Schultz and Nicole Auerbach of Levine, Sullivan, Koch and Schulz, and to Bob Lasnik, a good friend.

Dozens of other people helped in various ways at key moments in the evolution of this book. Thanks also to Sarah Kerr, Milt Zelermyer, Rebecca Young, Leslie Walker, Hans Toch, Terry Kupers, Joe Crews, Keith Curry, Jeffrey Brody, Dennis Lopez, Jennifer

Wynn, Jack Beck, Bob Gangi, Betsy Sterling, George Marlow, Elsie Butler, Bryce McCann, John D. B. Lewis, Elizabeth Koob, Joan Magoolaghan, Sue Burrell, Judi Milosevich, and Gary F. Wilson.

Thanks to my agent, Rob Wilson, for his many efforts on my behalf; to my editor, Doris Cross, who read the manuscript with an eagle eye; and to C&G's Adelaide Docx, who helped in many ways.

Thanks also to my husband, Rob Miraldi, who heard every word of this book several times over and actually listened. His commitment to this endeavor was as strong as mine; I am blessed to have so devoted and supportive a spouse (who cooked many dinners while I pecked away at my keyboard). I am grateful, too, to my children, Sara and Robert, who heard me complain more times than I should have and cheered me on. Thanks to my mother, Helen, for giving me a strong sense of indignation and for being there for me, and to my father, Charles, who taught me the values of hard work, family, and service, and whom I miss every day.

CRAZY
IN AMERICA

PART ONE

SHAYNE

—❦—

Shayne Eggen left prison the way most people do. She was given a bus ticket and a check for $100 and let go, on August 6, 2000, to the freedom she desperately craved. It was one of those mistakes that bureaucrats make a thousand times a day, an act that was wrong in simple and obvious ways but one that came naturally to the Iowa prison system. Shayne, who was a week shy of thirty-seven years old, wore her prison uniform: blue jeans and a blue shirt. She carried two bottles of pills and had been injected with Prolixin, an antipsychotic drug that would stay in her system for about a month. A pretty, gregarious woman with long brown hair, bright blue eyes, and a fetching figure that had broadened with age and starchy prison food, she had lived from the ages of fourteen to thirty-four mostly in institutions with people who were mentally ill. For the last two and a half years she had been in prison for stabbing the police chief in the small Iowa town where she lived.

Shayne's diagnosis had varied over time, but the predominant, recurring label affixed to her was paranoid schizophrenia. Hers was a paralyzing and brutal illness that had, time and again, held her back from the life she wished to lead. She wanted to live in her own apartment, to manage money, to be with people who she thought were normal. Instead, since adolescence, her life had been a fog of locked hospital doors, drugs she did not want, screaming fits and padded cells, a life of beliefs and fears that no one else shared.

Shayne had been deemed incompetent and incapacitated at a dozen different points in her life and she had tired of it long ago. In prison, she had taken control of her life in one key respect: she had decided not to seek parole even if it meant doing more time. When she left prison, she decided, there would be no parole officer to report to and no conditions to meet. She was well enough and smart enough to figure that out. Today, as she walked through the gates of the Iowa Correctional Institution for Women in Mitchellville and into a gloriously sunny and warm day, Shayne was determined to find the life she was destined for. And so, she boarded a bus for a settlement in central Iowa inhabited by the Meskwaki Indians, a tribe to which she believed she belonged.

CHAPTER ONE

The Eyes of an Indian Princess

SHAYNE ELIZABETH EGGEN WAS BORN on August 13, 1963, of a Greek mother who immigrated to Detroit at the age of fourteen and a Norwegian father who grew up in Decorah, a small city of tow-headed children and church-going Protestants in northeast Iowa's farm country. They met in 1961 while working in the Federal Housing Authority office in Detroit. Elizabeth Vou Vakis was nineteen, an exotic new secretary who captured the attention of several office males. Donald Eggen was twenty-six and a U.S. Army veteran who had been recruited as an appraiser trainee after he graduated from college.

Elizabeth was a petite and shapely size six with long auburn hair parted in a way that often obscured one of her brown eyes and added a sense of intrigue to her exotic looks. The daughter of a Greek-born psychology professor who'd been educated in America and spoke many languages, and a mother of Norwegian ancestry who sang opera, performed in theater, and gave music lessons, Elizabeth was an outgoing and confident young woman despite her sheltered upbringing. When she was fourteen, her father Yanni died, and so did her expectation of an arranged marriage. Her urge to nurture and have many babies in the Greek tradition did not.

Don was a head taller than Elizabeth, a well-built man with coarse dark hair and blue eyes whose parents were of stiff, working-class stock. His mother was a career clerk in the local Sears, Roebuck and his father was a truck driver who delivered Sears goods and hired out. Vivian Eggen was the antithesis of Elizabeth's mother, Ruth. Where Ruth demanded a warm hug after an absence, Vivian stiffened under it. Harvey Eggen was a no-nonsense kind of man who had once punished Don, who was perhaps six at the time, for mischievously stealing flags from the headstones at a local cemetery by making him put on a dress and then tying him to a tree.

Don offered Elizabeth a ride to work every morning, arranging for his two roommates to sit in the front seat while he sat in the back with Elizabeth. It may have been a case of opposites attracting— Elizabeth demonstrative and sensuous, Don reticent and insecure— a meeting of Mediterranean heat and Northern chill. The match likely had disaster written all over it. After nine months at the FHA, Don was fired for lying on his application; he had indeed, it turned out, spent a night in jail years earlier for disorderly conduct while drunk in Decorah.

Elizabeth had five children in eight years—Shayne came first— and she surrounded her babies with family, food, and, particularly, music. A stunning woman with long silky hair and an air of bohemian youthfulness, Elizabeth belly danced in flowing skirts, sang, and played guitar. When her hands weren't strumming or wiping dirty fingers, they were making clothes, quilts, or crafts. Donald was a gambler and a drinker, a real estate salesman who occasionally made nice commissions that were followed by irresponsible purchases and long dry spells. Mostly he was absent, emotionally and otherwise.

Elizabeth had her own circle of friends with whom she'd go on weekend forays to a local lake and once on a cross-country trip, always without her husband. Don was stern and detached with the children, more apt to express himself by yelling, say, over a bad report card than in any other way.

When Shayne was eight and Elizabeth was fully pregnant with their last child, a son among four daughters, the bank foreclosed on the Eggens' tiny three-bedroom bungalow in Royal Oak, Michigan. Elizabeth, as disconnected from their financial straits as she was from her husband, was furious. They divorced when Shayne was eleven, but Don stayed in the house for another year before Elizabeth suggested that he go back to live with his parents in Decorah. She thought he might cope better in the environment he'd grown up in.

The family's separation didn't last; the Greek idea of the primacy of the family was so deeply embedded in Elizabeth's bones that she soon followed Don to Iowa. They settled in a nineteenth-century corner Victorian on tidy, wide West Broadway, directly across from the Lutheran church, where the romantic Elizabeth swore she heard sleigh bells outside on her first Christmas. She was quite in love with this Currier-and-Ives kind of town; nonetheless, when the couple remarried, she wore black.

Shayne was her mother's daughter, a nurturer who wiped her siblings' spills and kept them away from electric sockets. She was also a bright and engaging young girl who sat around with the adults, captivated by philosophical discussions. She had a vivid memory and, inexplicably, seemed to know things without being taught. She once pointed to a tree during a forest walk and recited its medicinal uses. Family friends, startled by Shayne's awareness and maturity, remarked that she was a kind of angel from another realm. To Elizabeth, these were manifestations of Shayne's immortal past. She had long believed that mother and daughter had been together in past lives, back to the beginning of time, sometimes with Shayne as mother and Elizabeth as daughter.

As the primary parent-in-residence, the ever unconventional Elizabeth raised her children on a sort of Montessori model: a belief that children thrive in a stimulating environment and wilt under rigidity. Discipline was not her strong point; respect for children was. Except for Don's nonparticipation in most family affairs, the Eggen family was close, loving, and functional. When Shayne was eight years old, her sister Marcy, three, was diagnosed with leukemia. Elizabeth had long held firmly un-Western ideas about health and well-being so that when she was told that the child had a month to live, she considered rejecting chemotherapy in favor of alternative therapies. When she was advised by friends that the baby would surely be taken from her, she opted to do both, immersing Marcy in "color therapy" and natural foods as well as a regimen of traditional drugs. After a siege of several years, Marcy survived.

A photograph of Shayne at age nine shows a budding young girl with a round face, blue eyes with large black pupils, and long straight hair, brown at the crown and deep blond at the shoulders, suggesting long days in the sun. Adult teeth peek through a demure, childlike smile. If there were signs in her childhood that Shayne was heading for a lifetime of illness, they were of the subtle, developmental kind common to many children. Elizabeth had been a Girl Scout leader for several years, but there came a time—roughly coinciding with Marcy's illness—when Shayne became unwilling to share her mother with other girls and insisted that Elizabeth quit. Elizabeth, always trusting of her children's instincts, complied. At age eleven, during a walk to school, Shayne saw that her younger sister Alana, nine, was wearing her jeans, and she became enraged. She viciously attacked Alana, to whom she'd been an otherwise caring and protective sister, leaving her traumatized and with a black eye. When her third-grade teacher asked Alana what had happened, she lied and said she had fallen.

Later that year, Shayne made a sexual pass at an adult family friend who was driving her home. He was horrified and refused to be alone with her again. The incident was written off as an unfortunate upshot of the impending divorce and the pressure on Shayne as the eldest sibling. Elizabeth was not told about it. After Shayne's illness was fully in bloom, this developed into a pattern. She would make inappropriate comments at social gatherings. She would tell her cringing father of her exploits in masturbation or her sexual fantasies, embarrassing even the free-spirited Elizabeth. Where did these expressions come from, she wondered?

Thoughout her childhood, Shayne considered herself Native American, notwithstanding the Greek-Norwegian ancestry reflected on her birth certificate. She told her siblings that they had been deceived about their origins. She gave them Indian names and assigned animals to them—one was a turtle, another a dolphin. She wore moccasins and turquoise jewelry and braided her hair. She invented an Indian language and performed chants and whoops. The feeling that she was of Indian heritage seemed to have always been with her. It was there even when, as a small child, she put a hand to her mother's stomach, felt her sister move, and saw a vision of an Indian child in a swing. The feeling was there when at age three she demanded a horse, uncommon in the suburbs of Detroit, and cried about it in a way that was out of keeping with her age and experience; there when she made Indian vests out of brown paper bags in the first grade; there at age twelve when she dreamed of marrying a Native American man. Shayne's attraction to aboriginal culture was so strong that Elizabeth, a woman who embraced mysticism, believed that Shayne had lived as a Native American in a former life. She repeatedly questioned her ethnic roots, a strictly European melting pot, in search of an ounce of Navajo or Cherokee blood. It was not a fantasy, Elizabeth would say, it was an awareness.

Shayne's institutionalized life officially began with what Elizabeth came to call "the inquisition." Shayne was introduced to marijuana when she was eleven by the worldly older sister of a friend, and she became a discipline problem in school for smoking cigarettes and the like. Two years later, when the family moved to Iowa, she seemed to settle down. She was a polite and attentive B student in seventh-grade English, well-adjusted and unremarkable in eighth-grade social studies. In ninth grade, things changed. Shayne was the city-girl-gone-country who wore makeup and matured sexually long before her Iowa counterparts. She found an older crowd to hang with and smoke pot, at least once laced with PCP, an addictive anesthetic that can cause delusions. Teachers noticed. She would laugh inexplicably in study hall, seemingly at something that wasn't there, or defiantly blow bubble gum. She was sometimes glassy-eyed and seemed vacant and apathetic. This wasn't earthshaking stuff, but Decorah, a town from a Hollywood back lot replete with colonnaded courthouse, wide tree-lined avenues, and brimming flower boxes, was a cliquish community of mostly blond Norwegians. Newcomers, particularly of Greek descent from urban climes, were viewed with suspicion. Shayne was ripe for the rumor mill, and it was spinning. One afternoon at recess, a young boy stole the hat off little Marcy's head with the taunt, "Your sister's the druggie."

In December of Shayne's ninth-grade year, Elizabeth was summoned from her job as a secretary in an insurance office for a fateful meeting at Decorah Middle School. Shayne was in distress, she was told; come immediately. When she arrived, Elizabeth entered a room where the school principal, vice principal, several teachers, a guidance counselor, and a representative of the police department sat in a semicircle. Shayne was in the center. They were grilling her. Why was Shayne smoking marijuana, they wanted to know. What was troubling her? Why was her behavior so poor? Elizabeth chafed at the tenor of the questions, at the ferocity of the attack on her daughter, a child. Her instinct was to shield Shayne, to rescue her. Shayne was typically uncooperative—sullen and adamantly silent, incapable of analyzing her own behavior for a roomful of adults who expected the worst from her. Elizabeth was told to take her to the local mental health center for a consultation. It was the first indication that Shayne had mental problems.

On December 22, 1977, after one missed appointment, Elizabeth and Don took Shayne to Decorah's public mental health clinic "on an emergency at the referral of local school people and the police department," according to her record. It was an encounter that would forever change Shayne's life. Paperwork from that day describes a fourteen-year-old girl who refused to respond to simple questions, was sneaking out in the middle of the night, and getting failing grades. She had been found in a park with a young man who was in possession of beer. She smiled inappropriately. She was withdrawn and "had expressed the idea that people could read her mind." Her record listed no extensive history of worrisome symptoms, no voices heard or visions seen. Based on this single evaluation, the rebellious, drug-using Shayne was deemed by the assessing physician to have a condition of "psychotic proportions," and to be in the midst of an "acute schizophrenic episode." Hospitalization was recommended.

The next step was to sign Shayne over to the state, making her a ward of Iowa. That's the way it was done, at least when a family did not have the money to provide an alternative. The Eggens' finances had long been precarious. Elizabeth, recalling her friends' warnings when Marcy was sick, feared the authorities would take her daughter even if she did not consent. The sheriff came for Shayne the next day. There really wasn't any choice.

For Don Eggen, this may have been a solution, deliverance from a hellish year of trying to manage Shayne. He was tired of it. While Elizabeth had been passive in the face of Shayne's rebellion—part of her laid-back style of parenting—Don had been angry. He had been brusque at Shayne's evaluation, telling an interviewer that he needed to leave to take care of his trucking business. After Shayne had climbed up a trellis and slithered through a second-floor window late one night, he had slapped her face. She had thrown a radio down a flight of stairs at him. Things had gotten so bad that Don slept with his door locked, fearful that Shayne would do something to hurt him. Moreover, the house had been filled with tension. When Shayne failed to come home one night, she was found asleep beneath the stairs to her grandparents' apartment; she had been out for a night of drinking. There had been shouting matches. "You can't tell me what to do," she had told her parents. "I can do what I want."

Elizabeth signed the papers.

Shayne was taken from the Eggens in 1977, twenty-three years after the state's esteemed medical society had endorsed lobotomy as a way to reduce the anxiety of mental patients and stretch hospital labor.

In 2000, a national report identified six states that most often asked parents to relinquish custody of their children—institutionalize them—in order to receive mental health care. Iowa was among them. "No state agency should exact the heavy price of custody relinquishment before providing mental health services to a child," the report, by the Bazelon Center for Mental Health Law, concluded. "Such a policy destroys families and exacerbates children's behavioral health problems." It would be five more years, however, before Iowa passed a law to let parents retain custody of their mentally ill children who receive state-subsidized care. At the bill's signing, the state's director of human services, Kevin Concannon, said that the old law had been passed in the 1960s "when it was believed that if you had a child with mental health problems, it somehow reflected poor nurturing on the part of the parents."

At the conclusion of the 1977 meeting that led to Shayne's lifetime of dependence, she did show one reaction, the assessing physician noted. There were tears in her eyes.

As a young adult, Shayne Eggen was a small, pretty woman who wore peasant blouses, fringed vests, and flared skirts. When she was well, she was fastidious about looking good, her long, flowing hair fixed just so. Shayne was beautiful, people would say, especially her eyes, so piercingly blue. When Shayne was sick, it was obvious; her hair became stringy and her clothes disheveled. The confidence that defined her dissolved. She became cross.

As part of her Native American persona, Shayne called herself Shay-lee-sha, and considered herself a warrior. She spoke her own language and sang her own songs. If fellow residents of whatever facility she was in dared to challenge her authenticity, she would lash out with her arm, quickly, decisively. She would bluster and curse in group therapy sessions, and participants knew to steer clear. Family members had long been targets of Shayne's aggression. At sixteen, Shayne, home for a weekend from a state mental hospital, discovered that Alana, fourteen, had helped herself to her eye shadow. Shayne berated her and pushed her; Alana, who was tired of Shayne's histrionics, pushed back. After a two-minute scuffle through the house, Shayne grabbed Alana by the hair, threw her up against an antique cabinet, and grabbed a knife from a drawer. Shayne was a tower of anger and strength, and Alana wisely gave up the struggle. Two years later, when Elizabeth went to hug Shayne in the hospital, Shayne locked her hands tightly around her mother's throat. When Elizabeth fell to her knees, Shayne let go and fell into a swoon beside her, kissing her mother over and over. "Mami, whatever I do, please know that I love you!"

Everything gelled for Shayne in the summer of 1981, when she was in her fourth or fifth commitment at the Mental Health Institute at Independence, Iowa, a state-run psychiatric hospital. Shayne was eighteen and quite lovely then—her blue eyes radiant inside a fringe of shiny dark hair, her skin clear and supple. She had gained weight from her medications but her proportions, within a five-foot, two-inch frame, were shapely. Like her mother, Shayne was ebullient by nature and unflappably sure of her allure, and she left in her teenage wake a string of boys with unfulfilled crushes.

At a hospital dance one night, Shayne met a man who was very tall and dark. He wore blue jeans, short in the ankles, and a tight T-shirt. Shayne was dressed in a blue Levi's shirt tucked snugly into her jeans, with a blue bandanna tied fetchingly around her knee. The man was ten years older than Shayne and had been hospitalized for treatment of alcoholism. "Are you Indian?" she asked him. "Meskwaki," he said. They danced. At another dance a week or so later, she met him again and they went outside and talked. Oldies music played and they flirted, but the couple never so much as kissed. Over the years, he married and had children, and except for an occasional cruelly encouraging letter or call, he had put Shayne behind him. She could not do the same for him. She was an Indian princess and he her chief. She raged at the distance between them and the failure to consummate their "marriage," wrote hundreds of letters to him and about him, and played out a life with him in exquisite detail. In phone calls, she would tell his wife she had no right to be with him; she'd strike up conversations with his children. When she jumped from a second-story hospital window, fell hard, and crushed her arm, she was in pursuit of this man. She believed he was her soul mate, and wherever she was for the next two decades, he dominated her thoughts.

When Shayne was nineteen, she was discharged from the Mental Health Institute and landed on her mother's doorstep in Michigan— Elizabeth had recently returned there—hopeful as always that she could stay and that she would be well. She spent two frenzied days rocking in a chair, then, in a psychotic state, fled the house. As far as anyone could tell, she was raped and sodomized by more than one man before she was hospitalized again days later. In the hospital they strapped her elbows to her waist and locked her in a room for weeks with nothing but a mattress.

Over the years, Shayne became what one psychologist called "a lost soul who cannot cope in life outside institutions." She did not lack for hospital care. Often, the problem was the times in between. At age twenty, she was discharged from Independence again and given a bus ticket to Dallas, where Elizabeth, separated from Don, had relocated. This was known cynically in the mental health business as "Greyhound therapy"—it amounted to Iowa's attempt to unload a frequent and costly patient. Shayne did not know exactly where Elizabeth was, and Elizabeth did not know she was coming. Police managed to unite them after Shayne was found rolling around naked on the edge of a highway, wrapping herself in what she thought were beautiful sunlit shards of glass. She was hospitalized in Texas for a couple of months, then let go again. She landed in Flagstaff, Arizona, where she was treated at a hospital emergency room for scratching at her eye in a worrisome attempt to pluck it out. From there, she hitchhiked to Phoenix, where she would later talk disjointedly about several men, three days, a knife, a series of coerced sexual encounters, and an escape. "They controlled me," she said simply. Finally, four months, one hospitalization, one gang bang, and one emergency-room visit later, some folks in a soup kitchen sent her back to Iowa.

A social worker once asked Shayne why she was so angry. She said it was because she had been locked up for so long. As always with Shayne, it was a succinct but incomplete explanation, one that left out the demons that drove her and the frustrations of a life unlived.

Shayne lived an existence of irrational fears and unchecked emotions. She fretted about being alone and having no one to care for her. She worried that she was rude and disliked, yet she was aloof from and disdainful of the institutionalized people around her—they were part of an identity she rejected. She read insults and slights into the most innocent of comments made to her. "I want to feel bad," she once wrote in a letter, "so I can feel good." Her solace was in her Indian chief, a creation almost totally of her imagination. She would fill letters to her family with proclamations of undying faith in him. She would cling to the slightest sliver of encouragement that he cared—a letter from him five years earlier or a family member's comment that somehow rekindled her hopes. "He is my comfort when I lay my head on my pillow," Shayne wrote in 1999 of an unrequited love then eighteen years in the making. But even Shayne's ironclad fantasies sometimes crumbled. Her chief's absence and silence—and on several occasions his crude and callous rejections—told her he did not love her.

It was just a matter of time before Shayne became involved in the criminal justice system. Her tendency to be violent, often mixed in a stew of confused thoughts and paranoid fears, had been too consistent and too pronounced. "I get so scared people are going to hurt me," she once explained, "I have to hurt them first." And times had changed for people like her.

It was on September 16, 1997, that Shayne crossed the line from disturbed to dangerous. She was living in a supervised apartment house for mentally ill people in Decorah then and had been smoking marijuana, which often caused her delusions to return. She had been sad about the recent death of Princess Diana and the departure, after a visit of several days, of her parents, two sisters, and their children. She did not like being alone in her apartment and had been hanging out, day and night, in the apartment below, where four mentally ill men lived as part of the supervised housing program. She was expecting to be kicked out at any time—an expectation she invariably helped to fulfill—and asked a staff member if she could have her collection of small decorative knives, in particular, the knife with a gleaming turquoise handle. These were her warrior's knives, part of her Native American identity. When the staff member refused, Shayne exploded and jumped through a plate glass window. Police Chief Ben Wyatt arrived to find her on the lawn, dressed in jeans and a tank top, her hands bloody from a small cut. She refused to speak, and scooted up an exterior staircase to her second-floor apartment.

When Wyatt followed and opened the storm door, Shayne lunged at him with a steak knife in her hand, aiming for his chest. He turned reflexively and it sank into his shoulder. She was an Indian warrior who could kill if she wanted to—in this case kill someone she believed had come to take her to the mental hospital. "Oh my God," she said, when she saw what she had done.

Shayne was charged with attempted murder and felony assault on a peace officer. When it was determined that she had likely been too disturbed to form the necessary intent for attempted murder, she was allowed to plead guilty to assault and interfering with a peace officer. She received two concurrent five-year sentences, which under Iowa law were automatically halved.

"I was proving the warrior that I am inside," Shayne said of the incident that transformed her from merely a mentally disturbed woman living in the community to Inmate 0808309A in the Iowa Department of Corrections. If she disliked the mental hospitals, juvenile facilities, and adult homes she had been cycled through as a teenager and young adult, the thirty-four-year-old Shayne had not seen anything yet.

> *You are not my god and you are not my parent. You are a department store making money off people's lives with your lies. Institutions of the world hear this. You should for all time after eternity be at the bottom of the bottomless pit. Hit the ground and when the walls come tumbling down I will laugh in your calamity.*
>
> —Letter from Shayne to the head
> of the Iowa prison system,
> October 1998

CHAPTER TWO

Creature of the Institution

SHAYNE ENTERED THE IOWA CORRECTIONAL Institution for Women in Mitchellville in early 1998 as a mentally ill woman with a profile that spelled trouble. Diagnosed with schizophrenia or its equally troubling variant, schizoaffective disorder, she had been hospitalized for acute care some two dozen times. In hospitals, she had picked fights and hurt herself and had often been restrained. She had long ago signaled her unwillingness to submit, from refusing medications to throwing tantrums to brazenly escaping from the institutions that contained her. It was in one of these that she had jumped through the bars of a second-floor window at age eighteen, losing partial movement in her arm and leaving her with a slightly misaligned right eye. This imperfection came to drive her efforts at self-harm, which were obsessively directed at her loveliest feature: her translucent eyes.

Shayne would prove as difficult an inmate as a patient, a disciplinary problem who similarly refused to toe the line and who, when upset, "can be very violent," her keepers had noted. When she wrote to the director of Iowa's prisons in 1998, she was in solitary confinement, a place she would come to know well. "They are keeping me in the hole under unlawful orders," she told the prison chief. "I am not a possession. The state of Iowa does not own me." In Shayne, as in many mentally ill inmates, a battle of wills had begun, fed on one side by a relentless need to control, on the other by a sickness that defied every effort at it—the two sides fighting at cross-purposes, each ultimately as helpless as the other.

When she committed her crime, Shayne had been insane in every sense but the legal one, a standard that in a post–John Hinckley era had become nearly impossible to meet. (In 1981, Hinckley had attempted to assassinate President Ronald Reagan in order to win the love of the actress Jodie Foster and was found not guilty by reason of insanity; many states subsequently passed laws that sharply limited the use of the defense.) If there was a worse place than an Iowa prison for her—for any person with serious mental illness—it was hard to imagine. People with mental illnesses lack the basic tools for prison survival. They see things that others don't, yell out to silent voices, think in chaotic patterns. They are often crippled by irrational fears or weighted down by profound feelings of sadness. Yet the hallmark of prison life is regimentation and control. Obedience is expected to be instantaneous and unquestioned. When inmates are counted several times a day, they must stop in place wherever they are and wait for a signal to proceed. Failure to follow directives can result in "tickets"—and punishment. "I am written a major Class I ticket every time I turn around," Shayne complained. "It keeps adding days to the hole."

Beyond this, meals, wake-up time, phone calls, mail, and medical care are all tightly controlled. Necessary hygienic products may be rationed and withheld according to the proclivities of those in charge, and in unjust and punitive ways. Corrections officers vary in their approaches, but many express outright disdain for their charges, whom they see as human beings caged for the sole purpose of punishment. It is an environment of tension, conflict, and control, ideally suited to pick at the inmates' scabs of paranoia, depression, anxiety, and delusion.

At Mitchellville, Shayne thrived in one respect: she attended an art therapy class in which she produced beautiful pastel-colored drawings of green, snow-capped mountains, golden teepees, prowling wolves, and quivers filled with feathered arrows. In one picture, a rainbow arches gloriously over the head of an Indian maiden who sits atop a richly patterned blanket on a chestnut horse, her long hair tucked demurely behind one ear. The pictures reflect a certain kind of knowledge, of art or life, the kind of knowledge that family friends saw in the youngster that was Shayne. She seemed to know things, they said. Her art therapist, Roberta Victor, delighted in Shayne's skills and in her persona. She was smart, intuitive, and talented. Her art bared her soul. She often drew pictures of Chief Tomahawk Moon, which consisted of a moon, an ornate suspended headdress, and a raised tomahawk. Missing was the figure beneath the headdress, the man of Shayne's dreams. Likewise, the feet of her horses were often buried in the grass, unseen, a sign of Shayne's own powerlessness.

> *I have dreams of running away to the mountains with him. You know how much I love the mountains. I would like to go live around Buena Vista in the forest. I want him to build a log cabin and he can hunt and stuff and we can go for walks and find fruits and berries. Maybe I can learn about different leaves and roots. I can do all my things I do and we can sell stuff in town.*
> —Letter from Shayne, age thirty-five, to her mother, January 25, 1999, while at the Iowa Correctional Institution for Women

In class once, Roberta asked students to draw their dreams. Shayne, who was teetering on the edge of sanity, drew a bunk bed in a psychiatric unit with her in it. She used vibrant colors and began to tell a sad, disjointed story, her thoughts a slurry of memory and fear. She told of getting pregnant in prison in 1997. She said she had a dream that someone was trying to kill her baby and steal things from her. Then she abruptly left the class, ran to her cell, and returned with a Bible and some photographs. She tore them up and threw them in a trash can.

Of the humiliations and indignities that mental illness had brought Shayne, the birth of her baby may have been the most haunting. She had become pregnant in the psychiatric unit at Iowa Medical and Classification Center in Oakdale where she was being evaluated to see if she was competent to stand trial in the police chief's stabbing. The tryst, as Shayne tells it, consisted of a quickie in an unlocked laundry room off a corridor with male-female access. "I bent over and got pregnant," she said. Shayne chose not to abort and approached pregnancy in the same way as other prospective mothers, fretting that her smoking would hurt the baby and that she was not gaining enough weight.

Throughout her labor in a hospital, Shayne's hands were cuffed in front of her and her legs were shackled until the moment of birth. Officers stood guard nearby. When a son, Angelo, emerged, he was quickly taken from her because a psychiatrist reported that she planned to kill her baby. "I never had that thought," Shayne told her aunt. "I never got to hold him. . . . I believe that man will die and so will the judge that made Mom and Pop bring me to MHI [Mental Health Institute]." For the next two days, Shayne, in shackles and with a round-the-clock police guard, could only peek at her son through a window of the maternity ward. Her sister Marcy, who had given birth two months earlier to her third child, a son, breastfed them both in a room provided by the hospital until Angelo could go home. She and her husband, Jeffrey, adopted the baby.

Before her release in 2000 from Mitchellville, a medium-security prison of about five hundred women, Shayne had lived on her own just once, in 1995, not counting hospital escapes and ill-planned releases. It was a brief and unsuccessful experience. Given $200 of her government check to buy food for a month, she instead bought a cockatiel, a small bird with a crest on its head. On three occasions of fleeting liberty, she was raped by groups of men, twice over a period of days. She related these events to family members matter-of-factly and with little obvious trauma, except when she was pressed for details. Then she became anxious and agitated, regretting the mistakes she believed she had made and fearful of the memories they carried.

To Shayne, the details were unimportant. What mattered was self-determination and freedom. Her sexual power, regardless of the terrible consequences it sometimes brought, was a form of expression and control. She used it liberally, having perhaps fifty liaisons, some of them while she was in facilities of confinement. She was perhaps the only inmate in the history of Iowa prisons to be impregnated by another inmate—another of the myriad ways the Iowa prison system proved itself unable to come to terms with Shayne Eggen.

Releasing Shayne from prison without a place to go or a plan for her care was something akin to leaving a six-year-old alone in Times Square. One of those people whose mental illness was never well controlled, her life consisted of fleeting periods of peace in a minefield of mania. Often filled with fear, she sought to strike before being struck—as when she arrived in prison in early 1998; she determined who was the most feared inmate at Mitchellville and promptly assaulted her. Shayne was fierce, yet vulnerable. She had little ability to survive on her own, and she was not the only person who could be hurt by her freedom.

Back in Decorah, a tidy northeastern Iowa town surrounded on three sides by a wide loop in the Upper Iowa River, Jan Heikes was aware of Shayne's impending release and had been assured that plans were being made for her care afterward. Heikes, the county's coordinator of mental health services, had been a social worker years before at a residential facility where Shayne had lived. She had watched the chapters of Shayne's illness unfold until it brought her to the gates of an Iowa prison in 1998. Heikes knew Shayne's "incredibly sweet and caring side" as she called it, the side that caused her to watch over a profoundly retarded fellow resident like a mother hen and help out in the facility's rehab department. But she also knew the Shayne who flaunted her sexuality in a way that could get her into trouble and who could turn on a dime, lashing out at fellow residents who crossed her in any way. In twenty years of illness, Shayne was a known quantity around Decorah. She'd been an uncontrollable teenager who ran with an older crowd, got into illicit drugs early, and was consigned to state care at the age of fourteen. She had been known to run through town naked on occasion, once stopping traffic on Main Street and another time prompting a protective pastor to throw a blanket over her. She'd been taken to mental hospitals in the backs of squad cars, delusional, angry, and defiant.

The Sac and Fox Settlement in Tama, Iowa, sprawls over seventy-four hundred acres of wooded lands and cultivated river bottom in central Iowa along the Iowa River. Despite the opening of a casino in 1992, the settlement had a per capita income in 1995 of less than five thousand dollars a year, and a quarter of the populace was unemployed.

When Shayne arrived there from prison in August 2000, she had two things going for her, at least for the moment: she was a woman and she had a hundred dollars. She used them both over the course of the next three days in an overdue course of joyful partying. She played designated driver for a group of drunks, although she'd never

before driven a car. She sucked in marijuana for the first time in
three years. She slept in three homes on the settlement and with
three different men, two at the same address. Every time, when
morning came, she was asked in various ways to move on, something
she had come to expect from experience.

Once, years before, she had gone to the bathroom and come out
to find that her Indian friends had left her. Another time, a group of
men who had had their way with her over the course of several days
dropped her at a bus station on the pretext of checking the cost of a
ticket. "I knew they were going to leave me there, and they did," she
said in that way of hers that begged for more information. On her
third night on the settlement, Shayne's head was reeling from too
much pot, so she left the party to wander the byways of Tama in
search of her chief, the preoccupation to which, sooner or later, she
invariably returned. She did not find him. Her tall, dark Indian man,
whom she had not seen since she was eighteen, was in a halfway
house in Cedar Rapids for people with addictions to drugs and
alcohol. When she returned to the party, the door had been locked
behind her.

On the fourth night, Shayne slept in the woods. Her last fifty-
seven dollars had been snatched from her hands by a woman friend,
and Shayne had not objected. She had always given generously to
the people around her during these delicious forays into freedom,
small price for acceptance and camaraderie. The next day, the
woman drove her the twenty miles to a Salvation Army shelter in
nearby Marshall County. Iowa has a policy called "legal settlement,"
which holds that county governments are responsible to provide
mental health services only to people who are bona fide county residents. The policy is a notorious tactic of shifting costs elsewhere,
in a state where some counties provide generously to people who
need help but most do not. Folks in Marshall County quickly determined that this unkempt former mental patient turned inmate did
not belong. And so they made arrangements to send Shayne back to

the small Winneshiek County city from which, before prison, she had come.

Several months before Shayne's discharge from prison, Heikes had received a call from a prison social worker who was planning for Shayne's release, making sure that she would have housing to go to and that Medicaid and Social Security benefits would flow. Heikes was relieved. Things seemed to be moving along. She didn't learn that none of this had materialized until she got a call from Marshall County after Shayne's four-day odyssey on the settlement. She was indignant. Shayne had been institutionalized twenty-five times. She was likely among the sickest mentally ill inmates at the prison in Mitchellville. She had spent her last month there confined to a cell for twenty-three hours a day—crying, pacing obsessively, and often shaking uncontrollably, a sure sign that her illness, or medication, was out of control. Then, when the appointed day came, the system shed Shayne Eggen—and she shed it, like a butterfly sheds its cocoon.

> *What I was thinking the day I stabbed you was that I was going to lose my Indian boyfriend if I wasn't really careful and when I get to thinking that way that everybody doesn't know they love me I'll do all most anything I think.*
> —Letter of apology from Shayne, age thirty-four, to Chief Wyatt, October 1997

Pat Jewell was a spectacled woman in her mid-fifties who wore athletic sneakers and loose-fitting clothes and had eyes that became thin crescent moons when she smiled. She had been a loving aunt on the periphery of Shayne's life, a born-and-bred Iowan who visited her on occasion in hospitals or prisons and sent money to underwrite her cigarette addiction. Shayne was a prolific letter-writer, and many letters begged for checks.

By now, Pat was the closest relative of Shayne's who remained in

Decorah, and so, on August 11, 2000, Pat received a call: could she collect Shayne at the Nashua bus depot upon her return from prison—by way of the Meskwaki Indian settlement? Pat's role of affectionate detachment was about to end, to be replaced by that of sometime case manager, therapist, support network, and chauffeur. For Pat, a plain and dutiful woman who helps run a family organic soybean farm and works part-time doing laundry in a nursing home, assuming responsibility for her brother's daughter was the right thing to do. "There are people in this world that we're meant to take care of," she has been known to say. "They're kind of put here to give the rest of us an opportunity to earn our way to heaven." In short order, however, caring for Shayne became more than a way to earn grace. It became Pat's education in a tattered mental health system pressed to its limits by a sick, uncooperative, unstable young woman. Pat had signed on to do her duty. She was appalled at how unwilling society was to do its.

In the month after Shayne's return in August 2000, Pat set Shayne up in a motel and then rented her a small apartment for one hundred dollars a month from an understanding and compassionate landlord. She helped round up an array of hand-me-down furniture— a mattress for the floor, a donated television, a discarded TV stand, and a cushioned chair with wooden arms that harkened back to the 1950s. She helped her apply for Medicaid and Social Security, get her medications in order, go to the mental health clinic, and enroll in a group therapy program—all the things that should have been arranged before Shayne left prison and without which she would have been vulnerable to homelessness and worse. Pat ferried her from appointment to appointment, wondering all the while who did this for people who were estranged from their families. What happened to the other people released from prison or mental hospitals without a plan?

Everything seemed to be going well. But this was, after all, only the second time in Shayne's adulthood that she had lived in an apartment on her own after a lifetime of being brought her meals, given her clothing and medications, and taken to therapy of one sort or another.

One day, just a couple of weeks into this new life, Shayne stopped in to see her landlord, Stan Fullerton, a low-key Midwestern pharmacist who uses phrases like "holy buckets" and believes that mentally ill people deserve to be given a chance at a normal life. Fullerton had purchased the two-story brick building a year earlier after operating his pharmacy on the first floor for a decade. He did not have to advertise the eight apartments above the store because they were cheap and centrally located on Decorah's main street. Pat had approached him to see if one was available. Fullerton knew that Shayne had been in prison but agreed to rent to her, having had little trouble with other tenants who had psychiatric problems. That day, Shayne told Fullerton she had stopped taking her medications. "But I'm okay," she said. "I'm going to take care of things." Fullerton didn't think so. She seemed unwell. Her long brown hair was unwashed and disheveled. Her hands and eyes were in constant motion, and she was rocking back and forth. "I've been doing bad things," she told him. He reminded her about the building's smoking prohibition, which Shayne had flouted, and she left. Later, Fullerton would remember this exchange.

On her return to Decorah, Shayne had met up with Rick Sorenson, a thirty-eight-year-old man she had known for twenty years, from the days when they had both lived at the old Winneshiek County Farm. The farm, now called the Oneota Riverview Care Facility, was a nursing home at the edge of town that had a population of younger people who, like Shayne, were the otherwise homeless overflow of shuttered psychiatric centers. They would often sneak off, go beneath a bridge over the river nearby, and emerge glassy-eyed and silly. Throughout her twenties and thirties, Shayne was in and out of the bland, one-story facility, which provided little therapy and had the hospital-like trappings of the institutions she had long known. It was a way station, not a place to live, and people like her were anxious, though seldom quick, to move on. When she reconnected with Sorenson, Shayne found both a boyfriend and a quick and easy high. She had begun a fateful slide to the place that marijuana invariably took her: psychosis.

On September 18, 2000, Shayne got high and embarked on an Indian "vision quest." It was something she had done before as part of her Native American persona, a ritual in which she sought wisdom and enlightenment by overcoming challenges in the natural world. In a previous quest, in 1997, Shayne had dived headfirst off a tree and hurt herself. In this one, Shayne believed she had spent three days in the woods living with wolves. The trouble started when she emerged from the forest. At 2:06 P.M., a resident of South Mill Street in Decorah called the police to report that a woman with long dark hair and wearing jean shorts and a light blue T-shirt was in her backyard trying to kill her little black dog. Shayne was intent on breaking the howling dog's neck and emasculating it. She had also smeared mud on cars in the area.

Ten minutes later another call came in: a woman of the same description, her hands and arms bleeding badly, had knocked on the door of a two-story wooden house on Maple Avenue, pleading for blood for her baby. When a woman at the house refused, Shayne broke the storm door and three small windows in the main door and called the woman a bitch. By the time police arrived, Shayne's delusions had turned to desperation. She attempted to get into another house, slamming herself against the door. She screamed that she was Geronimo, that she had attacked a dog and wanted to kill it. In her bloody, bitten hands Shayne held what looked like a knife. Police, alarmed, drew their guns and trained them on a panting, delusional Shayne.

She was holding a feather. A cycle had begun that Pat Jewell tried mightily to stop.

I know I really messed up again. I got in a fight with a little shit of a dog because I was high. Yes, I did break out some windows too. Pop, I'm going to prove it to you that I can do something with my life. In all my years now I see what getting high does to me.

Please don't be ashamed of me, Pop. I'll prove it to you that I can do well with my life. I know I can . . . Pop you once said you were proud of me. I hope you are not disappointed. I never meant to disgrace you or myself. I'll be good. I promise . . . They are giving one last chance . . . I'll make you proud of me again. You'll see.

—Letter from Shayne to her father, September 2000,
while at Covenant Hospital in Waterloo, Iowa

At the recommendation of the police, Shayne was involuntarily committed to the mental health unit of a private hospital in Waterloo. She was filled with remorse and shame, emotions she knew well. She wanted to be good. She tried very hard. She had every good intention. After a week in the psychiatric ward she was released on a magistrate's order that she receive outpatient drug treatment. Pat thought the move was highly inappropriate for someone as unstable as Shayne, who suffered from both mental illness and an addiction to illicit drugs, with the two dynamics intimately entwined. Marijuana had proved her downfall from her first hospitalization at fourteen. She had returned to it time and again, thinking, always, that this time it would make her feel good. Pat knew that Shayne needed a program that would address both the addiction and the mental illness. The outpatient drug treatment program wasn't it.

Three days after her release, Shayne called Pat at 4:30 in the morning, obviously high and locked out of her apartment. She had had a fight with Rick Sorenson and thrown her keys away. He was not very nice, she told Pat. She thought she had married him, she said. She was calm, at least, when Pat let her in, only wishing to walk around the apartment naked. She asked at last if a worried Pat would ever leave. Things did not get better.

Later that day, Shayne turned up at St. Benedict's, a Catholic elementary school on Rural Avenue in Decorah, her skin red and blotchy, her breathing labored. She relieved herself in the bushes. She had come to the school in search of a little boy whose stepmother, Shayne's cousin, was a second-grade teacher. She began peering through classroom windows in the preschool wing and eventually found Dana Spry, who was startled to see her sweaty, overwrought cousin. Dana recalled stories of Shayne's family sleeping with their doors locked, of the time their grandmother woke up in a blackened room to find Shayne leaning over her, having scaled the balcony to her second-floor bedroom. Shayne had an announcement: Great-grandmother, who slept in the next room, was dead. (She wasn't.) Dana recalled Shayne as the cousin who always reminded her, in a way that was patently annoying, about her perennial battle with her weight.

Dana realized that Shayne wasn't right; her speech was disjointed and filled with fearful allusions. She'd seen a bird dive straight into a pond, she said: "It committed suicide." She hated the people at the mental health center. She wanted Pat. This was enough to worry Dana. But then Shayne approached a class of first graders in an outdoor gym class. She caught a ball, threw it back, and settled onto a bench, with the class in view, repeating a saying that was spinning inside her head: "Kill them all," she said vacantly, menacingly, "and let God sort them." Here was a woman who had already served two and a half years in prison for stabbing the town police chief, a woman who had been out of prison just forty days, and she was clearly unhinged. I need to get her out of here, Dana thought.

When Pat and Dana got Shayne to the Winneshiek Medical Center emergency room, they thought she would be hospitalized. She was pacing, sitting, standing, crossing her legs, playing with her hands, and swaying back and forth. She took a cigarette lighter and attempted to cauterize a wound she'd sustained a few days earlier. They learned that earlier in the day she had abruptly left the mental health center after talking of knives, suicide, and killing people. Shayne was medicated in the emergency room, and she soon calmed down. The crisis had passed—and so had the need to keep her at the hospital. Being no danger to herself or anyone else, the standard of commitment around which these things revolved, Shayne was released. Pat was incredulous.

By that time, it was after 5 P.M. and the courthouse where Pat would have to go to obtain an order of commitment was closed. She knew that Shayne's calm demeanor was temporary but she nonetheless took her home. Over the next two days, Pat watched as Shayne grew increasingly unstable and all attempts to get help were thwarted. At one point, Shayne spotted the shriveled remains of a rabbit killed by neighborhood cats and seized on it, insisting on cutting the feet off. She set fire to a towel at a friend's house. Pat called the police for help, warning them that something bad was going to happen. They told her they couldn't do anything until it did, and thanked her for the heads-up. Pat took Shayne to the mental health center, where a psychiatrist wrote in her chart: "I do not believe she is a danger to herself or anyone else at this time." The next afternoon proved otherwise.

Shayne met up with Rick Sorenson at a friend's house, where he broke up a "Betty," a marijuana cigarette, and they smoked it through a pipe. It was very strong. Shayne asked Sorenson to marry her, and he declined. When three other people arrived, Shayne announced that she wanted to be alone with Rick. She was miffed. She had been planning to reject him if he'd agreed to marriage but she hadn't gotten the chance. They walked to her apartment above Stan Fullerton's pharmacy and started to have sex. Shayne was distracted, agitated, and stoned. She thought of her Indian chief, whom she had not seen in nineteen years and who was now in a rehab

center. She thought of the Native Americans who hated her and
wanted her dead. She became terrified and suddenly knew: she had
to kill Sorenson.

Before they were finished having intercourse, Shayne got up,
went to the kitchen and found a five-inch bread knife with a ser-
rated edge. Holding it behind her back with both hands, the blade
facing down, she returned to the mattress on the living room floor,
where Sorenson was still erect. She bent over him, screamed, and
with both hands, plunged the knife into his chest above his left
nipple. She pulled it out and moved to plunge it in again as
Sorenson sprang up. She swung it at him several more times, cutting his arm, before Sorenson grabbed the knife. He fled the apartment, and Shayne reeled. She was panicked, thinking in staccato
bursts. What to do first, what to do first. Burn the house, burn the
house down, she thought, how to burn the house. She got matches
from a tin and set a blanket alight, then, inexplicably, lit a cigarette
from the fire. She would burn herself to death, she thought. She
wrapped the burning blanket around her body. When it singed her
left thigh, she changed her mind. She ran from the apartment
naked, down the outside stairway and onto the street, up the stairs
and down again, screaming "Fire!"

When police arrived, a naked Shayne was screaming incoherently
on a second-floor balcony of the apartment building. When they
placed her in a squad car, a sweater thrown over her, she began
speaking rapidly in a language that did not seem to be English. She
then blurted out that there was a baby. She was hysterical and difficult to understand, sometimes speaking in gibberish. People were
asking, Is there a baby? Is there a baby? Is it in the apartment? Yes,
Shayne told them, in the apartment. Firefighters searched but were
driven back by intense heat and flames. A skylight in Shayne's apartment collapsed on the back of one fireman, injuring him. They did
not find a baby.

There had been ample warning, in the days before, that Shayne was coming undone. Now she had stabbed Rick Sorenson and set a fire that caused four hundred thousand dollars in damage and risked the lives of her fellow tenants and the firefighters. She faced charges of arson, going armed with intent, and assault with a dangerous weapon. Shayne was taken from the fire—naked, delusional, and screaming that a baby was inside her burning apartment—to the state's Mental Health Institute in Independence. It was the first place where she had been hospitalized, at the age of fourteen, and the place where she had met her Indian chief at eighteen. Since then, a new order had taken hold at the hospital, whose bed count had been whittled from eighteen hundred people in the 1940s to ninety-five. There was not only far less room for difficult and aggressive patients like Shayne Eggen, there was also far less tolerance.

The Mental Health Institute discharged Shayne in six days, her second hospital stay in twenty days. "It seems she was too aggressive and MHI didn't feel they could deal with her," Pat Jewell wrote in the diary she kept of Shayne's comings and goings. Shayne was sent to the Winneshiek County Jail, where she was assigned to a glassed-in suicide observation cell next door to the control room, so that officers could keep a close watch on her.

Thirteen days later, Gregory Torgrim was on duty. He was a trim and compact man with slightly salted balding hair who had been a sheriff's deputy for seven years. He knew Shayne's history well—in particular, her naked prances through town and the prison stint she had finished only six weeks before for stabbing the chief of police. As he put it in a way that only Iowans can, Shayne was what you'd call "half a bubble off." That night, Shayne's condition worsened. She refused her dinner and medication and got upset when a phone call to Pat was disconnected. At 8:30 P.M., Pat arrived at the jail and, in the casual way of a small-town lockup, was permitted an off-hours visit with her niece. Shayne had been scratching at her eye again, which was red and tearing; she told Pat she was going to pluck it out.

Pat, concerned, alerted jailers on her way out. They were aware that Shayne had attempted this before, and she was under close supervision. Kim Bohr, the jailer on duty, checked Shayne at 11 P.M. and found her sitting on her bed in her black-and-white striped jail uniform, her hands folded in her lap. Ten minutes later, Kim heard a scream and went for the intercom button to Shayne's cell. "I plucked my fucking eye out!" she heard Shayne say. Bohr called for help. "Something's happened," she told Deputy Torgrim.

When Torgrim looked through the narrow window in the cell's steel door, he saw Shayne lying on the thin mattress of her metal bed, her back facing him. He asked her to get up, and she quietly complied. When she stood up, Torgrim saw Shayne's right eye hanging from its socket by the cords. Shayne was playing with it. She was not crying and did not seem to be in pain. "It actually made me feel good," she would later tell a psychologist. "It was an adrenaline rush." Torgim entered the cell. As he placed a compliant Shayne in handcuffs so that she would leave the eye alone, she began to recite a Bible verse. "And if thine eye offend thee," she said, "pluck it out." The scripture, which is from Mark 9:47, continues: "It is better for thee to enter into the kingdom of God with one eye, than having two eyes to be cast into hell fire." In her tortured logic, a remorseful Shayne was making amends and asking for forgiveness, acceptance. "If I dug my eye out," she said later, "this magnificent feat would make me a part of the tribe again." When Pat arrived at the hospital, Shayne, parked on a gurney, matter-of-factly pulled back the covering over her face. There on her cheek sat a tethered blue and white orb, almost like one of those cartoon characters whose eyes are attached to springs, Pat thought. Shayne was all satisfaction. She had gotten it out, and she did not want it saved. Pat waited to go home before she cried.

The tiny Winneshiek County Jail was ill-prepared for an inmate like Shayne and this was the result. When she had stayed there before her prison stint, the sheriff would offer Shayne a cigarette when she refused her medications, sitting with her, in violation of a no-smoking policy, as she smoked it. This was the jail's sum total of mental health care.

Shayne's life is a series of tragic chapters, a litany of a person, a family, and a system that was helpless against an illness. To be mentally ill like Shayne was to live a life of indignities and incapacity, of helmets and restraints, shackles and handcuffs, needles and pills. She was held against her will. She was used and thrown away. She was discharged so that she might be someone else's problem. She was not protected from herself. This was the life of a woman with schizophrenia, a strong will, and a hazardous yearning to live.

A one-eyed Shayne pleaded guilty to arson and assault with a dangerous weapon and began her second stint at the Iowa Correctional Institution for Women in Mitchellville in April 2001. In June 2002, Shayne "attacked someone again," as she put it in a letter to Aunt Pat, and she began five months of isolation in Mitchellville's segregation unit—in what inmates called "the hole." It was the one tried-and-true tool for inmates who could not otherwise be controlled. Shayne fit the bill. She had assaulted inmates three times in recent months, including a vigorous attack on a seated African-American inmate on whom she had a crush. "Bam-bam-bam-bam-bam," she described it, before officers wrestled her to the ground, tearing open her shirt in the process.

"At this time it is imperative that she is secured from assaulting others and causing any harm to herself," a prison psychologist noted in placing her in solitary confinement under what was called "intractable status"—a detail meant to connote that Shayne was not being punished. "Inmate's mental capacity does not allow for adequate comprehension of issues relevant to disciplinary case." If she had become assaultive in a hospital, Shayne would have been contained for a matter of hours or days until the crisis was past; at Mitchellville, it would stretch on for months.

This was the beginning of an end for Shayne. "They have taken everything from me," she wrote in her first days there. "I have to eat with my hands and I only get to use toothpaste on my teeth once a day with no brush. I can only have crayon to write. I am very sad at times." It would be another week before Shayne earned a pen to write with, six weeks before she got a Walkman, and two months before she could participate in a program that would let her earn her way out of isolation. "A miracle just happened," she wrote joyously to Pat when told of the program in mid-August. It would take another eight weeks of good conduct before she was released from the hole.

Throughout this period, Shayne was stoic. She completed "anger management assignments" and comforted her aunt several times when divorce was about to end her twenty-year marriage. "I know that you must be going through a hard time," she wrote. But the ordeal was wearing on her. According to a psychologist who recorded Shayne's demeanor once every week or two, she was "paranoid and guarded" at one point, displaying "distorted thinking" and "illogical thought process" at another. She expressed "considerable anger and resentment." "Aunt Patti, I don't want to suffer anymore. I've had enough," she wrote in early September.

By mid-October Shayne was released from the hole; by November, she was back in. "I don't mind being here," she told the psychologist on December 5. "I'm communing with God. I'm trying to get rid of the demons in me; I think I have one big one, can you imagine how Jesus felt when everyone abandoned him?"

The psychologist noted Shayne's "rambling thoughts" and, ironically, that she was not stable enough to return to the special needs unit—the unit where mentally ill inmates were, in theory, to receive the best care. Treatment for Shayne was the four walls of the hole and a regimen of deprivation. Karen Cox, an inmate assigned to watch Shayne through a tiny window in her steel cell door, saw the result.

Shayne had slept through most of the morning of December 21,

2002, a favorite preoccupation of inmates in solitary for whom day and night were virtually indistinguishable. When Cox checked her at 11:30 A.M., however, she noticed a change. Shayne had gotten up and was pacing the length of the small cell, back and forth, back and forth. This went on for about ten minutes. The next time Cox looked, Shayne was standing in place, her back to Cox and her hands on her face. She was moaning, almost like a woman making love. "Oh, oh," she said repeatedly. But she did not move. Cox put in check marks on the log she had been given: inmate standing, twice.

Then the moaning accelerated. Now it was like a woman in ecstasy, Cox thought, like a woman having an orgasm. "Yes baby, yes, yes," Shayne was saying. "Oh baby, oh baby." Karen peered in through the window and was not prepared for what she saw. Shayne was covered in blood. There was blood on her face, on her shirt, on the floor. Cox screamed wildly for help and banged on the walls of a raised glass control room nearby. Officers saw what happened on the unit's security camera. One officer arrived, looked in on Shayne, and threw up on the floor. Then a funny thing happened, at least as far as Cox was concerned. No one rushed into Shayne's cell to help her, no doctors or nurses or aides with gurneys. Instead, the officers of Building 6 got all dressed up, outfitted like they were going to a raid, with masks and shields and other protective gear. It took them twenty-three minutes to open the cell door. Shayne was known to be assaultive, sure, but a report of the incident would later suggest pointedly that officers needed to find a quicker, less confrontational method of responding to such emergencies.

Cox knew what awaited them. When she went back to the cell window, Shayne was holding her eye, the remnants of tissue and veins draped across her bloody face. It was an image she would never forget.

In 2004, Pat Jewell, who as the only family member in Iowa had been named Shayne's guardian, filed a lawsuit against the state of Iowa. It contended that Shayne's prolonged periods of isolation, combined with the refusal of jailers to protect her from her "mad self," had led to her mental deterioration, blinding, and assorted acts of self-mutilation. Incredibly, in the months after Shayne "enucleated" herself, as the lawsuit puts it, she was once again returned to the hole. There, she was so sick that she attempted to chew off her pinky, losing four teeth in the process. She also chewed a hole in her cheek and stuffed it with feces and vaginal secretions. Iowa prison officials "failed to transfer Plaintiff Shayne Elizabeth Eggen to a care facility which was equipped to provide care and treatment for her immediate serious and urgent medical needs," the lawsuit charged. Shayne was alleging "cruel and unusual" punishment in violation of the Eighth Amendment to the Constitution. These abuses had occurred in a solitary confinement cell. At this writing, the state has informally agreed to care for Shayne for the rest of her life.

A blind Shayne was released for the second time from the Iowa Correctional Institution for Women on May 2, 2005. This time, although she had also served her full sentence and had no parole officer to answer to, she did not walk to freedom with a hundred dollars and a couple of bottles of medication. Instead, she went to the Mental Health Institute in Independence. Her sentencing judge, who was not taking any chances, had ordered her civilly committed on completion of her prison term. Ironically, Shayne had been deemed sane enough to go to prison but too unbalanced to be let out.

CHAPTER THREE

Bedlam in Iowa

SHAYNE EGGEN NEVER GOT BETTER, not with each passing year, not with the transfer from mental hospital to juvenile facility to adult facility and back, not with the addition of Haldol, Prolixin, lorazepam, and many other drugs. Her illness made her feel "like being buried alive," she had written in a letter when she was twenty-five. "Like the movie about the little girl who fell down the well." A smart woman who understood more than she got credit for, Shayne became angry. Hospital staff blamed her for being sick. Doctors were concerned only with her mood and her medications, which incensed her. Her mother told her over and over that the illness was not the problem, the drugs were.

Shayne's education effectively stopped when she was institutionalized, and she did not graduate from high school, much less college. Her parents ceased to make any decisions for her. Don was characteristically detached in the aftermath; Elizabeth was overwhelmed by guilt and sorrow.

In giving Shayne up, Elizabeth came to believe that she consigned her daughter to an eternity of adolescence, allowing the state
of Iowa to medicate and confine her during her formative years.
Elizabeth never believed that Shayne was mentally ill—not after
Shayne gouged out both her eyes, jumped through windows, rolled
naked in shards of glass, or tried to strangle a barking dog. She was
endlessly patient with Shayne's musings about being an Indian and
having many husbands and hating herself intensely because she was
white. This wasn't illness, Elizabeth would insist; this was Shayne,
after a life of mind-altering drugs as dangerous as the illicit ones
they replaced. In Iowa, a state that once embraced lobotomy, where
state-of-the-art therapy once meant injecting mental patients with
enough insulin to cause coma before reviving them, where mental
patients had been wrapped in a cocoon of wet sheets so that they
could not move for hours, Elizabeth's theory makes a certain
amount of sense.

> *Of our 104 patients, 79 have shown some degree of improve-*
> *ment. We therefore conclude that a lobotomy program is*
> *worthwhile for state hospitals. It reduces the load on the*
> *attendants by decreasing violent behavior, it eases the lot of*
> *the patients by reducing tension and anxiety, and it allows*
> *the elimination of restraints to a considerable degree, thus, in*
> *effect, increasing the supply of institutional labor.*
> —Article in the Journal of the Iowa State Medical
>   Society, June 1954

As Shayne was growing up in the mental health system, a new
dynamic was emerging. From 1955 to 2005, Iowa went from having
204 psychiatric beds for every 100,000 residents to having six. It was

a relentless, half-century contraction in supply that left mental patients adrift and, by default, drove them into the arms of the law. In just the last half of the 1990s, when Shayne entered the Department of Corrections, Iowa prisons saw the proportion of inmates on psychotropic medications double, from 4 percent to 8 percent. By 2005, 16 percent of inmates were mentally ill; a year later, corrections officials revised the figure to 34 percent. A classic example of this hospital-to-prison shift was a male inmate in the early 2000s known as the Shoe Thief. The Shoe Thief could not help but steal shoes; he once took all the boots from a firehouse. He was in his late sixties and had spent two decades in Iowa mental hospitals for treatment of schizophrenia. Pushed into the community, he lived in facilities with little supervision or care. When he assaulted someone over a pair of shoes, he was imprisoned.

The closing of hospital beds, in Iowa and across the country, was prompted by the magic of medicine, the power of legal precedent, and the prodding of legislation. Mostly, however, it happened because state governments saw an opportunity, as these events unfolded, to save money. Federally-funded Medicaid would pay for psychiatric patients in nursing homes like Oneota in Decorah where Shayne lived for several years. It would not pay for their care in state psychiatric centers. Similarly, federal Supplemental Security Income, signed into law in 1972, would support ex-patients living in communities—often run-down adult homes or single room-occupancies—allowing states to shift costs elsewhere.

The Community Mental Health Centers Act was adopted in 1963, the year that Shayne was born. It was supposed to fill the void left by hospital closings. Evolving legal standards had made hospitals anachronistic; they gave patients the right to refuse to be hospitalized and to demand treatment in less restrictive settings, which new drug therapies made possible. The act was to help states offer services in communities to former psychiatric patients—to make sure they had housing, work, therapy, and support for their daily needs. What happened in Iowa, where only the barest patchwork of programs replaced the once-mammoth hospital system, was typical across the country.

In 2006, the National Alliance for the Mentally Ill gave the state an F in mental health care. "Iowa is a prime example of what President Bush's New Freedom Commission on Mental Health meant when it reported [in 2002] that the nation's mental healthcare system is 'fragmented and in disarray,'" the organization reported. At least Iowa was in good company.

Ben Wyatt, the police chief into whose shoulder Shayne had plunged a five-inch steak knife, had come to Shayne's small town in northeastern Iowa in 1992 after a twenty-four-year career as a police officer in Rochester, Minnesota. In 1982, when Wyatt was serving on the narcotics and vice squad, a state mental hospital closed in Rochester. Wyatt watched as mental patients turned up on the streets, pushed out of the hospital and abandoned by the system. They often ended up in jail. He never believed that Shayne was in her right mind when she stabbed him; he knew that she was one more victim of what he had seen in Rochester. "The reason she was prosecuted was because she was mentally ill and the criminal justice system was only way to get her into a facility of any kind, at least for a determined period of time," he said. He harbors no ill will toward Shayne. "I've healed but she never will. So I'm really the lucky one."

In the late 1980s and 1990s, other Winneshiek County police began to notice what Wyatt had. When they'd pick people up who were threatening suicide or were psychotic, they had increasing problems finding beds for them in a state mental hospital. Taken to private hospitals with psychiatric units, these people would be let out after a few days with no follow-up care, increasing their chances of a return trip. It became inevitable that when illness drove mentally ill people to destroy property, become a public nuisance, or assault someone, jail was where they ended up. There was simply no other place to put them.

In this milieu, in the era of abandoned mental patients, it was by sheer good fortune that Shayne stayed out of the criminal justice system for as long as she did. She had abused drugs. She had failed to take her medications. She had been prone to lash out violently. The time finally came on September 16, 1997, when a delusional Shayne demanded a turquoise knife, shattered a window, and attacked a police chief who was just trying to help.

While control is paramount in modern prisons, programs are scarce. The belief that inmates can be reformed in prison—through drug treatment, high school and college courses, and vocational training—ended in the mid-1980s, when the size of prison populations nationwide starting ticking relentlessly upward. In Iowa, the prison population more than tripled from 1985 to 2005. Four new prisons were built, including two on the grounds of former mental hospitals, and there were additions built to existing facilities, among them the women's prison in Mitchellville. From 1983, when a state correctional agency was established, to 2005, the prison budget quintupled from $59 million to more than $300 million. Growth was fierce, but it could not keep up; the system operated at 20 percent over capacity in 2005. More money spent to house inmates meant less available to help them. From 1991 to 2004, the education budget was slashed by two-thirds. Substance abuse programs were also cut, so that by 2004 they served just half of the inmates in need.

While hospital closings pushed the mentally ill to the streets, other forces drove them into prison and kept them there: the war on drugs, mandatory and longer sentences, and a trend away from early release through parole. Iowa prisons performed fewer than eight hundred psychiatric assessments in 1992 and spent just fifteen thousand dollars on psychiatric medications. By 2002, it provided nine thousand consultations and spent $1.2 million on drugs. Still, it was not enough.

Iowa, like many states, was not prepared for this onslaught, nor

had it attempted over the years to make much effort to accommo-
date it. It was a posture that would cause untold grief and suffering
for sick inmates and embarrassment for the system. It was also one
that would be deep rooted and difficult to change.

For thirty years, Iowa's prison mental health care was in the
hands of a man named Paul L. Loeffelholz, a psychiatrist who ran
the Iowa Security Medical Facility in Oakdale. Oakdale had three
missions: to evaluate inmates new to the system for mental and
physical problems; to perform court-ordered competency evalua-
tions for people awaiting trial; and to care for the system's most seriously mentally ill inmates. Care was a word that only vaguely
applied. At Oakdale, obstreperous inmates sometimes had their
mouths taped shut and slept on the floor in their underwear. If they
refused to get up, talked out of turn, or swore, they would be
injected with apomorphine to induce vomiting for up to an hour.
One prisoner, who had not been convicted of a crime but who was
being evaluated for competency, was locked naked and hog-tied in
an air-conditioned room for hours. Another was locked in his cell
around the clock, routinely denied food, and allowed to flush his
toilet only six times in a month. A state official described Oakdale as
"Iowa's version of Dachau," the Nazi concentration camp. It may
have been more apt to liken it to Bedlam or Bellevue or other asy-
lums with shameful histories of abuse of the mentally ill.

Loeffelholz's philosophy toward mentally ill criminals was an
unabashed mixture of disdain for coddling and insistence on responsibility. "Mental illness is no bar to a person's doing time," Loeffelholz would say, which meant two things: Regardless of their ability
to cope, convicted mentally ill inmates belonged in prison, not in
long-term psychiatric care, and few needed medication for their illness. The upshot was that mentally ill inmates were placed in the
general population, but not before nine out of ten were first taken
off their psychotropic drugs. In 1991, that is what happened to an
inmate named Craig Gardner, a six-foot, four-inch father of two,

who had taken monthly shots of Haldol for six years for schizo-phrenia. Gardner initially adjusted well at Iowa State Penitentiary, where he worked in the furniture factory, played guitar at weekly church services, and was a model inmate. Five months after his med-ication was withdrawn, however, Gardner became anxious, lost his appetite, and began to believe that officers were trying to kill him. One night, he snapped. He heard trains running through his head and saw legions of people peering through the window of his cell door, their faces pressed to the glass. He took apart his bed to make room for company he believed was coming and, using his clothing, plugged the toilet and flooded his cell.

As is typical in prisons, psychotic breakdowns are not cause for medical intervention but for overwhelming shows of force. No attempt was made to talk Gardner into leaving his cell. Instead, in order to force him out, an entire can of Mace, ordinarily used in one-second bursts, was emptied into his cell through a food slot in the solid metal door. Even the officers became disabled when the chemical shot back out through the slot. Gardner was left with severe burns across his abdomen and groin and he had disciplinary problems for the remainder of his prison stay. A report by the Iowa Citizens' Ombudsman concluded that the system's response to Gardner was "unreasonable, unprofessional, and unwarranted." It also likely wasn't isolated. Loeffelholz, with his insistence on treating mentally ill inmates just like all the others, was a huge part of the problem. Just 2 percent of Iowa inmates were diagnosed as mentally ill under Loeffelholz, while systems around the country had triple or quadruple that figure at the time. Clearly, mentally ill inmates were left to fend for themselves in Iowa's prisons, and here was one result.

In 1999, the Iowa Board of Medical Examiners concluded that Loeffelholz was negligent and incompetent. In ten of thirteen cases from 1983 to 1996, Loeffelholz routinely "exhibited a pat-tern of minimizing symptoms of mental illness and assuming that all aberrant behavior is a result of a rational choice by a responsible individual even in the face of extreme symptoms of psychosis." The psychiatrist, who had finished his third decade with the system by then, agreed to retire. But his philosophy of care was well established. For the inmates whose illnesses were never diagnosed or who were taken off medications and sent to the general prison population, it meant a prison stay marked by delusion, anxiety, and clashes with authority. Far too often, it also meant doing time in the one place where prison administrators could control them: solitary confinement.

Karen Cox has nightmares about her first and last day as an inmate monitor in the solitary confinement unit at the Iowa Correctional Institute for Women. Cox was fifty years old and a mother of four who was in prison because of a penchant for gambling that ran in her family. Her father had run poker games behind a truck stop and hosted a game for his buddies on Saturday nights, when the kids knew not to come home. Now Cox herself had stolen checks, forged her sister's name, and dearly regretted it. She wanted to do her time at Mitchellville as quickly as possible and get out. She had spent her first four months as a house cleaner in her dorm when she heard about an opening for a job in Building 6—otherwise known to inmates as "the hole." It was the place no inmate wanted to live in, where prisoners were locked around the clock in tiny cells with solid doors for disturbing the prison peace, fighting, or perhaps assaulting a guard. The monitor's job paid two dollars a day and would get Cox off her unit. She liked that. All she had to do was park herself at a table between two cells and every five minutes look in on two inmates who were under suicide watch. Peek through the window and check a box: Sitting on bed. Standing. Reading. Sitting on toilet. Easy. She could even read a book between rounds.

When Cox reported for work at 8 A.M. on December 21, 2002, she knew nothing about Shayne Eggen—not that she suffered from schizophrenia and had been hospitalized dozens of times. Not that two months before, she had tied the belt from a robe around her neck tight enough to have to be cut off. Not that she thought she was an Indian princess who performed chants and had gouged out one of her eyes in jail two years earlier. Cox had trained for a couple of days with another inmate, who had told her how to track inmate movements and get help if necessary. She was also told what not to do: Under no circumstances was she to talk to the inmates she was watching. Her predecessor had been fired for that; the idea of solitary confinement was to deprive inmates of human contact. House rules. Cox found this prohibition cruel. If anything, she thought that a little conversation could only help someone who was suicidal. Nonetheless, she complied.

On this day in 2002, Karen worked in the newest, most secure unit at Mitchellville, where corrections officers presided over three clusters of cells from a central console in a raised glass enclosure known as the "bubble." It was all very tidy and seemingly efficient, the video cameras in each inmate room, the electronically controlled doors that clanked and buzzed, and the panic button in case of a problem. Solitary confinement was something that Iowa prisons had honed and crafted over the years and had come to use increasingly as a place to put troublesome inmates who were mentally ill. These inmates often acted out in bizarre ways, refused orders, or got into fights; the surest way to contain them was the four walls and isolation of the hole.

Researchers have long known the effects on the human psyche of sensory deprivation, of long periods without talking to other people, without experiencing the normal buzz of human endeavor. The first prison in New York State had tried solitary confinement for eighty of its worst offenders in 1821 and abandoned it two years later after inmates became suicidal and psychotic. More than 150 years later, a study found that inmates kept in isolation at a prison in Massachusetts displayed alarming psychological changes. They became hypersensitive to prison noises, heard voices, and had panic attacks.

Some became obsessed with fantasies of torture, particularly of guards. Others hallucinated and engaged in self-mutilation. The conditions, it was concluded, were toxic to their functioning.

In 1990, an inmate named George Goff filed a federal lawsuit against the Iowa State Penitentiary in Fort Madison, the nation's oldest prison west of the Mississippi River, over its use of solitary confinement. Goff, joined by 190 other inmates, alleged that his time in the ISP "hole," also called Cellhouse 220, constituted cruel and unusual punishment in violation of the U.S. Constitution. The lawsuit took seven years to decide and shook the foundation of the Iowa prison system. The physical circumstances of Cellhouse 220 were purposefully extreme: confinement for twenty-three hours a day in rooms as small as forty-eight feet square with an area to stand in about the size of a dining table for four. There was little personal property, the barest of materials to keep an inmate busy, and virtually no human contact. No recreation occurred on weekends and none at all during the winter months.

> *I am still in the hole. . . . I spoke to [the prison psychologist]*
> *last week. She doesn't think it is healthy for me to be in here*
> *this long. She said she was going to say something but I*
> *think she forgot. . . . I don't really get a lot of attention in*
> *here. Day after day hour after hour I sit in here alone. I*
> *don't usually talk much anyway but it would be nice if*
> *someone would stop by my door. . . . People just don't seem to*
> *have time for me. . . . Being alone is torment.*
> —Letter from Shayne, age thirty-eight,
> to Aunt Pat, August 3, 2002,
> while serving four months
> in solitary confinement

Inmates were sentenced to the unit under a policy of "rigid consistency"—the judge's words—that lacked both logic and compassion. In one case, an inmate was sentenced to a year and a month for assault after spilling juice on an officer; another inmate got the same term for calling an officer Satan and spitting in his direction. An inmate could accrue multiple sentences for a temper tantrum, leading to sentences that stretched to three, nine, ten, twelve, and even fifty years—terms so long that they ceased to have any corrective benefit, which was the purpose of a prison disciplinary program. This consistency applied regardless of an inmate's mental health. Offenders who had grown up in mental institutions, who had been civilly committed many times, or who were known to spread feces on the walls and mutilate themselves were considered sane enough and responsible enough to do time in solitary. As a result, the prison's Cellhouse 220 was like an old-time madhouse with "yellers" and "head-bangers" who rose up in a cacophony of noise and were sometimes released directly into the streets—"walking time bombs," a prison expert called them.

Paul Loeffelholz, the system's foremost mental health official before he was charged with professional incompetence, found little problem with these conditions. Extraordinarily long sentences, he testified in the Goff lawsuit, were the inmates' way of saying "screw the system." He told the judge that people who cut themselves and smeared themselves with feces were not mentally ill but mentally disordered. In a strange display of circular logic, he testified that an inmate who said he banged his head against a wall to keep his dead father out may simply have been acting in a delusional manner as a way to avoid punishment for head banging. Loeffelholz was adamant: He would not accept violent inmates, however ill, into his psychiatric unit: "There is no alternative place for those kind of inmates," he said: no place but Cellhouse 220.

Like Karen Cox, the U.S. District Court judge in the case, Donald E. O'Brien, was outraged. "Iowa should be ashamed," he concluded. Care for mentally ill inmates—who then constituted 20 percent of the population in solitary—"falls astonishingly below" the Constitution's guarantee against cruel and unusual punishment, he found. He described conditions as "horrendously loud," the cells as "claustrophobically small," the units as places of "pandemonium and bedlam." He ordered a major overhaul.

O'Brien's decision was rendered in 1997, the year Shayne Eggen received her first prison sentence. In 2002, around the time that Karen Cox reported for work, the system opened a new 150-bed unit for mentally ill male inmates at the Iowa penitentiary—a direct result of O'Brien's ruling. The so-called clinical care unit was to solve the problems of solitary, the place where seriously mentally ill inmates would be sent to avoid putting them in the hole. In the unit, teams of professionals would counsel mentally ill inmates in a therapeutic setting, and inmates would have formal treatment plans that went beyond the provision of medication. This ideal, years in the planning, would prove illusory.

From February 2003 to November 2004, four inmates killed themselves in the unit. One stuffed toilet paper and underwear down his throat, another placed a plastic bag over his head, and a third swallowed hoarded pills. A fourth, who had been known to insert eating utensils in his rectum to stop his intestines from falling out, hung himself. Despite the trappings of a state-of-the-art facility, the culture of prison had not changed. The inmates' behavior had been viewed as so much acting out—"manipulative or attention seeking and not as the product of significant mental illness," counselors believed.

In a report following the deaths, an outside consultant found that the clinical care unit gave "virtually no professional therapy," had an unresponsive mental health staff, offered treatment plans on paper only, and relied almost completely on medication as a form of treatment. More broadly, just one psychiatrist served the entire system of nine prisons and eighteen hundred mentally ill inmates. Despite the investment of $26 million at the behest of an angry federal court, Iowa was still failing miserably in the care of its male mentally ill inmates. Things weren't much better at a twenty-five-bed special needs unit for mentally ill women at Mitchellville, where Shayne's case would be a prime example of vastly inadequate care.

In 2005, the Center for Public Representation, a legal advocate for the disabled, studied a small sample of records at Iowa's four mental health institutions and came up with an amazing finding. Aggressive patients at the hospital were being arrested for minor attacks on staff, sometimes due to the staff's clumsy attempts to restrain them. One case involved hair pulling, another pushing—the kind of thing that has long gone with the territory of caring for intensely ill people in mental hospitals. To the center's staff, this seemed an unconscionable abrogation of the hospital mission. It was also a sign of the times. By this time, jail was an accepted alternative for people with psychiatric disabilities, even among mental health professionals who should have been resisting such trends.

<hr />

On her release, Shayne did not look at all like the blue-eyed thirty-six-year-old who had left Mitchellville with so much enthusiasm five years earlier. Her hair had begun to show streaks of gray and her figure had lost its shape. Her eyelids hung like silent curtains over empty sockets. Her cheek was pocked and scarred. She had a large gap in her mouth from the teeth she had dislodged when she tried to chew off her pinky.

It was many months before I met Shayne while I was researching her life. Her sanity was too precarious, and her aunt and lawyers, not to mention those of the state, feared to test it. I got to know Shayne through her letters, her records, and her family, friends, and associates. Pat also asked Shayne questions on my behalf at their weekly visits to the hospital in Independence. Shayne's answers, as transcribed by Pat, were often succinct ("I bent over and got pregnant") and poignant.

Once I asked her through Pat to talk about her relationship with her parents. Her father, who died in 2003, hit her several times, she said, but she understood his anger and frustration in the face of the uncontrollable being that was Shayne. They both said mean things to each other. She believes he was afraid of her. "One time Pop came into the room and got down on one knee in front of me. He said, 'Shayne, I love you.' His eyes filled up with tears, and he left the room. I was so wild." As for Elizabeth, the answer was more complex. "I think she is so very, very beautiful," Shayne began. "I've decided not to feel guilty because I know I did the right thing with my life. . . . Pop was aggressive and I acted back with aggression towards him. Mom was just there," she said. "Mom never acted upon her deep feelings. Never really brought anything out."

Elizabeth understands these conflicts in Shayne. She was passive in the face of Shayne's rebellion and her husband's rage. She let the state take her daughter. Then Shayne said something else that wrapped this subject up in a beautiful, peaceful package: "To whom much is forgiven there is much love," she said, quoting from the Gospel according to Luke. "That applies to both Mom and Pop."

I visited Shayne at the Mental Health Institute in Independence in early September 2006. We sat at a picnic table with Pat and Elizabeth under an open pavilion, in the shadow of the first building opened at the institute in 1873. It was an imposing four-story edifice with lofty, arched windows, bracketed eaves and a mansard roof, the first of many at an institution through which more than eighty-six thousand patients would pass. On this day, it had fewer than one hundred. Shayne was dressed on our first meeting in dark blue jeans, a stretchy gray shirt that showed her belly rolls, and an unbuttoned pink overshirt. Her voice was strong and clear, her laugh hearty. It had been sixteen months since her release from prison, and she was, for Shayne, well.

She had not been told I was coming but was delighted to be the focus of such attention. For several hours over two afternoons, Shayne told me about her extraordinary life, about her crimes and her vision quests and her days of smoking pot, about her Indian chief and taking out her eyes and giving birth in handcuffs and being raped. She remembered a dead bird that had been put in her locker at school when people knew she was sick. She told me that she knew she had conquered her illness because she would not beat me up. As she spoke, she often rubbed her legs and arms excitedly. She wrung her hands and ran her fist through the long ponytail at the nape of her neck. She became especially animated when she spoke about a hospital carnival that week at which she had flirted deliciously with a resident named Jimmy. "I put my arms around him and looked into his eyes," she said, her arms raised to an imaginary man, her face uplifted in a swoon. "He's smooth," she kept saying, like a teenager in love. Elizabeth had picked up Chinese food, a favorite, and Shayne ate it voraciously.

I asked her about regrets. "Every once in awhile I get thoughts over and over and over," she said. "I hear people say, 'We didn't mean any harm by it.' They didn't mean any harm." Shayne believes that harm has been done to her. Shayne would like to see. She would like not to carry the scars of illness and incarceration. She did not choose this. Her eyes shuttered to but a hint of light, she performed for me a beautifully haunting Indian song that she had composed. In 2001, a mental health counselor summarized Shayne's history and the system's failure. Shayne needed treatment for both her mental illness and drug abuse, yet no such facility existed for women in Iowa, he said. "I do not believe we have ever found a set of services that have effectively met Shayne's needs." Typically, he went on to blame Shayne, three separate times, for her "unwillingness to accept" her diagnoses and to stay on her medications. Except for her illness, the counselor seems to say, she might even be well.

Shayne has felt this, felt blame for emotions more powerful than herself. "I think mental illness is the excuse we're not allowed to have," she concluded, before going back to her Chinese food.

When she isn't sad or terrified or angry or crazy, when she is not being contained or confined or punished, when she is Shayne the person and not the patient, Shayne Eggen, a blind, damaged Indian princess, does indeed know things.

PART TWO

LUKE

—◦◦◦—

For five years, Tricia had been Luke's fixer. When he took too many pills, accidentally or otherwise, she'd walked him in a loop from room to room, over and over, his bulky mass on her feathery shoulder, until he was straight enough to sleep. When thoughts nibbled at the inside of his skull, telling him that he was slipping away, losing it, she calmed him, reasoned with him, made appointments for him. When her twenty-year-old, six-foot-three-inch bear of a kid with size 14 shoes cried, she held him and cried inside with him. This was the younger of her two children, her only son, a boy who'd hugged her in elementary school in front of everyone, a boy who'd raised guinea pigs and wanted to be a paramedic. A boy who, much later, took to taking Ecstasy and smoking pot and hearing voices that weren't there.

Tricia Ashley was a small Texas woman in blue jeans with salt-and-pepper hair that flowed down her back like tumbleweed. She had a pretty, chiseled face with a delicate aquiline nose, a quick smile, and a throaty laugh. She was nothing if not tough. If she didn't know how to fight the thing that was fighting Luke, she'd find out. She'd do what was necessary in that can-do native-Texan way of things.

When Luke fell apart, Tricia knitted his frayed emotions. She took a course and learned all she could about the diagnosis that Luke had been given: bipolar disorder. She worked the phones and e-mail, called lawyers, and visited counselors and probation officers. She could always find something to do to keep things moving forward or to at least make it seem that way. Take Luke to the remote-controlled car races and away from unseemly friends. Write him letters that beseeched him to fight. Find him a job. Get him out of bed. Give him a hug. She could always do something, until now. Now her Luke was twenty-four, a grown-up man. Despite all her warnings and trips to the mental health clinic, despite the dozen medications that never seemed quite right, despite the breakdowns that had sent him to the mental hospital a half dozen times, his and her worst fears had been realized: he was in a cell at the Williamson County Jail.

CHAPTER FOUR

Fear and Ecstasy

LUKE HAD SPENT HIS FORMATIVE years, from six to fourteen, in Palm Springs North, a mostly Hispanic neighborhood in the sprawl that is Miami-Dade County. It was a low, dense suburb of strip malls, palm trees, and billboard-speckled boulevards sandwiched between I-75 and I-95 and criss-crossed overhead by the jets of Miami International Airport. Like many metropolitan areas in the early 1990s, Miami and its suburbs were at the crest of a two-decade crime wave during which drive-by shootings and drug trafficking were common fare. Palm Springs North was a small oasis—a decent neighborhood and one that the Ashleys could afford on David's salary for fixing elevators and Tricia's substitute teaching.

Luke was a cute kid with hazel eyes, a toothy smile, and thick blond bangs who initially thrived in PSN, as it was known. He played flag football, soccer, and Little League baseball, happily and without the competitive edge expected of boys. He was a little spaced-out, but so what? He'd zone out in the outfield or run the wrong way in soccer. He'd hit the ball and forget to run to base. Clumsy and big, he'd place last in the sack races at the annual union picnic. But he would always come back for more. David Ashley coached most of the teams he played on, hoping, as fathers do, to develop a winning athletic prowess in Luke. There were scattered moments of triumph, as when a diarrhea-challenged Luke, the football team's center, slogged through a championship game with intermittent visits to the bathroom. The ensuing victory ranks as a golden Ashley family memory.

More typically, Luke was the kid who did not fit in. He soon grew too big to play football with kids his age but was too young to play with older kids. At the age of ten he was overweight, had poor eyesight, and wore size 12 shoes; he was tantalizing prey for bullies. They let the air out of his bicycle tires and taunted him about his thick, horn-rimmed glasses. A sensitive boy who could be crushed by the merest cross word, Luke was easy to play.

What David called his own "rough and tumble" ways—cultivated during a tough Miami upbringing—were passed on not to Luke but to his sister Dena, a pretty girl with long honey-blond hair, blue eyes, and a sharp tongue. While Luke quaked at the bogeyman that was Miami, Dena stuck her finger in its eye. Dena, almost four years older, was the champion of her stories; Luke was the chump in his. Once, when a boy at school grabbed her backpack, Dena wheeled around, caught him by the neck and told him to get his hands off her. When it was Luke's turn to have his knapsack snatched, a well-placed punch from the boy sent him stumbling to a bathroom where a teacher accused him of skipping class.

Fearless and outgoing, Dena became Luke's protector, as well as his friend. After school, the siblings and their friends would hit the pavement on skateboards, riding the curbs, streets, and sidewalks like a pack of wild dogs. They'd order breadsticks brushed with garlic butter at an Italian fast-food chain, then head to a friend's backyard skate ramp. With Dena, Luke would be free to be his uncoordinated self, safe from the hazards of the 'hood. He'd tell silly middle school stories and mash Cheetos on his face. He would laugh uproariously on a candy high. These were the treasures Dena would take from PSN. Luke would remember the fear.

In 1992, Luke, thirteen, began his freshman year at American High School in Hialeah. Part of the sprawling Miami-Dade school district, American was a place where students went through metal detectors, German shepherds sniffed lockers for drugs, and students died with some regularity. A girl was killed by a jealous boyfriend, a boy died when he was hit by a train while spraying graffiti, another boy perished in a gang shooting. Dena had witnessed a boy getting shot during lunch hour in front of the school. There were routine drug busts and knife fights, and police were a constant presence. The school and its environs were no place for a kid like Luke, who was wound so tightly that he once dove for the bushes at the honk of a passing car—with Dena in it.

Tragedies in the Ashley circle compounded Luke's natural apprehensions. When Luke was eight, a close family friend named Brian, twelve years old, was skateboarding across a street in the neighborhood when he ran into the back of a truck and suffered a brain injury. He remained in a coma for several years, then died. Dena visited Brian often in a rehab center; Luke went occasionally. A year after the accident, other close friends—a father and his daughter, five years old—were killed in a horrific car crash just before Christmas. Dena helped the girl's mother, who had been driving the car, unwrap the presents that had been placed for them under the tree. The Ashley family prayed together and cried together and questioned why such things happen. Luke's response to these events was to withdraw into the safety of the family's beige-and-brown ranch house on NW 185th Terrace, content to play with his Transformers and Star Wars characters and to watch cartoons for hours.

That first year at American High, Luke began to ask his parents if they could move back to Texas, where he'd been born and had lived until kindergarten. He wanted to live someplace where it wasn't so scary, he said, where he wasn't afraid to go to school. The Ashleys wanted to do right by Luke, and they thought he had a point. Besides, Tricia's family was in Texas. She had met David after moving to Florida at the age of twenty and they were married eighteen months later. They had lived in Texas for several years and knew they would return sometime. So in 1994, the Ashleys pulled up stakes and settled outside Austin, where office buildings were going up and David could find work installing elevators.

Things did not work out as Luke had hoped. In Miami, he had played second-string varsity football in ninth grade. In Round Rock High School outside Austin, he rarely got to play. In Miami, he had studied Italian, which he loved, but it wasn't offered in Round Rock. He had to start from scratch with Spanish, which left no time to take computer science, a subject he was so good at in Miami that he'd been the teacher's helper. In Miami, he'd aspired to join the photography club, but Round Rock didn't have one. Once again, Luke was a misfit who stood out even for his clothes: oversized shirts and precariously perched jeans that weren't yet the style in the Lone Star state. He was as discontented in Texas as he'd been in Florida— though none of his friends ever knew it.

The Luke Ashley his friends knew was funny, easygoing, larger than life. He'd drive into the school parking lot blaring Beethoven on the stereo one day and Notorious B.I.G. the next. A slow, three-hundred-pound lineman on the football team, he would put a hairnet or underwear on his head for a guaranteed laugh. He would make light of his outsider status, playfully drawing out "y'all," or insisting, "Steers and queers come from Texas," a line from the film *Full Metal Jacket*. Luke was a gentle friend to legions of girls, who thought him charming and sweet. Safe, they called him; a teddy bear. The Luke they knew took two girls to the prom when one's date fell through, and he so loved things in a black-and-white cow motif that they called him Mookie (a variation on Lukie). Their Luke gave them rides, smelled sweetly of the clove-laced cigarettes he smoked, and always had pot and shared it. He had first tried it at the age of ten in Miami. In Round Rock, his consumption was legendary. While friends toked on skinny joints and quit early in the evening, Luke did cigar-sized "blunts" well into the night. Afterward, he'd boast about it, belying what many saw as an adolescent insecurity behind his thick glasses, jowly cheeks, and intermittent acne. What his friends did not know was that Luke was wracked with self-doubt. He suffered at the least slight, was afraid a lot, and could not concentrate for long on anything. They did not know that he would go home and cry like a baby after football games, so frustrated that he hadn't played.

"I stay very withdrawn," Luke later wrote on a mental health questionnaire that asked if people around him were supportive. "They don't know much." To his parents, Luke was a work in progress, a kid—like many—with bad habits and imperfections that were supposed to be worked out in adolescence. At least that was what they hoped.

In October 1998, police were called to an unsupervised party of minors at which Luke had just arrived. He hadn't even had time to have a drink, and, besides, he didn't much like alcohol. Other kids fled in panic, but he was confident that he would not be arrested. The law, he found, didn't work that way. He and a couple of dozen others were hauled off and charged with "minor in possession of an alcoholic beverage," a misdemeanor. Luke pressed both palms to a fingerprint pad; turned in his clothes, pager, belt, necklaces, earrings, $1.64, cigarettes, and shoes, and was held overnight at Williamson County Jail—the longest night of his life, he would later write. He was fined, sentenced to six hours of community service, and made to write a research paper on the evils of alcohol. He did so dutifully and without derision. He was nineteen, old enough to vote and enlist in the army, and an age at which alcohol consumption is legal in most countries in the world. He even worked legally at the time as a bartender. The experience was one of several encounters with the police that multiplied his fear of the law and of jail.

At the time of his first arrest, Luke was a young man who loved his car, had worked from the time he was fourteen, smoked too much pot, and had the vaguest sense of impending disquietude. The summer before, he had taken a magical trip with a high school girl-friend, Allison Olofson, and her family to New Mexico, where he relished the scenery and culture—the caves of Carlsbad, the aliens of Roswell, fishing in the sparkling rocky pools of Rio Ruidoso. One night, sitting on the porch of a cabin overlooking the river, Luke confessed to Allison that his marijuana smoking was more than just an exercise in getting high. It made him feel better; it made him feel clear, he said, in a way that Allison, a straitlaced country girl to Luke's hip-hop cool boy, would not forget.

When he was nineteen, Luke discovered a new passion at the pulsing dance parties of Austin's legendary Sixth Street. If the clothes, lights, and camaraderie of these raves were the sweetest cake, Ecstasy was the icing. "With Ecstasy," said a friend of Luke's from that time, "you love and love and love some more." Luke fell hard. But while marijuana mostly made him friends, Ecstasy would cost them.

Around this time, Luke took up with a high school friend who had long been the object of a crush. It was a tender interlude after a lifetime of flirting, the fulfillment of a longing. On the night of their first kiss, five years after their meeting, Luke told her he had dis-covered X. What an awesome high it was, he said. They made love twice after that, and they seemed to share the belief that this could go somewhere. Luke was never the type to take what he could get from a woman and move on; it was part of the whole Luke that so many women loved. But this time, he simply stopped calling her. Later, he dated another woman and was taking a thirty-day breather from drugs so he could pass a urine test for a job. He kept telling her how much he liked being straight; he was going to try it for a while. After he passed the test, Luke turned on a dime. He reveled in the wonder of being high again as if he'd never considered going straight. The woman ended the relationship.

Soon Ecstasy was running Luke. It cost $20 to $25 a pill at the time and required more and more hits with each use. Luke had always had a tendency to exaggerate his illicit endeavors in that insecure way of his. But when he told several people that he sometimes took twenty Ecstasy pills a night, they believed him. He wasn't bragging. He was confessing. He had gone too far and he knew it. He told a couple of friends that he had overdosed one night and that his mother had nursed him through it. He wondered if Ecstasy had "short-circuited" his brain, he told another. He was also occasionally selling X to finance his habit, once getting into debt to a dealer he feared. Money had long been an issue between him and his parents because he couldn't stay employed and make payments; now, his need for cash was relentless. It made him do things he would otherwise not have done.

Good, years-long friends accused him of taking money from a wallet. They cut him off, argued with him, took him back. When a close female friend rebuffed him, he followed her home from work and pounded on her front door, demanding to be let in. He was desperate to explain himself, but she was too scared to listen. He was too strung out. She had loved him before he got like this. Many had.

Luke's family saw the changes, too. In November 1999, the Ashleys took a trip to Disney World with Dena and her new husband, a belated, bring-the-family-along honeymoon that says a lot about the Ashley family. Luke was now twenty; Dena, who had eloped the previous July, was twenty-four. On other such trips, the family had camped or stayed in cheap motels in nearby Kissimmee. This time, in celebration of Dena's birthday and marriage, they took rooms within Disney World. Luke was not himself. He slept until noon while the family toured the park. When he finally did get up, he wanted to go off by himself. When anything whatsoever went wrong, he would announce, "The trip is ruined." Dena thought Luke had been smoking too much pot, that he was in a sort of withdrawal. His drug use became a source of friction between them, and for the first time in a lifetime as best friends, a reason to hide things from her. Things did not get better on the trip. While they were away, Tricia's father died in a nursing home and the family headed to Houston. Luke walked into the wake, looked, walked out, and threw up in the bushes outside the funeral home.

Luke began to lose weight. In high school, he had weighed over three hundred pounds and had a puffy Pillsbury Doughboy sort of physique, his eyes recessed above fleshy cheeks and a double chin. By his twenty-first birthday, he had shed more than one hundred pounds and was long, lean, and chiseled. When a friend asked him how he'd lost the weight, he laughed and said that eating dulled an Ecstasy high—typical Luke.

Far more was going on. Luke's life by then had become a cycle of highs and lows—spurts of mania when he would be awake for days, and bouts of depression when he would stay in boxer shorts all day, his unbathed body leaden and unresponsive. He told one person that he'd developed anorexic eating habits. As he lost pounds, he also lost jobs, going through thirteen in the three years after high school graduation. He would oversleep and not show up; he would fall asleep at a computer. He would be gung-ho one day, lackluster the next. During one manic phase, he believed that a coworker had intentionally tripped his girlfriend, a waitress. He pinned the man to the wall, one of few times that Luke had shown any aggression. He was fired on the spot.

In the spring of 2000, Tricia helped Luke to get a job as a computer technician in the watch manufacturing company where she was an office manager. Luke had always been a whiz at computers, solving his friends' software problems and speaking the arcane language of computer geeks. This, he thought, could lead some-where. "Computers have caught my interest time and again," he wrote on his résumé, "and it would be great to have a career in a field I am so intrigued by." Luke's enthusiasm quickly soured. He would forget tasks, call in sick, or be unable to sit still. He'd quit one day and beg for his job back the next. When he couldn't figure things out, he railed to Tricia that he'd been left to fend for himself and was underpaid to boot. He'd cry in frustration, shedding real tears, as he always had, when life seemed to turn against him.

In October 2000, a month after turning twenty-one, Luke took Tricia aside at work. He could not control his thoughts and feelings, he told her. He knew there was something terribly wrong with him, and he was terrified. Then he said, "Mom, sometimes I feel like I'd be better off dead."

Tricia had managed Luke for years—his moods, his tears, the dis-appointments that he showed to no one else. She made an appoint-ment for him at Bluebonnet Trails Community Health Center. When he left Bluebonnet on a November day in 2000, he had a ten-tative diagnosis of bipolar disorder, a disease that, he was told, was chronic and would need long-term management. He had a pre-scription for Depakote, a drug meant to soften the mania associated with the disorder. He was assured that if the drug interfered with his ability to perform sexually (the only side effect he inquired about) it could be changed. He was relieved in a way that some of his ques-tions had been answered, and unsettled by others that loomed. When he got home, he called Dena in Houston and said, "It's offi-cial, I'm crazy."

The entry in Luke's file for his first visit to Bluebonnet Trails reads: "21 year old male living with parents, suffering with depres-sion, irritability, weight loss, hopelessness, memory loss (long + short term), anxiety, anger, rages, excessive guilt, confusion, sleep-lessness (up for 28–48 hours at time), loss (grandfather last year), crying spells, paranoia, no present thought suicide (have cross [sic] mind in past), no recent attempt, nervousness, suddenly scared for no reason, restlessness, worthlessness, feeling lonely."

Chrissy Malson was a newly minted social worker at Bluebonnet when she met Luke Ashley, by then a young man who was broad and tall, with a thick neck, hazel eyes, and wire-rimmed glasses. He had a straggly goatee, cropped brown hair, and a small stud earring in each ear. He wore baggy jeans low on the hips, an orange nylon shirt that seemed a bit loud, and what Texans called tennis shoes, better known to the easterner Chrissy as sneakers. Chrissy was twenty-three and just out of college, a petite young woman with long, thick red hair swept up in a clip and blue eyes behind wire-frame glasses. She, nonetheless, knew a thing or two about disorders of the mind. Mental illness had made an indelible mark on her childhood; it ran in both sides of her family. She immediately felt protective of Luke for the demons he suffered, internal and external.

For some clients of Chrissy's, especially the homeless ones and those abandoned by their families, mental illness had become a way to get things—a bed for the night, some cigarettes, a cold drink. Some came in when the rent was due, others to escape the Texas heat in an air-conditioned hospital room. Luke wasn't there yet. He was more than an illness, especially to himself. He was twenty-one and struggling to live the life he thought he should—a job, girls, parties, family. He had ambitions of working with computers and getting his own apartment. He wanted to get married someday. Mostly he wanted not to be such a burden to his parents. But he could not hold anything together. He had always had highs and lows, but they'd been like the gentle shift of a pendulum compared to the wild trapeze ride he was on now. He was so anxious about everything, so unable to cope even in the least challenging of circumstances. He was either ridiculously energized or terrifyingly inert. He had thought about killing himself.

Chrissy scribbled notes as the Bluebonnet psychiatrist took Luke through the paces. He sat in a metal frame office chair, his butt slumped forward on the black vinyl seat, his huge legs and feet fairly filling the office's small patch of cheap, all-season carpeting. The furnishings were symptomatic of Bluebonnet's thin resources. The staff cared, they tried, but there was so little money and so many patients. Chrissy's pay was terrible, and the clinic hadn't seen a budget increase in years. Psychiatrists came and went like burger flippers at a fast-food joint, tired of running patients through a mill.

Chrissy thought that Luke was scared out of his mind. He offered nothing until asked, but it was clear he'd answer any question, give any information, if it might lead somewhere, might make him feel better. She'd seen a lot of people chafe at the time and the paper-work of the intake process. The give-me-drugs-and-let-me-go types. That wasn't Luke. He talked about his girlfriend, Stephanie, his sex life, his desire to be normal.

Over the next tumultuous year, Chrissy held Luke's hand, worked on his medications, reserved hospital beds, and made referrals. She worked hand-in-glove with Tricia, who was a rarity among the people on her caseload—a mother who was energetic, organized, and involved. Other families made it easy for the system to treat their charges like so many numbers. Tricia would have none of that, a trait that Chrissy admired. She was an advocate who would not let anyone forget that Luke was loved, that he had a history long before he had an illness.

An ever-changing mixture of drugs, legal this time, made him gain weight and lose his sex drive. He was still manic at some times, depressed at others. His hands shook and his head twitched. A friend who ran into him after his diagnosis saw what seemed like a veil over his once-vibrant face. He hugged her, but there was no emotion there.

Luke's path to the Williamson County Jail began seven weeks after his diagnosis when he was stopped for driving 42 miles per hour in a 30-mph zone. He was behind the wheel of his snappy green Pontiac Sunfire, which had a supercharged stereo system that had often attracted the attention of Round Rock's vigilant police force. Luke was struggling mightily at this point, staying awake for two to three days at a time, then crashing for twenty-four hours straight. He was still having mood swings and anxiety attacks, and he was frustrated because the medications they'd prescribed at Bluebonnet were not kicking in. He was missing days of work and had failed to show up for therapy at Bluebonnet so many times that his file had been closed. Moreover, he had been using Ecstasy and marijuana because these were the things that made him feel better. If there could have been a worse time for him to be arrested, it was hard to imagine.

When an odor of pot wafted out of the window, Officer Robert Mata requested backup and informed Luke that he wanted to search the car. The felony complaint describes Mata's discovery of some marijuana and, in a black backpack, a clear plastic Ziploc bag with two pills, one green with the number 88, and the other white with a Mitsubishi trademark. Mata knew, "through my training and experience," that this was 3-4 methylenedioxymethamphetamine, better known as Ecstasy. Ecstasy, also called the "love drug," is a potion with a punch, a chemical sister of the stimulant methamphetamine and the hallucinogen mescaline. Its possession, concludes the stock-issue complaint form signed by Mata, was "against the peace and dignity of the State." It was December 28, 2000, in Round Rock, Texas, a rapidly growing Austin suburb situated in Williamson County, which had a reputation for being tough on crime. It had the lowest crime rate among Texas counties with more than one hundred thousand citizens—a statistic that prosecutors intended to uphold.

Luke spent a terrifying night in the Williamson County Jail, hysterical and convinced that he was going to die. He tried to choke himself and passed out. Three weeks after that, having gone for days without sleep or food, he was hospitalized for the first time at Austin State Hospital. "I want stuff to make sense," he said when he was admitted.

During the next three years, Luke's entanglement with the law would be a determining factor in the course of both his illness and his addiction, a burden so great that it undeniably made the thing it was meant to address—his drug abuse—far worse, and with it his psyche. America is a bad place for anyone, mentally ill or not, to become addicted to illegal drugs. This nation does not suffer its weak citizens lightly, nor do its drug laws make much distinction, in terms of criminality, between the people who traffic in illicit drugs and those who use them, something the Ashley family would come to learn.

If December 2000 was a bad time for Luke to be arrested, Williamson County was a bad place, with its take-no-prisoners attitude toward crime in general and drugs in particular. Take Ismael Velasquez. Velasquez, forty-seven, was released from Williamson County Jail in January 2005, after serving ten months for cocaine possession. He made the mistake of immediately coking up and getting caught. A plastic bag with a trace amount of cocaine was fished by pursuing police from a toilet, an offense that normally would have drawn six months to two years. But Velasquez had seven previous felonies for auto theft and drug possession, and prosecutors did not like that he had tried to ditch the drugs. He rejected what the district attorney thought was a real deal: a plea and a thirty-year sentence. Instead, a jury gave him twenty years for possession and eighty years for evidence tampering.

Williamson County's trademark prosecutorial toughness was pioneered by Ken Anderson, who had been district attorney for fifteen years when Luke Ashley was arrested in 2000. Under Anderson, the county had become known as being so heavy-handed in its plea bargaining that some defense attorneys from Austin refused to practice there. Defendants and their lawyers were treated with an equal measure of contempt. "The defense attorney takes on the persona of the defendant," Betty Blackwell, a former president of the Texas Criminal Defense Lawyers Association, told a reporter for the *Austin Chronicle* in 2004. "This doesn't exist almost anywhere else where they recognize the Sixth Amendment right to be represented by an attorney." In Williamson County, defense attorneys were expected to be cooperative and accepting of both plea agreements and long prison sentences. After all, the alternative, as in the Velasquez case, might be quite a bit more unpleasant.

When Luke was arrested in 2000, he didn't have much choice but to cop a plea. The knapsack the Ecstasy was found in wasn't his, he said, but it was in his car and he declined to say who it belonged to. Besides, he did have some familiarity with the drug. In his favor, his record was clean; his only other arrest, two years earlier, had been sealed. That had been another case of Williamson County's zeal to uphold legal and moral codes; but for a harrowing night in jail, Luke suffered few serious consequences. That would not be the case this time.

CHAPTER FIVE

Ten Days

LUKE'S CRIME WAS THE POSSESSION of two pills of Ecstasy, a felony that got him four years' probation, $3,000 in fines, and three hundred hours of community service—mountains too steep for a guy on a bigger hill. Luke's drug use was what twentysomethings did in the hip-hop/rap/techno scene that was fashionable in downtown Austin. He loved to connect with friends, wear outrageous clothes, and dance with abandon on an Ecstasy high. But for him, taking drugs was far more than a social experience—it was also inextricably linked to his psyche, a frenetic, and usually private, struggle to escape the voices that taunted him, telling him he was worthless and going nowhere because of his infected mind. His depression was paralyzing, his mania exhausting, his fears relentless. He stayed in bed or stayed awake for days on end. He lost jobs and racked up bills. He got addicted, got clean, relapsed, and contemplated suicide. He was ill enough to be deemed disabled by the federal government—not an easy sell—the first time he applied for Social Security.

After two and a half years on probation, in late 2003, Luke's urine tested positive for methamphetamine, Vicodin, and marijuana. It was a time when his depression and anxiety were out of control; he sometimes could not tell if he was hallucinating or dreaming. As a result of the violation, he was sentenced to a special program for people with drug and mental problems, a regimen that might actually do him some good. The question was whether Luke would survive the four-month wait for an opening. During that time he would be held in a small cell at the Williamson County Jail in an effort, it seemed, to prevent him from popping pills or smoking dope—at a cost to taxpayers of seventy-five dollars a day, or roughly nine thousand dollars. It was an all-expenses-paid trip to a place that terrified him. "The client has an increased panic response when he deals with the law," a counselor had written in his file eighteen months earlier, including fears of "being behind bars," and suicide.

At twenty-four, Luke was a far cry from the nineteen-year-old of his first arrest. This Luke had an ornate tattoo on his back of red, blue, and green dragons—colors that often matched his hair—intertwined inside the characters of the Chinese calendar. He had tongue and nipple rings; he had inserted bars into his eyebrow and the skin between his shoulders and stretched the holes in his earlobes to the size of dimes. He had driven nails through his ears and cut designs into his arms. "The physical pain takes his mind off the mental pain and emptiness somewhat," a counselor wrote in 2001. "Said he feels hollow and frozen inside." This Luke had been diagnosed, hospitalized, and medicated.

Five days before he entered the Williamson County Jail, Luke sat scrawling away during one of his long interludes without sleep, writing in choppy cursive waves on two sheets, front and back, of a 5-by-8 notepad that the Ashleys kept by the telephone on the kitchen counter. In this disjointed tract, Luke was turning his problem over in his head, analyzing it, trying to figure out where in the scheme of things he, his troubled mind, and his drug habit fit.

He had failed a drug test and knew what awaited him. He was angry and scared. The words poured out of him in a jumble with the tiniest glimmers of clarity and insight:

> *I am crazier than I thought For my safety could mom stay home with me Ive held back my thoughts of society and the way things are and what effect they have on me and at last what repercussion's those effects endure me when still I am misunderstood as criminally minded which in no case am I at all criminally minded . . . this is simply not a legalize drugs campaign it's a example leading to this question theres two kids both know right and wrong they both do wrong simple equation heres where it gets tricky where they both know right and wrong one knew why right and wrong was acceptable to society and right on the other hand the other kid knew not of this society . . . this boy understood but couldn't help to notice this society was not right (to him) no generalizations or attacks being made also this has nothing to do with drugs at all!!!!*
>
> *Like being the first foreigner of a distant land to a place of fear based people who hate and destroy and exhile things of difference or defect where the non sentient have no fight in disposal the sentient have to fight with all they have to make people feel their a part of society till one day the fight becomes harder and harder.*

The family found Luke's musings the next day. How would he ever survive in the Williamson County Jail?

Jail was a place tailor-made for Luke's depression to flourish, for his worst inclinations about himself to be proven true. He was a twentysomething mental case, the child from whom all family strife flowed, while his older sister met the normal goals of adulthood—marrying, working, living independently. A young man with manic depression and a burning urge to escape from himself, Luke was now officially a criminal, jumpsuit and all. It was an identity he loathed, a label like flypaper that he'd peel off one finger only to find it stuck to another. His probation officer had said he was a manipulative drug user, a thief whose parents should throw him out. The Ashleys had rejected that—though they had moments when they were tempted. There had been many battles with Luke, over money, motivation, madness. They had put locks on the valuables. They had paid off his irresponsible credit card bills, carried the car loan that his father had cosigned. They'd threatened, goaded, and tried to engender guilt, once even throwing Luke out for a night after he pawned his PlayStation, their gift to him. Ultimately, they didn't see the point of abandoning him. "All this country needs is one more homeless mentally ill person," Tricia would say.

But now, his fate was out of their hands. Luke was one more jailed mentally ill person, among the imprisoned legions who couldn't conform. The schizophrenics who assaulted cops in the midst of paranoid delusions. The deeply disturbed whose breaks with convention should have landed them in hospitals. The bipolars, like Luke, who depended on illegal drugs to get them through the day. In the end, Luke's mental illness would not be the thing that would break the Ashley family. It was the convergence in 2003 of two social revolutions—deinstitutionalization of the mentally ill and the war on drugs—that would come home to David and Tricia Ashley's two-story frame house in a subdivision at the edge of a six-hundred-acre ranch in the Austin suburb of Round Rock.

Tricia was all done in. There was no one else she could call, no power her determined force could muster. All that was left was to keep Luke together by visiting and writing him in jail, giving him what money she could for supplies from the commissary, lining up friends and relatives to support him, and accepting his daily collect calls. On these, she would counsel him as she always did, be his cheerleader, coach, and confessor all rolled into one.

The phone was ringing at the Ashley residence at 4:55 P.M. on

December 4, 2003, just after Tricia returned home from her job as an office manager at a manufacturing firm in Austin. As usual, it was she who answered. Luke's father, David, was devoted and loving in a traditional way, breadwinner to Tricia's nurturer. David had taken the young Luke fishing, and coached him at soccer, football, and baseball. He had enforced the rules when necessary, particularly over Luke's failures at finance, with his sheer physical presence—six foot five, barrel-chested, and baritone voice. But when Luke was hurting or needed something or wanted to talk, it was Tricia he turned to. She was his rock. And now Luke wanted Tricia to fix this, to get him out of this cell where he had driven his fist into a wall, where someone had punched him and, he believed, was trying to kill him.

Luke's calls, which were taped by the jail, were played for Tricia in a grand courtroom in Austin. Her son's electronically recorded voice lingered briefly among the warm maroon draperies, the brass eagle on the paneled wall above the judge's head, the hard pewlike benches where Tricia's sister and cousin and a few other interested people sat and listened. The audio was scratchy, but the inflections, the desperation, were clear. It was a December day in 2005, and Tricia was on the witness stand, the first witness on the first day in the case of *Ashley v. Williamson County*. Her hair was ironed and silky and she wore a smart, tapered pants suit that she had bought for this day. A defense lawyer was cross-examining her. Although she knew of the tapes, and even had copies of her own, she had not ever listened to them. She could not go there. For that reason, her own attorney in this lawsuit would not play them.

It was Luke's tenth day in the Williamson County Jail, and something had happened, something had broken loose inside him. Over the next few hours, corrections officers would hear the same voice, and in it they would hear anger, willfulness, and defiance. But they did not know Luke, nor did they know about this illness of his. Like a claustrophobic passenger on an airplane who in midflight simply has to get off, Luke is panicking. He is paranoid, believing that

people are out to get him or to abandon him. And he is overwhelmed with a debilitating, irrational fear, the kind he has lived
with for the past two years.

Tricia presses the obligatory number to indicate she will accept
Luke's collect call.

Tricia:	Hey. *(Silence)* Luke?
Luke:	What!?
Tricia:	Oh. What's going on? Dad said you called like three times today.
Luke:	I haven't talked to nobody.
Tricia:	No, the phone kept picking up—the answering machine answered.
Luke:	Yeah, why didn't you pick up?
Tricia:	Luke, we've been at work all day.
Luke:	It's pretty much an emergency, Mom. . . . OK— basically, I've been in three fights today.
Tricia:	What?
Luke:	*(Shouts)* Yes! I've got another guy trying to beat down the door to try and fight me right now!
Tricia:	Why? I mean, I don't understand.
Luke:	OK. You need to do this for me. Right fucking, now! You need to call the jail—request an emergency meeting with the psychiatrist for me right now. I've already been punched in the jaw once today—
Tricia:	Do they know that?
Luke:	Yeah. They're not doing shit about it. I already told you I want the fuck *outta* here. I'm seeing things. I can't even see straight lines, Mom. The walls are curved right now. I just had a fucking attack on the floor where I had—I just fucking basically passed out, woke back up and snot and fuckin' tears and bubbles and shit coming out of my mouth. And no

one came in to check on me. I was like basically
drowned in my own drool and snot. That's why
these guys are yellin' at me right now because
they're like, "Why are you cryin', bitch?" I—I don't
even know what the fuck happened to me. I just
fucking fell on the ground and started going into
one of those attacks like I had that one day when I
called you and said I had a seizure? Well, I had one
of those. Right here on the floor.

Tricia remembers. Luke had called these events seizures, but they
were really anxiety attacks. He would pant and his chest would hurt
so much he felt like he was having a heart attack. Sometimes he
would fall to the floor shaking and writhing, an overwhelmed
muddle of baggy blue jeans, turquoise or yellow hair depending on
the day of the week, piercings and tattoos, visible and otherwise, and
a strong, square jaw rimmed with youthful facial hair. She remembered. But now is not the time to soothe and commiserate, to com-
plicate Luke's ability to cope. Besides, she wonders how much of
what Luke is saying is imagined and how much is real. Now Tricia
needs to hold Luke together, to make it possible for him to stay in
jail, which is where he must be. When he unraveled before, it was a
simple matter of taking him to the mental health center and then,
usually, to Austin State Hospital. This is different. She is winging
this, thinking on her feet, mixing tough love with motherly admo-
nitions and a dash of changing the subject. He tells her of his messy
seizure; she asks if he cleaned up the puddle. He tells her his hand is
bloody; she asks if he has been picking fights. He complains that the
jail's medical officer, a bitch he calls her, does not believe he is sick;
she warns him not to make enemies. In the end, he extracts a
promise: Tricia will call the jail and ask for an emergency consultation with a psychiatrist. He says he will call back. She says no, no.
"Mom, I'm going to call you back!" he screams into the receiver.

Luke is calling again. Tricia hears the incessant beep of call waiting as she talks with the jail's duty medical officer, whom she has called as much because she promised Luke she would as because she is worried about him. Her conversation is a frustrating exercise with an obfuscating female bureaucrat by the name of Mary Suarez who tells her more than once that Luke did not sign a release form; therefore she cannot tell Tricia anything about him. As if that's what Tricia's purpose is, to snoop, to violate Luke's privacy. She tells Suarez that Luke is "crawling out of his skin" and needs help. Suarez tells her that the jail psychiatrist will be in on Saturday, two days from now. It has been nine minutes since she hung up with Luke, and Tricia hears the beep again.

Luke is frantic. He fears many things, but chiefly he is terrified that he will be returned to what is called the "VC," or Violent Cell. He had been put there last week, on his fourth day at the jail, after a bout of crying and hearing voices telling him to hurt someone. The decision was made by a medical officer named Johnna Rister, after Luke looked her "in the eyes," as she put it, and said, "I am going to kill myself." Rister, a large woman with shoulder-length strawberry blond hair and an air of supreme confidence, had thought that Luke was "actively angry," rather than actively suicidal, a "manipulator" who did not want to be in jail. That would be her testimony later. Nonetheless, a suicide threat was a suicide threat. Luke was stripped of his clothing and put in a padded cell with only a drain in the floor, and left there overnight. He banged furiously on the walls. He was humiliated and shaken. To Luke, this was more than an effort to protect him from himself. This was a warning that in the power struggle that is jail, inmates will always lose. Luke did not forget the VC, did not forget Rister, whom he called Ristoris, and did not forget the price of threatening suicide.

When Luke finally gets through to Tricia, he wants to know what she has found out, whether he will go to the hospital. They play another game of verbal ping–pong, with Luke lobbing and Tricia deflecting. He is paranoid and disconnected; she is frustrated. All the things Luke hasn't followed through on, the warnings he didn't heed, the predicament he is in because he returned to using drugs— it all wells up in Tricia, a woman for whom the use of a foul word is a singular and extraordinary occurrence.

Tricia:	OK, I called. I gave them all this information. I don't know what'll happen. That's what I've done.
Luke:	What did they say?
Tricia:	They can't talk to me! You never signed any kind of medical release or anything like I told you to. They cannot talk to me. All I can do is tell them my story.
Luke:	What is, did they say they were going to check into it?
Tricia:	They could not give me any answers or information back. You are an adult, Luke, I have, they have no right—
Luke:	I'll sign the medical form then.
Tricia:	They still won't talk to me. Not like, I mean it's like, Luke, you, you are in a place that we kept telling you you didn't want to go. OK. I can't—
Luke:	Yeah, but I thought I was going to Special Needs SAFEP [a drug treatment program]; I didn't think I was going here.
Tricia:	You are going to Special Needs SAFEP if you don't fuck up in jail and get yourself—thrown into an insane asylum jail facility.
Luke:	Well, Mom, if I keep getting jumped by people and have psychotic officers come at me and shit like that I'm not going to have much of a choice. Now I have two other people down the hallway from me that want to kill me.

Tricia: Well, I can't understand what in the—why anybody would be mad at you if you haven't done anything. I don't understand why people—

Luke: Because, Mom, I'm different! You can't be different in jail. You have to be one of these hardcore gangster people. I'm not. I actually had the head sergeant down here—helping me. And then they called medical to see if they could get a doctor down here and that Ristoris bitch came down and that's when everything went awry. Everything was going very well. I thought I might actually get a chance to go to ASH [Austin State Hospital]. And then that Ristoris girl came down and started messing everything up.

Tricia: Well—

Luke: And then she had that she wanted to lock me down in the fighting cell with all the people that fight with all, with a whole bunch of other people. That's where she wanted to put me.

Tricia: And they refused?

Luke: Well, of course. I mean, they're not that stupid.

Tricia: Well, good.

Luke: But I mean, honestly, that's the medical officer's response for a schizophrenic kid who's freaking out? Put him in the fighting cell? I'm just telling you right now, Mom, I'm not going to get through it! In one day I've been in three fights and I have a broken hand.

Tricia: And yesterday everything was fine.

Luke: And yeah, Mom, one day three fights, broken hand. I think I win.

Tricia: OK, well—Luke you know what I—my hands are tied. OK. I can't do anything. Your dad and I did everything we could to keep you from putting yourself there and you wouldn't listen to us. There's nothing that I can do beyond calling and asking them to please check on the situation. You know?

The phone call ends with Luke's plea for her to call his sentencing judge, "as a pleading mother," he says. Tricia knows that won't work, that the judge was very clear when he sentenced Luke to the drug treatment program. This was his last chance, he had said. She begs Luke to get it together, not to call officers names, not to threaten and be difficult.

Luke: You know, Mom, that also goes along with the fact that I'm schizophrenic.
Tricia: No, you know mental illness is not an excuse for that, Luke.
Luke: No, your whole excuse that mental illness isn't an excuse is bullshit. You don't know what mental illness is because you don't have it!

Tricia hangs up. She knows she has not said the right thing. There is no right thing to say because she has no control. Her son is now the property of the Williamson County Jail. He sits in a cell where the lights are never fully extinguished and there is the constant din of banging, shouting inmates. She recalls how he slept with his windows darkened by cardboard and aluminum foil and how the slightest noises jarred him, how he couldn't even be around little children for the chatter. She remembers when he went before Judge Carnes ten days earlier to have his probation revoked. It had been impossible to get him out of bed that morning; she tried cajoling, patting, putting the telephone to his ear with his father at the other end, screaming and pleading. He finally got up. Then, as they got nearer the courthouse, Luke started to cry long, deep, uncontrollable sobs. She begged him to pull himself together; court was starting. Finally they were in the courtroom, Luke stoic, her hand patting his knee as each case was called. Then he was up there, sentenced to up to one year in a drug treatment program, four months of which might be spent in the jail awaiting a bed. Two years before this, Luke had been hospitalized after being told he would have to go away to a drug treatment facility. "Mr. Ashley admitted that he became suicidal at the thought of separation from his parents," the hospital record states. "He stated he had a plan, intention, and the means to accomplish his suicide."

After his sentencing, Luke was led to a corner of the courtroom, a cordoned-off holding area, to await an escort to the jail. There he sat, staring into space, sticking his pinkies through the dime-size holes that he had made in his earlobes, one of his many exercises in self-inflicted pain. In and out. In and out. He dropped his head. He didn't seem to be aware of anything or anybody—even his mother, the tears rolling down her face.

After her unproductive phone call with Luke, Tricia is comforted in one small way, at least. She had spoken with his jailers and told them that he was in trouble, "crawling out of his skin," she'd said. They were on notice. What she did not know was that the message she left would not be passed on to anybody who mattered. Instead, it would be filed away as one of so many duly transcribed incident reports in the jail's medical records, records that often went nowhere and nobody read. She would not learn this until two years later, when Johnna Rister took the stand.

When Luke called for the third time on December 4, 2003, a sort of unsettled calm had overtaken him, the way the sky turns black and the air becomes still before a storm. He wasn't getting anywhere, wasn't going anywhere, and he seemed to know it. He persisted in his quest to get Tricia to get him out of there, but his tone had changed. A psychologist, hired as an expert witness in the Ashleys' lawsuit against the jail, later testified that had Luke been his patient, "I would not have let him leave my office."

Luke begins the call by rehashing a particular fight he believes he has had, in which an inmate attacked him and "everybody jumped up and got up like they were all behind him . . . cheering and everything." He tells her he is now locked alone in a small segregation cell, which is fine by Tricia, because she feels he'll be safe.

Luke: I just wanted to see if there was anything, I don't know. There's gotta be something we can do like call human rights and make a grievance or something like that. This is ridiculous.

Tricia: All we can do is wait for you to get into SAFEP. I have made calls, I have made calls to lawyers, everywhere I can make. And the fact is that we have to just hang in there. I'm just real confused because yesterday you were doing great and today you're not.

Luke: Mom, Mom, you don't think that I am confused?

Tricia: Right. No. I know you are. I'm saying, we are confused too. And that we're powerless.

Luke: I don't need you to be confused. I need you to help me.

Tricia: (Laughs a sad laugh.) The fact is, Luke, that we're pretty—

Luke: You used to be this advocate for mental health and shit like that and be able to do all kinds—

Tricia: It doesn't matter if I'm—you know what, Luke? I'm still an advocate. It's just that I'm powerless because for the last two years we kept telling you: Luke, just do what you need to do to stay out of jail, do what you need to do to stay out of jail. And you know what? You coulda cared less what we told you and now we are powerless and you seem to think that we should be able to make things different.

It always comes back to this. As it has for months—or is it years? "This is the third time I've talked to you," Tricia intones, "and I really don't know what I'm supposed to do, Luke."

Luke: Yes, Mom, because I don't want to die.

Tricia: I don't want you to.

Luke: Then help me. Then don't give me this "I don't know what to do." Figure out something . . . why don't you help me?

Tricia: You act like I have some power over this whole situation.

Luke: Mom, you used to be the person that never gave up, that never backed down and shit like that. You need to call somebody and talk to them and make them believe me. Now you act like there's just no hope. I still have faith in you I still have faith that you can help me but you don't . . . I can't even see straight right now, Mom. Everything is like a fish-eye lens. My distortions are so bad that I don't even know what's going on.

Tricia: Like I said, honey—

Luke: I don't feel, I feel like I'm on acid. But nothing is wrong with me. I'm just BS-ing the lady. And there's nothing wrong with that? That's what I need you to help me with.

There is more of this, the back and forth that has been their relationship, and then the automated voice announces, "You have one minute left." Tricia again tells Luke, "I can't change everything anymore." He again asks her to call someone. Then the line goes dead in midsentence, once and for all and forever.

It is 8:58 P.M.

Luke's last afternoon and evening can be pieced together from the antiseptic words of jail incident reports and the answers of jail officers to questions from Joe Crews, the Ashleys' lawyer. It looks something like this: flat, disjointed slices in time from the life of a twenty-four-year-old with bipolar disorder who made the mistake of getting arrested.

At 3:40 P.M., Luke asked Officer Richard Tooley for help. He told Tooley that he had schizophrenia—the diagnosis he had given himself—and was having vision problems. This was Tooley's first shift with Luke and he tried over the course of the night to help him out, taking him to the telephone and going out of his way to keep him calm.

At 3:44 P.M., Luke appealed to Sgt. James Curtis, who had been called in by Tooley. He said he wanted to be taken to Austin State Hospital. The sergeant believed that Luke was upset and agitated, but not suicidal. He was "an angry young man who wasn't getting what he wanted," Curtis said.

At 4:20 P.M., when Rister arrived on the scene, Luke appealed to her, again asking to be sent to the hospital. He repeated that he'd been punched in the face and said he would rather "bite someone's ear off" than tell who hit him. Rister concluded that he was angry and possibly a threat to others—"He was a manipulator," she said—so she ordered Luke moved from a group cell to a closet-sized segregation cell on the same floor. She didn't think he was suicidal, but nonetheless put Luke on a standard fifteen-minute suicide watch. The other inmates in his cell cheered as the hapless, tearful Luke was led out.

At 4:30 P.M., Rister heard a loud noise come from Luke's cell and found him with bloodied right knuckles. He had punched the wall. She ordered him to wash his hand, and he complied. "At no time did the I/M [inmate] state that he wanted to hurt/harm or kill himself," she wrote in her report a week later.

At 4:45 P.M., Luke was noted to be in his cell with his back to the bars. He was holding his hands over his ears and crying. Three other inmates were furiously banging on the walls of their cells; when

Luke yelled at them to stop, they banged harder. "The walls are closing in," he told an officer. The officer asked if he had ever attempted suicide. "Which time?" Luke responded.

At 4:55 P.M., Luke spoke to Tricia for the first time.

After her phone call from Luke, at 5:03 P.M., Tricia called Mary Suarez to tell her that Luke was "crawling out of his skin." Rister was not told of Tricia's call.

At 5:11 P.M., Luke called Tricia for the second time.

At 8:43 P.M., he called her for the last time.

At 10 P.M., Luke called the control room officer on the intercom and told him, "I can't take it anymore."

When Officer Tooley did his 10 P.M. round he saw Luke sitting on the floor of the cell, his back against the wall opposite his bunk, which sat on a high shelf. A white towel—a jail-issue cross between a hand towel and bath towel—was draped over his head and his hands were covering his ears. Tooley assumed Luke was trying to cope with the racket of another banging inmate, and he made a comment to Luke to the effect that he didn't blame him for doing that, it was so loud. Luke didn't respond.

At 10:15, when Tooley made his next round, Luke was in the same position, the towel loosely draped over his head.

At 10:28, when Tooley returned for another look, Luke had tied one end of the towel around his neck and the other to a nine-inch brass hand grip, sixty-seven inches from the floor, which was used to climb onto the cell's raised bunk. He was hanging there, shirtless and facing the door through which Tooley peered, his chin resting on the towel. Luke was balancing on his heels; his feet were a deep purplish hue. His glasses were still on. All hell broke loose.

"He's hanging himself!" Tooley shouted. Keys were obtained, doors rolled.

At 10:31, a radio call went out for help. Tooley struggled to untie the towel's knots, which had closed tightly under Luke's 190-pound bulk, while one officer lifted his torso and another held his legs.

At 10:33, CPR was started.

At 10:44, "strong carotid pulses and femoral pulses" were noted.

At 10:48, an ambulance arrived.

At 11:02, Luke was rushed to Georgetown Hospital, about a mile, and four minutes, away.

At 2:15 A.M., on December 5, a doctor noted Luke's condition: "No purposeful movement . . . unresponsive to pain . . . pupils fixed/dilated . . . episodes lasting 1-2 sec w/ twitching/opening of eyelids and jerking of body."

At around 3:30 A.M., the phone rang in the Ashley home, but by the time Tricia got there, the line was dead. At about 4:00 A.M., five hours after Luke was rushed to Georgetown, a deputy sheriff knocked on their door. When the Ashleys arrived at the hospital, they saw their son enmeshed in wires and tubes, blood coming from a large tube in his nose. He had shackles on his ankles. As they passed four officers guarding Luke, Tricia said bitterly that she wished they had watched Luke as closely when he was in the jail.

At 7:55 A.M., Luke's heart rate and blood pressure suddenly dropped. At 8:00 A.M., he was asystolic—his heart had stopped.

At 8:05 A.M., a doctor's note recorded, "Pronounced dead— mother at bedside."

CHAPTER SIX

Crazy in Texas

THE TAPES OF TRICIA AND Luke's jail conversations had been played on the first day of testimony in the Ashleys' lawsuit against the Williamson County Jail, and they had led the newspaper article that followed in the *Austin American-Statesman*. On the second day of testimony, a sixtyish woman in a dress and heels, her hair coifed into a neat combed-back puff, slipped into a first-row bench in Judge Lee Yeakel's second-floor courtroom on Eighth Street. Catherine Kelly wanted to see what this was about, to meet another mother like herself, to hear how the jail defended itself. It had been six years to the day that her daughter, thirty-five years old and suffering from bipolar disorder, had killed herself in the jail, where she was being held on charges of "engaging in organized criminal activity." She and her boyfriend had been found to have accidentally overdosed on heroin, and both were arrested.

Julie Town had had her troubles. Like Luke, she had had

symptoms of a mental illness long before she had a diagnosis. Sometimes she'd be incredibly vibrant and joyful. Other times she'd rant and rave and castigate her husband and two young sons because of the perceived slights of others. At thirty-two, her condition was given a name and a medication. At thirty-four, her marriage to a navy careerist was over, and at thirty-five, she became involved with a man with whom she shared heroin. Her mother discovered the pair unconscious one day and called for help, prompting a search of the home and ending in her daughter's arrest. Town had been on an antidepressant medication for four years and was also taking prescription drugs for asthma and cholesterol control, but none of them followed her into Williamson County Jail on December 10, 1999.

During the four days that Town was in the jail, various appeals were made on her behalf, and they fell into a bureaucratic void. Her ex-husband, who was a corrections officer in a neighboring county, called to warn his colleagues that Julie was depressed and had been suicidal in the past; they needed to watch her. The warning was clipped to her file. Catherine Kelly asked if she could bring the medications that her daughter had relied on for the past three years. She was told she'd have to wait until visiting day—five days away. "I've never gone this long," Julie wrote in a letter to her boyfriend. She grew frantic with each passing day, mutilating her wrists with a toothbrush and pestering guards, who, another inmate said, "kept blowing her off."

On December 12, she wrote to her son Jason, fifteen, "I'm not doing good—bad thoughts. I'm sorry." On December 13, while other inmates were at lunch, Julie Town ripped her jail-issue blanket and fashioned the strips into a garrote. She tied the noose to a handle used by inmates to hoist themselves onto an upper bunk, climbed up on a step that was affixed to the wall, stood precariously on a desk stool and then let go her five-foot-three-inch frame. Inmates discovered her when they returned from lunch. Town hadn't been checked on in more than five hours, although policy required checks every hour. Only one guard—half the required number—was on duty for ninety-five inmates. A week after Town's suicide, an officer was fired for falsely reporting that he had checked on suicidal and other inmates, telling a newspaper reporter that guards were trained to falsify logs when they fell behind.

Like Julie Town, the Williamson County Jail had had its troubles. From 1990 through 2003, the facility had failed ten state inspections. Eleven months before Luke Ashley was incarcerated, the jail had been cited for four key deficiencies, including a failure to document that inmates had been screened for suicidal tendencies and that suicidal inmates had been regularly checked. When Luke Ashley arrived at the jail in November 2003, another factor was complicating the jail's operation. Following a national trend to build more jail cells long after crime levels had fallen, Williamson County Jail was in the midst of morphing from a facility that housed about 425 inmates to one with nearly seven hundred. Six weeks earlier, 125 new officers had been hired, bringing to an already troubled facility a huge complement of inexperienced staff.

Keith Curry is a bookish, bearded psychologist from Washington, D.C., with dark curly hair who studied the Williamson County Jail as the Ashleys' expert witness. Curry had already analyzed the workings of thirty-eight jails and prisons in eight states and was a known quantity in Texas, having written a scathing report in 2002 on the care of schizophrenic and other mentally ill inmates in the state's prisons. Curry found psychotic inmates locked in solitary confinement without care, inmates whose medications were abruptly halted and who were too disoriented to object, inmates with "meaningless and outdated" plans for the care of their serious mental illness. The void into which Luke Ashley stepped on November 25, 2003, Curry knew, had swallowed many people before him in jails like Williamson County's, where the small-time ne'er-do-wells did short time for low-level infractions, and in the state's prisons, where the longer-term, tougher cases went. Curry's findings of lax care in state prisons were no small thing in a state with an incarceration rate a third again as high as that of the United States, in itself the highest rate in the world. On December 31, 2003, one hundred sixty-seven thousand people were in Texas prisons, of which about twenty-seven thousand were mentally ill. Another sixty-six thousand were in its jails, including almost eleven thousand who were mentally ill.

Keith Curry worried about the fate of such people. So did Joe Crews, the Ashleys' lawyer, a low-key, methodical man with combed-back silver hair, a neat gray beard, and a sharply tailored blue suit. He had agreed to take the Ashleys' case and invested hugely, knowing that the odds were against him. He operated in a judicial circuit and an era that offered little sympathy, legal or otherwise, to the troubles of imprisoned Americans. Over the years, Crews had taken personal injury cases in order to support the far less lucrative civil rights work that he loved. As usual, he took the Ashley case on a contingency basis. He'd be paid only if he won. He'd cover the considerable cost of the jail's defense if he lost.

Under Crews' deliberate questioning, Curry, often squinting under the courtroom's fluorescent lights, proceeded over the course of an afternoon to tell the story of the Williamson County Jail. The jail, he explained, had a mental health plan that referred to such things as a mental heath services division, a mental health director, and case files, in which counselors were to record symptoms, notes, and treatment plans. In reality, there was no mental health services division, no mental health director, no counselors, and no case files.

Under the plan, when Luke Ashley was suicidal, a formal assessment was supposed to be performed to answer specific questions; if necessary, an outside referral was supposed to be sought. It wasn't done, Curry testified. When Luke was placed in a Violent Cell, an incident report should have been written, with periodic checks and notes on his progress. It wasn't prepared, he said. And when Tricia called to report that Luke was troubled, the jail's separate health plan required that officers take "necessary steps to see the inmate's needs are immediately addressed." The steps weren't taken. The policies, Curry concluded, were "written for staff that did not exist for a mental health treatment program that did not exist."

The jail's expert witness was David Salmon, an earnest jail consultant with four decades of experience who had bypassed a master's degree and earned a Ph.D. through a correspondence course in the 1980s. A genial man who repeatedly used the word "mental" as a noun—as in, if an inmate is "a mental"—Salmon knew that Curry was right. "The plan overall was not implemented," he acknowledged. "It was in a notebook on the captain's desk. They never had the funding." Salmon was confident, however, that it didn't much matter. A document is a sort of wish list, something to aspire to, he indicated. "Should we have a plan? Yes," he said. "Follow a plan? Good idea. Do they hold them to it? No." The defense chose not to enter Salmon's written report into evidence.

From December 2002 to January 2005 at the Williamson County Jail, there were twenty attempted suicides that were serious enough to require transportation to a hospital—seven hangings, seven drug overdoses, three cut wrists, two falls, and one unspecified injury. Johnna Rister, the jail medical officer, was asked in a pretrial deposition about eleven of them; she knew of only one. That was another of the policies that weren't followed: the plan required meetings of "those directly involved in the delivery of mental health care in the jail" to improve care, including debriefing sessions after suicide attempts. They rarely occurred.

Curry sought to put into perspective what he had seen at the Williamson County Jail by comparing its mental health staff to those of other facilities across the country. The George Allen Detention Center in Dallas, with eight case managers, two social workers, one psychologist, and two psychiatrists, had a 1:54 ratio of mental health workers to inmates. The Manhattan Detention

Center in New York City, with 7.5 professional mental health staffers, had a ratio of 1:99. He put up a chart to make the point: a Virginia jail, 1:32; a California jail, 1:39; a Washington facility, 1:57.

Williamson County Jail's ratio was 1:2,907. Its mental health staff consisted of a psychiatrist who came in every Saturday for four to six hours. On November 29, 2003, Luke had spent fifteen minutes with the jail's visiting psychiatrist, Arvinder Pal Singh Walia, who had been licensed a month earlier. Walia had not been told of Luke's suicide threat the day before and had none of Luke's records. He diagnosed Luke as suffering from "schizoaffective disorder," a departure from hundreds of pages of Luke's outside records that listed him as having bipolar disorder. Walia also took Luke off suicide watch. Luke had spent the previous night in the Violent Cell, and he had gotten the message, Curry said; he was not about to tell Walia he was thinking of killing himself and go back there.

A meticulous litigator who knew every corner of his case, Crews worked methodically over the course of several hours to elicit the heart of his case from Curry. Toward the end of his examination, he asked Curry to rate the Williamson County Jail's care of mentally ill inmates. How does it stack up for people who are psychotic and in need of help? he asked. Curry shook his head slightly and leaned forward, knowing what this bottom line meant for Luke Ashley. "It's functionally devoid of mental health care. It goes way beyond grossly inadequate," he said. "I've never seen a facility that has this problem. I've never seen a facility that approaches this problem. It's orders of magnitude beyond what I would expect."

On the evening of December 4, 2003, the two officers directly supervising Luke were Tooley, a fortyish man with thick, receding hair that was graying at the temples, and Samuel Delarosa, a young ex-Marine with an erect bearing and a black crew cut. Tooley had worked security and fire prevention at the IBM plant back when the computer giant employed ten thousand people in Austin. Delarosa had provided support to soldiers in the wake of the bombing of the USS *Cole* in Yemen in 2000 and had worked for a few months as a security guard after the service. Both men, hired after the jail's expansion, had been on the job just two months, including a month of training. Tooley made the rounds of Luke's cell block and Delarosa worked the command center.

The other person with direct responsibility for Luke on December 4 was his nemesis, Johnna Rister, a three-year jail employee and nominal medical officer. She was not a nurse or physician's assistant but an emergency medical technician, an EMT. Her only formal training in mental health care had come in paramedic school and in the four-week training for corrections officers. More than anyone, Rister was responsible for deciding whether Luke Ashley was sick enough to merit an emergency call to a mental health center. She was the one to assess whether he was on the brink of committing suicide.

Rister had little doubt that she was qualified to make these judgment calls. Under questioning by Joe Crews, she described the mental health care she rendered to Luke. "I spoke with him, but—you know, I—I would ask to talk to him, and you could call that mental health care," she said. "You can talk to a person and provide mental health care without, you know, sitting him—sitting him down. You can—talk to a person and provide health care to the person. So, yeah, he was cared for and he had mental health services. Whether they were technically by a psychiatrist or by a doctor or whatever, he was cared for in—you know, in a manner of, you know, 'Hey man, how are you doing?' or, 'What's going on today?' or, you know, 'What's up?' or, you know . . ."

That, apparently, was the Williamson County Jail's definition of providing for its mentally ill inmates.

The report on Luke's death by the Texas Attorney General,

exactly ten lines long, lists the cause of death as anoxic encephalopathy. It recounts the events of December 4: his placement on suicide watch, his threat to bite someone's ear off, his transfer to a single cell. Officer Tooley was checking him every fifteen minutes when he found him, the report said; CPR was administered and so on. The key statement in this report, on which all responsibility turned, was this: "No outcry of Luke Ashley wanting to kill himself was made."

David and Tricia Ashley disagree. Luke, they believe, made many overtures. The jail's staff was too unschooled, too insensitive, or too unwilling to hear them. Beyond that, jail administrators had not hired the kind of people who could have discerned what Luke's pleas foreshadowed, and they made little attempt to carry out the written policies that might have prevented his suicide. David and Tricia filed *Ashley v. Williamson County* because they believed that someone should be held accountable for their son's death. They did not file the lawsuit to get rich. Making money would not have been reason enough for the indignities and anguish the trial process put them through: the press stories that were sometimes unsympathetic to Luke; the details of Luke's last days rehashed and relived; the jail lawyer who countered Luke's days in the Boy Scouts and his membership in a Christian church group with the assertion that he was a thief and a drug addict. When Joe Crews objected, the county's lawyer, Mark Dietz, presented a clumsy rationale that Luke wasn't the "great guy" the Ashleys made him out to be. Insults notwithstanding, David and Tricia filed the lawsuit because they wanted to expose the practices at the Williamson County Jail and what they meant for their son and all the future sons and daughters who might go there.

Jails are places of control, and the relationship between keeper and kept is inherently adversarial. Luke's jailers were dismissive and distrustful of his complaints, even as they recorded that he cried, had "multiple personalities," acted strangely and was "scizotophrenic [*sic*]."

They had a rational explanation for each symptom, each complaint, that allowed them to disbelieve the torment in his head. They thought he was angry. They thought he did not want to be in jail. They thought he was manipulative. Johnna Rister, acting in a capacity far outside her training, believed that Luke, though he had issues of the mind, did not have a serious mental disorder, which she defined as "something that cannot be controlled with medications." She contended that Luke was not "actively suicidal" even when she put him into a padded cell on November 27. How did she conclude that? "He didn't make an attempt."

Beliefs such as Rister's made it possible to ignore the flags that Luke was desperately waving. There were many things that could have made the difference, could have saved Luke's life. The jail could have sought Luke's mental health records, which identified him on his first day as suicidal and mentally ill. Had Officer Suarez followed the written procedure when Tricia called her on the evening that Luke hung himself, there would have been a formal assessment of Luke's situation. Bluebonnet Trails, the same mental health center that had originally diagnosed Luke, was under contract and on call for inmate emergencies. It could have been contacted. Luke could have been hospitalized.

The deciding factor, ironically, was the physical characteristics of the cell into which Luke was moved. Luke's raised bunk required a handle to get into it. Had he been put in the empty cell next door, with a ground-level bunk, there would have been no handle to hang himself from.

From the start, the Ashleys—and in particular their lawyer, Joe Crews—knew that the deck was stacked against them. Winning a case that alleged "cruel and unusual punishment" in violation of the Constitution would involve more than proving mere or even gross negligence. They would have to prove "deliberate indifference": proving that the officers at the Williamson County Jail knew that Luke was in danger of suicide—had "actual knowledge"—

but consciously chose to ignore the risk. It was a huge bar to jump over. Beyond this, Crews would also have to adhere to precedent in the Fifth Judicial Circuit, a conservative court in a conservative era. He would need to show not only that individual actors who cared for Luke were deliberately indifferent to his needs, but that the damage resulted from "a municipal policy or custom adopted or maintained with objective deliberate indifference"—essentially systemic indifference.

"Deliberate indifference is an extremely high standard to meet," the Fifth Circuit wrote in 2001. The *Harvard Law Review* said, more pointedly, that the standard was "a virtually insurmountable barrier for inmates who challenge the conditions of their confinement."

Predictably, the defendants in the Ashley case contended they had done all they could for Luke Ashley. "The evidence presented showed a concerned and caring staff that took a great interest in providing care for Mr. Ashley's known mental health needs and in protecting him from injury from himself or other inmates," their final brief maintained. "[L]iability only exists where a conscious decision is made to violate a person's civil rights or to disregard a known substantial risk. . . . [I]t takes a culpable state of mind."

On September 25, 2006, Judge Lee Yeakel agreed with the defendants. In two sentences that neatly sum up what Joe Crews was up against, the judge wrote: "The jail officials testified they harbored no animosity toward Ashley. Plaintiffs have presented no evidence to contradict such testimony." Judge Yeakel acknowledged that policies weren't followed, that the jail had no mental health facilities other than a padded cell. Dr. Walia may have been "wrong or even negligent" when he treated Luke on November 29, he wrote. But the jail was not indifferent because it apparently had shown no "animosity." The Ashley family's attempt to hold Williamson County Jail accountable had failed.

The Ashleys are comfortable but working-class people who own a modest three-bedroom tract home with small rooms and a tidy, lived-in feel. They have two cars in the driveway, and in the house, a small menagerie: three Persian cats, an iguana, a python, two tortoises, two turtles, and three dogs. One of the dogs is a 180-pound fawn-colored Great Dane named Aries that belonged to Luke. On the patio in back there is a hot tub that broke a few years back; it sits dusty and unused, its cover slumping forlornly after being jumped on by Aries. When the kids were small, family vacations were typically motor trips to see relatives in Texas or Florida. The Ashley kids never lacked for anything of consequence but were told early on that their future would be what they made it; they would pay for their own college education if they decided they wanted one. When Tricia reentered the work force after a six-year hiatus, she did everything from substitute teaching to working as a carhop at a fast-food place in order to make ends meet. Luke, one of those apples that did not fall far from the tree, got his first job, at fourteen, packing groceries.

When Luke Ashley's psyche became an overwhelming, unmanageable burden for him in the summer of 2000, he was like 46 million other Americans who have no health insurance, so the Ashley family sought care for Luke the way many people do—through publicly funded mental health programs. This would have been a dicey prospect in most states in America, where mental health care has long been the misbegotten stepchild of government largesse. It was especially so in Texas. The Texas system was then, and remains, one of the most cash-starved, overburdened mental health systems in the country, with a ranking of forty-ninth in spending per person—less than half the national average. From 1981 to 2002, per capita spending for mental health care dropped a disheartening 5.4 percent nationwide; in Texas it decreased a disgraceful 14.8 percent.

In 2003, the year that Luke died, the Texas legislature slashed another $50 million from the state's already anemic mental health programs. Medicaid coverage for counseling, except by psychiatrists, was eliminated, as was all mental health care for children served by a low-cost insurance plan for working families. The cut meant that Bluebonnet Trails, the agency that had treated Luke and had not had a budget hike in five years, would have to drop 1,000 of its 4,100 clients from care. The story was the same around the state. To cope with the cuts, a triage system was enacted into law: services would be limited to those adults with bipolar disorder, schizophrenia, or severe depression.

This was the system on which Luke Ashley depended for care from 2000 to 2003, and thanks in part to the advocacy of his mother, it gave him plenty of attention. He went to Bluebonnet Trails Mental Health Center dozens of times, and he was hospitalized at Austin State Hospital on at least six occasions. But in a state in which the need far outstrips resources, Luke got inconsistent, perfunctory care by an ever-changing cast of players. His hospital stays were emergency stopgaps. He was shuffled from one psychiatrist to another and put on a constantly changing regimen of drugs. Counseling was a commodity that came and went. "Pt stated he needed counseling but was limited as to what he could afford," a social worker wrote when he was discharged from the hospital in November 2002. He was referred to Southwest Texas State University, where a student finishing his psychology practicum took him on as a patient.

"I think my biggest problem," Luke wrote to his grandmother Mimi in December 2002, "is I go to the hospital get well get out let everything build up for six or eight months which seems to be my pattern with no counseling or working on my problems and soon I'm right back in the hospital or relapse."

The way of mental health care in Texas—and in America—is that those who need it get it in fits and starts or, more typically, don't get it at all. In 2005, mental health care was provided to just 27 percent of eligible Texans in need of it. The consequences of failing to help people with mental illness are enormous. After the legislature's round of cuts in 2003, jails and emergency rooms were flooded with a new influx of people with mental illness. Austin area hospitals and clinics saw a 79 percent increase in psychiatric cases in 2004. Mental health screenings nearly doubled at Harris County Jail in Dallas. Police calls involving people with mental illness soared in Tom Green County. A 2005 report commissioned by the Mental Health Association in Texas stated what has become an accepted and tragic reality across America: "Unfortunately, jails, prisons, and juvenile facilities have become a primary source of treatment for many people with mental illnesses. . . . It can be argued that deinstitution-alization really amounted to a 're-institutionalization,' as many persons with mental illness were simply shifted from state hospitals to county jails and state prisons." From 1970 to 1999, the number of people cared for in state mental hospitals in Texas dropped by 81 percent; the prison population rose 900 percent, and with it, the share of people who were mentally ill.

Luke Ashley's entry into the criminal justice system undeniably proved his downfall. He struggled with an overwhelming malady of the mind and a powerful addiction of the body. When he was arrested, his problems were compounded monumentally by the dictates of the court. He had to stay off drugs for four years while he was on probation. He owed a fine in the thousands of dollars. He had to pay court costs and a monthly fee for the oversight of his probation officer. He had to go to Narcotics Anonymous meetings. He had to perform three hundred hours of community service. These were all tasks for healthy, well people, and they overwhelmed him. He tried. He stayed sober for three, four, up to eight months at a stretch, joyfully telling his counselors of his accomplishments. Despite his fear of leaving his parents, he went through drug rehab twice. For his community service, he served Meals on Wheels, swept leaves at the county center, did filing at the mental health center, and pulled weeds outside the police department. He attended sobriety meetings and joined a Christian singles group to fill the void left by the Austin social scene he could no longer enjoy. But each time, the outcome was the same: he'd succumb to the lure of drugs because the pain was too great. "No one can be perfect for four years," Luke would tell Dena when the subject of his probation came up. Behind that statement was the fear, eventually realized, that Luke, a mentally ill, nonviolent, drug-addicted twenty-four-year-old, would someday go to jail.

The receptionists at a local mental health office loved the colorful, larger-than-life Luke. He would greet staff members with a hearty hello and engage in mundane social banter. He always smiled; he seemed to love people. He was charismatic. Once he had passed through the waiting room, however, Luke's bearing would change, and he would become the tortured soul that his counselor knew so well. Several times during his sessions, Luke stopped in midsentence and suddenly ducked like a boxer dodging an incoming punch. He would say he had seen something or, more often, heard something. The voices were relentless and cruel. They told Luke he was stupid and couldn't do anything right. They taunted him. They were quieted only by the drugs he was not supposed to take.

On his twenty-first birthday, Luke put a techno CD in his car stereo, turned the music up loud, and for the benefit of the Ashley family, went out onto their small front lawn and danced a wild dance. He wore a black velour shirt with flaming tongues that Dena had given him, and held little lights in his hands. He was like some crazy scarecrow in the wind, his arms and legs moving in a perfect, seamless wave. His mother was delighted. Where, she thought, was the chubby kid who had run the wrong way in soccer so many years before in Palm Springs North? Who was this magical performer on her grass?

That was one of Tricia's last good memories of Luke before his diagnosis and arrest, a moment, for Luke especially, of unfettered joy. Luke did not want to die. He told this to Tricia on the night he committed suicide, and he had said it at other times and in other ways. "Life is funny," he wrote in a journal from a drug treatment facility. "Sometimes one minute your on a crazy roller coaster ride like some rock star and boom like that your shut down back at the bottom of the food chain. I'm used to being down but this is ridiculous but I'm doing something good for my life for once.

"I believe I'm going to do it this time."

PART THREE

ALAN AND PETER

—∞—

Locals in the eastern sliver of Tampa between Bayshore Boulevard and the Crosstown Expressway knew Alan Houseman, the eccentric wanderer with the loud shirts and predictable routines, knew that there was something amiss in his gait, his demeanor, his mind. They would nod knowingly when he claimed to own all of the area's condominiums or cast a wary eye when he seemed out of sorts. They would swap stories about the time he chased a rooster that was left to wander the streets after the city's raucous Gasparilla Pirate Fest, how he'd shooed and clapped and made more noise than the pesky bird ever had.

Just about everyone knew Alan's funny, sad, and sometimes strange ways—everyone, that is, but the cop on patrol who caught him urinating in a parking lot near dusk one late winter day. Alan reacted out of a primal and irrational fear. The officer did not know what the sight of a uniform and a cruiser would do to him, that he thought it meant he would be taken away again. Neither could she have known that, on this day in 2003, he was on a steady slide toward psychosis that had prompted his family to petition a court to have him committed.

⚬⚬⚬

Peter Nadir was an adult who would never really grow up. At birth he had suffered a loss of oxygen and a doctor had pronounced him, using the language of the time, "dull-normal." The condition had consigned him to a childhood in which the ordinary milestones of running or tying shoes were to him titanic undertakings. As he got older, it had limited his understanding, though not his enjoyment, of the world around him. He loved to go to the theater and to travel. He especially loved to eat, and he looked it: He was a portly pear of a man with brown hair, hazel eyes, and a pronounced waddle. After two years of crying spells and mania, Peter had been diagnosed with bipolar disorder at the age of twenty-one, another unfortunate turn in a luckless life, and his medications had only added pounds to his well-padded physique.

To his neighbors in Clearwater, Florida, Peter was a strange but harmless young man who picked up trash, had few friends, and shared a two-bedroom condominium with his mother, Barbara. He loved to engage neighbors in conversation, in particular on Israel and religion. Curious and lonely, he would show up to watch as someone shined a model car or peeked through a telescope. When the space shuttle *Columbia* exploded in 2003, an invisible strand snapped in Peter's mind. The police were called to contain him, to take him to a hospital, but the frenzied, frantic Peter would not be contained.

CHAPTER SEVEN

An Uncommon Fury

Alan

For most of his life Alan lived on Plant Avenue in Tampa in a graceful three-story, twenty-room Victorian house with a sweeping front porch, a second-story terrace beneath a broad shingled arch, and wide overhanging eaves with lacy cornices. The house was just a stone's throw from the piers of the Davis Islands Bridge where he'd fished in the blue waters of Hillsborough Bay since he was ten. Alan's world was a small one, and it was centered on this house with the azalea bushes and giant century plants, the transoms and fretwork and fireplaces.

When Alan was eight he had moved to the house from Baltimore with his mother, Linda, his father, Robert, and his six-year-old brother, David, back when his sibling was his friend and well before David became his parent. The boys had an idyllic upbringing. Their father drove a taxi and came home every day for lunch, and their mother, who was kind and loving, spent afternoons in a rocking chair on the porch, watching Plant Avenue's business unfold. They shared the house with their mother's sister Jessica, who had been a burlesque dancer and B-movie actress in the 1950s. Aunt Jessica had flown Pan American Airways first class, had an agent, and posed for photos with tassels on her breasts. She and her three husbands were among the things that made the Housemans a little different from the rest of the folks in Old Hyde Park, a neighborhood of big, old Southern houses that in the coming years was to change as dramatically as Alan Houseman.

A lanky youth with straight sandy-blond hair, Alan had always been on the reserved side. Not exactly withdrawn, but not the type who had a gaggle of friends and a frenetic social schedule, either. Mostly, he hung out with David, the more extroverted of the brothers, and with David's friends, or with a girl from around the corner on Beach Place, pretty, petite, blonde-haired Judy Ryan. There were no girls in the immediate neighborhood for Judy to socialize with and no boys that Alan liked, so they were best friends of a kind. Alan wasn't boisterous or wild, and the naturally restrained Judy liked that. They would ride bikes, spend warm Florida afternoons on the back porch talking, or walk downtown to a movie paid for with saved-up RC Cola bottle caps. It was one of those relationships that are particular to childhood, the bond of two people who grow into adulthood side by side, witnesses to each other's journey.

Always a gentle child, Alan seemed to change in his teen years. His mother babysat for a pair of his cousins who were eight and ten years his junior. Linda Houseman was a doting aunt who loved having the girls around and lavished attention on them; Alan would do things like fart on them and tell them there was no Santa Claus. David sometimes joined in on this variation on sibling torture, but Alan's teasing was more intense, more personal. He'd tell one of the little girls, whose parents were divorced, that her father was right to leave her mother. He never wanted your mom, he'd say, cruel comments that the girl would write off to jealousy.

At four o'clock one morning, the Housemans were awakened by the sound of a small hand ax Alan was using to chop down a chinaberry tree in the backyard. "I'm chopping down the tree to let the moon shine," he told his parents, who called the police and had their gangly, handsome boy hospitalized. It was the official beginning of his lifelong journey into schizophrenia, but it had shown signs of emerging for a while. There were Alan's increasingly aggressive brawls with David; in one, their mother caught a fist and had to be taken to the hospital. Alan briefly dazed David with a swift left hook in a boxing match, and Robert Houseman warned his younger son to protect himself from his brother.

In his last two years in high school, Alan fell in love with a Catholic girl named Peggy who had moved to Tampa from Baltimore and was one of ten children. The girl's mother ended the relationship on religious grounds—Alan was Jewish—and after Peggy's graduation, the family left for California. Alan soon followed. Family legend has it that he arrived at the girl's front door, a lean and love-struck young man who had just hitchhiked twenty-five hundred miles, and Peggy's mother told him to get lost. Peggy was his true love, Linda was known to remark, and years later Alan swore that her rejection was what had made him sick. "I fell in love and the girl didn't love me back," he would say.

When he was twenty-one, Alan dropped out of college and began regularly to take off for points west, sometimes traveling by thumb, sometimes taking a junky car and leaving it behind when it would go no farther. Nobody knows for certain what he did on these trips, and in particular, what happened on one such excursion in the 1970s. It may be that he didn't share the details with anyone, or that he didn't relate them in a way that could be understood. What's clear is that he ended up in a ditch by the side of a road, missing some clothing and his wallet, and had no recollection of how he got there. His parents wired money and he came home, but after that he was never quite the same Alan the family had known before. He was angry and belligerent, and refused to take any advice from his parents. He went through a series of menial jobs and experimented with psychedelic drugs. Then, in a shouting match over a pack of cigarettes, Alan shoved his father, a man with a great sense of propriety and decorum. It was the kind of thing that was not done in the Houseman home.

Alan had always been the golden son who got A's without studying and was inducted into the National Honor Society, while David shunned books and got C's. Alan devoured literature, earned scholarships, and aced his math and science tests. He had an amazing memory; he could take an engine apart and put it back together. Since his early childhood, he had been the son to watch, the precocious one, the boy destined to achieve big things. When he reached his twenties, however, it was becoming painfully clear that Alan would not live up to his father's dreams and his mother's pride. In the era of marijuana, hippies, and the counterculture, no one was quite sure what was happening—whether Alan's mind had been altered by illicit drugs or if he'd been brainwashed, beaten up, or even raped in California. What the family did know was that they were losing Alan, and there was little they could do to reclaim him.

Peter

Peter grew up in the 1970s in Selden, a town in Suffolk County, New York, just beyond the edges of the encroaching suburban sprawl that was Long Island. The Nadirs, Barbara and Michael, ran a somewhat amorphous buy-and-sell business on the busy Jericho Turnpike, one day selling tires or a truck, the next day heavy equipment. They'd buy and sell houses and rent out a couple of stores and a garage on the property. Michael, a stocky Israeli immigrant of medium height with a no-nonsense intensity, did the dealing and moving. Barbara, a plain woman who married Michael to escape a mentally ill mother, took care of the clerical end of the business. She filed income taxes, kept track of leases, and balanced the books with quiet efficiency. Nonetheless, Michael told her that she was incompetent and stupid, a moron—and she believed it.

Peter was preceded into the world three years earlier by his sister Susan, his only sibling. Bright, outgoing, and normal, she was the standard by which Peter measured himself, and found himself wanting. He had been born with his umbilical cord wrapped around his neck three times, and it had left him with an IQ of 89 and a host of physical and mental problems. He was not toilet trained until he was nearly five years old and he had lifelong bowel problems. Though Peter was a normal-appearing youngster with a head of thick dark blond hair, he did not seem to know where his body ended and the world began. He walked into tables and fell down when he tried to run. He could not fold his uncoordinated self into a car without help or navigate a staircase without both hands on the railing. He was slow to grasp concepts but bright enough to ask his mother why he was in special education classes when he always got A's.

Barbara made a second career of nurturing Peter; she took him to special schools, formed a Cub Scout group for children like him, and signed him up to play on soccer teams for the disabled.

Michael Nadir was a different story. He had little patience for Peter's infirmities and found them difficult to accept. He chastised Barbara for babying and protecting him. When Peter cried, Michael told him to be a man. You're acting like a girl, he would say, the implication clear. Homosexuals were among many groups—blacks, women, Jews like himself—for which he had contempt. Beyond disparaging his son's efforts, Michael paid little attention to the boy. Peter so craved his father's approval that he blamed himself for Michael's behavior. "I'm bad," he would tell his sister in his simple way when the topic turned to their father. To Peter, it seemed the only explanation.

Michael Nadir's abuse was not just verbal. A school nurse once found belt marks on the young Peter's buttocks after he'd soiled his pants at school. She called Barbara, who, for fear that she'd lose Peter and enrage Michael, begged the nurse not to report the abuse. Susan was perhaps five and Peter was a toddler when Michael broke Barbara's nose, one of catalog of ugly incidents that included dislodged teeth and a bathroom wall spattered with blood. Police came to the door a couple of times a year, and Susan once came home to learn that a drunken Michael had slaughtered her pet rabbit. "Don't go outside," her mother begged her. He was barbecuing it on the grill. Michael's rationale was that the animal was ignored anyway and feeding it was a waste of money.

In the face of Michael's callousness, Barbara cowered and Peter was defenseless, but Susan, a sassy little girl, grew angry and defiant. She was quick to sense injustice and came to see her father's behavior as sometimes weird and often cruel. When she visited her friends' homes and made comparisons, she would not want to go back to the Nadir place on Alma Avenue. Although the Nadirs had money and property, they lived like paupers. Michael would send money to his siblings and mother in Israel but refused to let Barbara buy kitchen curtains. The living room of their three-bedroom ranch was furnished with a worn sofa and other junk that he had plucked from the side of the road. A couple of times, Barbara tried leaving Michael, once after Susan announced that she was leaving home, with or without her mother and brother. They went to Barbara's stepfather's in Queens, a borough of New York City, but got a chilly reception, and Michael hauled them all home. Another time, Barbara—her nose scarred, her teeth knocked out—went to the welfare office, where a male caseworker told the hapless woman that she might consider losing some weight. "You have high cheekbones," he said. She became so desperate that at one point she held a loaded shotgun to her husband's chest but was unable to pull the trigger, and Michael pulled it out of her hands. Susan would have shot him for her, but she never got the chance.

Life in the Nadir household was an ongoing series of shouting matches and physical and mental assaults. When Michael's fists or feet started flying, Susan sassed back or ran, while Peter cringed and got in the way. "Don't hit Mommy," he'd implore his father. "Don't hit Susie."

Peter's future was written in his childhood, in the act of his birth, and in his DNA. He was classically vulnerable to develop a mental illness. Barbara's mother was a woman with schizophrenia who spent much of Barbara's childhood at Creedmore State Hospital in Queens, then a sprawling center with thousands of patients. Peter's father was pathological, a man from a poor but functional Israeli family. His inner demons may have sprouted in the heap of bodies under which he was buried, a bullet lodged in his leg, in the campaign to take Jerusalem during the 1948 war of independence. He could be charismatic when he wanted to be, but meanness was his forte.

Beyond what Peter had inherited and been subjected to, he had also to contend with the damage done by his entrance to the world. Barbara did the best she could. She got him through high school with a special education degree and the ability to read at a fifth-grade level. She nurtured in him a love of drama and performance. He collected animation art—the sequential original drawings of famous old cartoons—and had an intense curiosity about the Bible and Judaism. He even got a license to drive, something Barbara never thought possible.

Michael Nadir was a man who was not to be trifled with. It was July 1983 and his fifteen-year-old daughter was out of control, sneaking out late at night to see a twenty-two-year-old man from Guyana named Sham Jetto—just the thing to pique Michael's intolerance. "I'm not scared of you anymore," Susan had told him after

the family's abortive flight to Queens. Her dearest wish, thinly dis-
guised, was for him to be dead. Now he was taking back control. He
locked her in her room, barred her window, and made arrangements
to ship her off to his family in Israel. Susan had other plans: she
feigned acquiescence—asking to shop for things she'd need and
dutifully applying for a passport—until Michael's guard was down.
Then, on the evening before she was to leave for the Promised
Land, she took off.

Michael had a mantra he would repeat over and over whenever
Barbara dared argue: "The gentleman from Palestine is always
right." What he did to get Susan back demonstrates his faith in that
concept.

Michael went to Jetto's house and, on the pretense of enlisting
him to search for Susan, took the young man to an empty garage he
had on the Jericho Turnpike. Jetto, a handsome kid with dark
shoulder-length hair and well-defined biceps, spent the next hour in
terror. Michael beat him, broke a broomstick across his neck and
knocked him out. He then forced him into a shopping cart, his legs
protruding awkwardly, and tied him up using a perverse assortment
of slipknots he had learned as a merchant mariner. He wrapped a
rope around the boy's neck with a knot that ostensibly would tighten
if he attempted escape. He then took Jetto's keys and went to his
house, which burned down that night. It was ruled arson, but a link
to Michael could not be proved.

A couple of days later, Susan turned up at a friend's house, having
learned that her father had been arrested for kidnapping and assault.
The escapade cost the miserly Michael Nadir fifty thousand dollars
and the efforts of a high-powered criminal lawyer to launch a
defense, which boiled down to: concerned father, rebellious
daughter, older (foreign) boyfriend. It was a sensational running
story in *Newsday*, a Long Island newspaper. The charges against
Michael were ultimately reduced to his theft of Sham Jetto's keys.

Susan moved in with a loving foster mother, a former high school teacher of hers, and remained with her through her college years. Her loss was a source of great shame to Michael, who forbade Barbara to speak with her. Peter was packed off, first to Israel, for an unhappy six months in a boarding school where he did not understand the language, and then to a special-education school in Yonkers to finish out the eighth grade in 1985.

In 1991, when Peter was twenty, Barbara finally moved out of the house in Selden that had been the crucible of so much family pain. She took Peter to Florida where Susan, now married, lived. Always the family man, two years later Michael followed, but the divorced Nadirs no longer lived under one roof.

Peter was a good son to his mother, a divorced survivor of domestic abuse who needed him as much as he needed her. They were like two sides of a balanced scale, each doing for the other. He took her to the supermarket; she lined up his medications. He accompanied her on cruises to Cozumel and Alaska; she took him to a weight-loss class and watched his diet. Barbara arranged a series of courses and activities to give purpose to Peter's life, perhaps even lead to a job, but they invariably ended badly. Long after everyone else in dog grooming class had moved on to clipping, Peter was still washing. Watch repair was a similar debacle. "I know, I'm a moron," he would say. What Peter was, however, was uncoordinated and simple.

In 1995, Peter and Barbara were on a four-mile hike through the Grand Canyon when Barbara's left leg began to throb. It was the beginning stage of an abdominal aneurysm that would cut off the blood supply and, a year or so later, require amputation of the leg. Barbara could not wear a prosthesis, and now that she was fifty-nine and wheelchair-bound, she needed her imperfect, overweight son more than ever. Peter, twenty-five, did not disappoint.

On Christmas Day 1998, Peter asked his father if he could come for a visit, but Michael demurred. He had a date. That day, Michael attempted to light a backyard barbecue with green wood and gasoline—he was always too cheap to buy charcoal and lighter fluid—and it blew up in his face. He lived a couple of days in a burn unit in Tampa before he succumbed. Peter, a needy, mixed-up twenty-seven-year-old who had ballooned from 180 pounds at his high school graduation to well over 300, was inconsolable. Dead along with his father were the unresolved issues of a son who had never measured up and who knew it.

Lacking as he was in so many ways, having no prospect of independence or long-term companionship, Peter was often restless and contentious. A couple of times a week neighbors could hear shouting from the Nadir household, Barbara and Peter sparring over the mundane bric-a-brac of life. He'd rail if they ran out of Diet Coke or nag his mother for money for ice cream, cigarettes, or a magazine. He pestered her endlessly to get his way like the dissatisfied and overgrown child that he was, the child born with brain damage, subjected to abuse, and burdened with the adult onset of mental illness.

—

Alan's brother David, the younger, wayward, and less promising Houseman son, had long stood at the margins of Alan's life, only vaguely aware of his sibling's tribulations. Reticent by nature, David didn't ask questions, and mental illness wasn't discussed much in those days, anyway. He had his own life. Alan was his parents' problem. That changed in February 1979, just a week after David, twenty-four, married a pretty, olive-skinned Cuban girl named Ceida: Robert Houseman suffered a heart attack and died at the age of fifty-six, a man broken by the illness that had claimed his son, now twenty-six. "Cry now," his mother told David when she broke the news, "because I'm going to need you later."

From that point on, David, a tall young man with a generous helping of seventies-style hair and a big mustache, became the family's financial manager; moreover, he became the cudgel over

Alan's head when he refused to take his medicine or see his doctor. "Your brother will come over and we'll have to do something," Linda would recite. David was now the face of authority and an object of his brother's resentment. He assumed the role, but reluctantly.

Through the next two decades, an uneasy truce held between Alan and his illness; Haldol kept him stable and his mother kept him together. He smoked incessantly, waited ritualistically for the mail each day, and, like clockwork, walked to the grocery store for his mother. When he became an uncle in 1979 to David's daughter Morgan, he took the responsibility seriously. He fried up cubed steaks and chopped onions for her, told her to drink her milk, and used her textbook to teach himself Spanish so he could help her with her verb conjugations. He advised her against smoking and chastised her when she impertinently said, "Shut up." Morgan, a chubby youngster with curly black hair, her mother's skin, and brown eyes, quickly gleaned that something was not quite right with Alan. She loved him nonetheless.

Alan had an occasional girlfriend over the years, including a Native American woman named Star with silky black hair that thrilled him. He collected music and went to bars every now and then, but mostly he was the solitary, itinerant walker of Hyde Park, the skinny mentally ill man who lived under the watchful eye of a tall dignified woman with a silver braid down her back and a will as strong as her son's illness. In 1999, Linda Houseman had her second bout of uterine cancer. She went in for surgery and the doctors pronounced the disease beyond their control. For Alan, now a graying middle-aged man with a slight paunch, receding hairline, and a visible drug-induced tremor, the inevitable was unthinkable. When Linda refused to eat or drink, Alan insisted that the family do more. "I could cure her," he persisted. "I could fix her." He was not irrational or incoherent. He was grieving. This woman had cared for him for forty-six years. They had visited the neighbors together for holidays and on steamy Florida nights; she had taken him to the doctor and sent him to the store and cooked his meals. He could not stand to lose her.

In the last weeks of Linda's life, Alan nursed his mother at home—feeding her, doling out medications as she had done for him for so many years—until the day before her death at the age of seventy-three. When she died, he took a pencil and scrawled the date—November 23, 1999—on the wall next to his bed.

Alan had always been a little bit on the edge and was hospitalized every now and again for a couple of weeks when the paranoia and delusions of schizophrenia got the best of him. He had gone to a state hospital, G. Pierce Wood Memorial Hospital, in Arcadia, until it got harder and harder to get in; in 2001, the hospital finally stopped taking patients. Soon after his mother's death, Alan's body became unable to tolerate the Haldol he had been on for years, and his medications were changed. This marked a second turning point in his life. He no longer had his mother to ground him and oversee his daily functioning. He no longer had the medication that had kept him on a mostly even keel for years. He stopped taking care of himself.

Alan let his hair grow long and he didn't bathe for days. He could be seen wandering the streets in his familiar now-wrinkled Hawaiian shirts or wearing clothing that was too heavy for the Florida warmth. He refused to let people into the house to clean or make repairs because he was afraid they would rob him.

Thirty years after their last meeting, Judy Ryan saw Alan sitting on a bench in front of his decaying house. He was thin and unkempt. He listened patiently as Judy spoke about living in Houston, about her job, about having two daughters. He seemed not to know her— not to remember the middle-school party she mentioned at which he'd won a dance contest so many years ago—and she felt as if she were talking to someone with Alzheimer's disease. Judy said good- bye and cried on the short walk back to her childhood home around the corner.

At the time of Linda Houseman's death, David was a Tampa building inspector who was living with Ceida and Morgan in Clearwater Beach, a forty-minute drive from Alan, whose job every morning was to wake David up at 5 A.M. with a phone call. "Hey, buddy, you up?" Alan would ask. "Call me back in five minutes, buddy," David would respond, and Alan would comply, at least when he was well. It was David's way of keeping tabs on Alan, who was often paranoid, jittery, and on the verge of a breakdown. David would take him to the emergency room and duly catalog his brother's symptoms for physicians, but nothing seemed to change. At one point, convinced that Alan's medication wasn't working, David called the physician assigned to him through the local public mental health center and urged him to change or increase what he was taking. He got a stiff response. "Are you a doctor?" he was asked. "Do you live with him?" David could claim neither. He wasn't Alan's guardian and had no other legal authority. He was just Alan's brother. After that, his calls were not returned.

With Linda gone, David was beginning to learn just how difficult it could be to get help, especially for a resistant and difficult patient like Alan Houseman. In April 2001, after he ran out of his medications, Alan began to act bizarrely; he threatened David and talked nonsense. The house was a shambles. David filed papers to have him hospitalized. Alan knew the process well and disliked it intensely; they did not call it involuntary commitment for nothing. For a week, Alan managed to evade the police by turning heel at the sight of a uniform or, when there was a knock on the front door, fleeing out the back way. When, after an afternoon of cat and mouse, the police, a physician, and the Housemans finally caught up with him, there ensued a debate, led by a disheveled but convincing Alan. He accused David, a man with a pony tail and a diamond earring, of being a drug dealer who was bent on taking his house away from him. Police eyed David warily. Alan had always been bright and somewhat canny, and he convinced the pair that, at any rate, he was

sane enough to avoid commitment. They extracted a promise from
Alan that he would visit his doctor as soon as possible, and left.

Three days later, on a busy street near his home, Alan chased a
thirty-eight-year-old African-American woman, wrestled her to the
ground, and punched her twice in the head. "He appeared to be
foaming at the mouth," the police report stated, "and was rambling
nonsensically about trying to save the city of Tampa from 'black
aliens.'" He was arrested and charged with battery. When he was
released on bail, David and the doctor were waiting for him.
Then—three days and one assault too late—the doctor had him
hospitalized.

The process of getting Alan into a hospital, and keeping him
there, was as frustrating for David as it was threatening to Alan.
Under Florida law, people with mental illness can be involuntarily
committed for up to seventy-two hours if they are in danger of
hurting themselves or someone else or if they are likely to suffer
neglect because of their refusal to accept care. Family members can
file sworn statements with a court to initiate commitment under
what is known as the Baker Act, a law designed to protect people
with mental illness from arbitrary commitment, to help them
through their crisis if hospitalization is warranted, and then to connect them with aftercare. In reality, the procedure often shuttles
people through hospital beds and back home long before they are
ready. Florida simply has far too few beds for the need. Since 1990,
the supply of psychiatric beds has declined by 35 percent, while the
population has gone up by 38 percent. Florida residents use state
hospital beds at less than half the rate of Americans nationally
because there are so few of them. Once patients go back home, the
care they get from overwhelmed community mental health centers
is typically late, curt, and incomplete. In a review by the National
Alliance for the Mentally Ill in 2006, Florida received an F for its
mental health infrastructure, a D+ for services, and a C- for mental
health care overall.

Alan was "Baker Acted," as Floridians call it, some eight times in the ten years surrounding his mother's death. On such occasions, he was hospitalized for a day or two, too short a period to monitor the effects of his medication. Typically he would be sent home groggy and hardly in much better shape than when he went in.

In years past, Linda Houseman had been there to make sure that Alan obeyed doctor's orders and got to his follow-up appointments after he was released from the hospital. After she died, he became like many other people with serious mental illness, adrift in a system that offers little support for those without the wherewithal for care for themselves. No supervised housing, no caseworker visits, no meaningful hospitalization.

In March 2003, Alan took to eating cat food and running into traffic. He talked of seeing space ships and aliens, and threatened to kill David. David knew Alan was not taking his medications and filed papers to have him hospitalized.

CHAPTER EIGHT

Out of Control

ON FEBRUARY 1, 2003, THE SPACE shuttle *Columbia* disintegrated on reentry to the earth's atmosphere, forty miles above the southwestern United States. On board was an Israeli astronaut named Ilan Ramon. In the knurly patterns of Peter Nadir's mind, this was a huge personal tragedy and a signal that he had to go to Israel. For days, Barbara kept saying no, it was too dangerous, they didn't have the money.

When Peter woke before sunrise on February 8, 2003, he was, in his mother's words, "nuttier than a fruitcake." He was screaming. He needed money for cigarettes. Where was the credit card? Where was some cash? It was 5 A.M. By 7 A.M. Peter had progressed through a series of demands. He wanted to call Israel. He wanted to go to Israel. He wanted to call his sister Susan in Tampa. He wanted to go to his sister's house and get money. Barbara was trying hard to manage him, as she always had, but she was scared. Peter weighed 365 pounds, easily twice the size he should have been for his five-foot, six-inch frame. He ate compulsively and trundled when he walked. He'd gotten mad before; a few months earlier in a heated argument he'd spilled a can of soda on Barbara and she had called the police. But he'd never been like this—manic, uncontrollable, and violent.

To escape Peter's rage Barbara wheeled herself into her bedroom and locked the door. Peter attacked the door, gouging huge holes in it until Barbara let him in. When she tried to call 911, he snatched the wireless phone from her hand and took out the battery. Finally, Barbara pushed her wheelchair out the front door and onto Rampart Circle, their tidy lane of semi-detached homes in the middle-class Clearwater development of Chateau Woods. It was about 7:30 A.M. on an overcast, chilly morning with temperatures in the 50s. A woman was walking a white dog. Barbara implored her to call the police, saying she was afraid of her son.

Nearby, Peter was pacing back and forth, a seething jumble of anger and agitation. "I hate you," he told Barbara again and again. A liar, he called her. "Fuck this!" he shouted repeatedly. The woman left and Peter pushed Barbara's wheelchair over, spilling his sixty-five-year-old amputee mother, still in her housecoat, onto the asphalt.

By the time Officers Tania Alich and David Koscielniak arrived in separate cars, passersby had helped Barbara back into her chair. Peter knew he had done something wrong and was afraid of the consequences. Before this, he had wilted from violence and was known to flinch reflexively when someone made a sudden gesture—a remnant of years on the receiving end of brutality. "I didn't hit her, I didn't hit her," he was chanting. It was about 7:40 A.M.

Barbara told Alich that Peter was mentally ill and on medication. She wanted him "Baker Acted"—committed. Alich, thirty-five, who had been a Clearwater cop for five years, asked Barbara if she would be willing to have Peter arrested. She said no, Barbara told me, knowing what Peter's chances were of surviving in jail. She wanted him hospitalized. Alich, in her subsequent testimony to investigators, said that Barbara said yes. It is one of many inconsistencies in the police report that Barbara would later identify. Regardless, Alich had all she needed to proceed to apprehend Peter—Barbara's account of Peter's assault on her. These were police officers, not social or psychiatric workers. Peter's actions—and not his symptoms or his need to be hospitalized—would determine how they treated him. Alich had probable cause to arrest.

As Alich went inside with Barbara, Peter, wearing gray athletic shorts and a white polo shirt with boats on it, turned right onto Rampart Circle and plodded down the street. He was carrying that day's edition of the *St. Petersburg Times*, and on his ankle, above his black EZ Strider sneakers, there was a gold bracelet that read PETER NADIR. Officer Koscielniak followed.

David Koscielniak, the officer who had responded with Alich, was thirty-eight and had been a Clearwater cop for thirteen years. He called for Peter to stop. Peter did not respond. The officer yelled again, then again. Peter kept walking for two, maybe three blocks more, as Koscielniak tailed him slowly in his cruiser. Finally he radioed Alich to ask if they had charges against Peter. Yes, she said. She was on her way.

Koscielniak was five feet ten and weighed 160 pounds; Alich was five feet six and weighed 150. They were two relative lightweights who, combined, weighed less than Peter. This was going to be a challenge. Alich began by taking out her notebook. She asked Peter his name, his date of birth, his height. He answered. When she asked his weight, he demurred. "Why do you need to know that?" he asked. "We just need it for the report," the officers said in unison. Peter was done complying: He leaned in and grabbed Alich's notebook, and the two cops went for him. It was a free-for-all. Alich and Koscielniak grabbed Peter's arms, his girth, anything they could get hold of. Peter grabbed Alich's expandable baton and cracked her over the head, then on the nose. Then he went for Koscielniak, who thought the odds would improve if Peter were off his feet, so he put his foot across one of Peter's legs and gave him a shove. All three of them went down in a pile in the middle of Rampart Circle.

Peter was on his back, kicking, turning from side to side, pulling his arms away, and grabbing at the officers. After a minute or two, Koscielniak and Alich managed to get the cuffs around Peter's fat and flailing wrists. Cuffed or not, Peter wasn't giving up. He said he was sorry, that he was fine. Whenever the officers let up on the pressure they were applying to his body, he would jerk spasmodically in an effort to get up. They requested backup, and Koscielniak squirted Peter's face with Oleoresin Capsicum (OC) spray, a pepper concentrate that causes the eyes to burn and tear. Peter registered discomfort but did not stop resisting. "Don't take me to jail," he kept saying. "Just take me to the hospital."

Officer Darla Wood arrived, took Alich's hobble (restraining belt) from her waistband, and secured it around Peter's legs while the other two officers held him down at the shoulders. Peter's hands and feet were now bound. Although he had been resisting for several minutes, he showed no sign of letting up; more than once he tossed the 140-pound Wood in the air like a bronco would a cowboy. A fourth officer, Benjamin Hailey, arrived, and Peter began spitting and rolling from side to side. By this time Alich and Koscielniak were spattered with blood, as was Peter, and the officers were unsure whose blood it was. There were bruises and scrapes enough to go around. Peter was yelling that he just wanted to go to the hospital, not to jail. He was sorry.

At six-foot-one and 205 pounds, Hailey was the biggest of the cops. He was twenty-seven and had been on the force for not quite two years. Nine months earlier, he and Koscielniak had been investigated following a complaint involving their use of force; it was ruled "unfounded." Hailey took over for Koscielniak, who wanted to clean the blood from his hands. Hailey kneeled down and grabbed Peter's left arm. Peter spat at him, and Hailey stood up to get out of the way. Peter spat at him two more times. Andrew Gaylord, a thirty-seven-year-old would-be cop who was riding with Hailey that day to size up the job, stood back as four police officers struggled with this heaving mass of humanity, and watched the scene unfold. He later innocently told investigators that as Peter spat at Hailey, the officer placed his boot above Peter's mouth as a shield—not on it, just hovering a few inches above it. When Hailey was interviewed, he denied doing this.

Hailey then asked the other officers if Peter had been sprayed. One of them said to "spray him again," Hailey told investigators, and the officer gave Peter his second burst of pepper spray. Peter reacted violently—he went "really nutty," in Wood's words—his body surging to the left, then the right. He kept throwing his hands around, Hailey told investigators, and "wanted to hurt us."

"Just Baker Act me, take me to the hospital, don't take me to jail," Peter kept saying, with his fists balled in his cuffed hands, his eyes shut tight. "You can take me to any hospital you want." According to the state attorney's version of events, Peter then went over on his stomach of his own accord. The department's internal investigation states that the officers rolled him over, a significant discrepancy. As he went over, the strap around Peter's feet came undone, and two officers moved quickly to secure it on Peter, who was now facedown. A fifth officer arrived and took over for the exhausted Alich.

Hailey straddled Peter, who was so big that he had to do so with a knee on one side and a foot on the other, alternating leg positions when he got tired. "The subject was still grunting, just grrrr sounds, you know," Hailey said in his interview with the state attorney. "'Get off me, let me go to the hospital, let me go be Baker Acted.' Stuff like that. He just didn't want to go to jail." Throughout, as Peter used his cuffed hands in front of him to push himself up, the officers kept telling him to calm down, calm down. "He just kept fighting us," Officer Wood told investigators. "I stayed, trying to keep his feet down, and the other officers were trying to keep him down. He was trying to raise up, raising his upper body. They were trying to hold him down by his arms and his shoulders."

What Peter was doing was fighting for his life. Unable to breathe, he struggled all the harder to get up, increasing his body's demand for oxygen. With every upward push he made, the officers pushed down.

The statements of officers and neighbors who witnessed Peter's last moments differ on precisely where Hailey was positioned on his body; hence it was unclear how much pressure was on Peter's back. Hailey said he was on Peter's buttocks, as did Officer Tom Rodgers, the last to arrive. "I could see the top of the crevice of his butt. . . . I was holding down right at the back of his love handles . . . nowhere near his sternum or anything," Hailey said. However, a resident, Richard Heaton, said he saw an officer—a "big mother," he called him—sit on Peter's back. Officer Wood, who was holding Peter's legs, said Hailey straddled Peter's back, and Andrew Gaylord, the ride-along, said he saw him on Peter's "middle to upper" back.

The officers would learn many things from this ill-fated encounter with mental illness and resistance. Chief among them would be never to put a subject facedown and hold him there, particularly if the person is agitated, obese, and has been sprayed with a chemical such as pepper spray. Their own policy manual stated as much.

As the five officers debated what to do next, an unpleasant odor wafted up from the prone Peter Nadir. Wood thought she heard a strange little "giggle" emanate from him. A stream of urine seeped out from under Peter's gray shorts, puddling in the street. The police used his newspaper, February 8, 2003, to sop it up.

"And he was still tense and still fighting us," Wood told investigators. "And then we realized there were no more tenses. He didn't tense." They rolled him over and realized he was purple. Fifteen to twenty minutes had passed from the start of the struggle to the end; it was about 8:15 A.M. Peter was hauled into an ambulance that had been standing by. He was pronounced dead just two minutes after his arrival at the hospital.

Later that day, a state investigator questioned Benjamin Hailey. "He ever complain about not being able to breathe?" he asked in a taped interview.

"No. No, sir," Hailey replied. Peter's repeated requests for the officers to get off him apparently did not count as overt signs of distress.

Suffocation is a terrifying way to die.

⁕

Barbara Nadir kept waiting to hear that they had taken Peter to the hospital. She wondered what was going on; all the activity seemed to have shifted down the street where Peter had disappeared just before 8 A.M. It was 10:45 A.M. when a detective arrived at her door and started asking questions about Peter. Barbara readily complied; she never tired of telling and retelling the circumstances and challenges of Peter's life, in that throaty, smoker's voice of hers, from a mouth of missing teeth. He was her project in life and she had done well by him.

Barbara and the detective talked about Peter's birth and neurological impairments and his difficulties managing money. She told him that Peter had been diagnosed a decade earlier with bipolar disorder, told him the names of the three medications he was on, told him that Peter had been hospitalized three or four times but not in the past several years. She told him about the schizophrenia in her family, the horrible death of Peter's father, and Peter's recent troubles sleeping. They went over the events of the morning.

Barbara said Peter had not hit her; he had just pulled her hair and knocked her chair over. She was firm; he had never hit her. At 11:25 A.M.—the very moment that Peter's autopsy was beginning at the medical examiner's office in Largo, seventeen miles away—the detective put his hand on Barbara's shoulder and said, "He's dead."

Peter had died some three hours earlier a couple of hundred feet from her front door. Barbara accused the police of killing her son.

Rebecca Bodamer was a thirty-nine-year-old cop with ten years on the Tampa police force when she reported for duty on Saturday, March 8, 2003. A slender woman of modest height, she was assigned to District 1, which stretched along Tampa's central peninsula, with Tampa International Airport to the north and MacDill Air Force Base to the south. Bodamer was known as a "firehouse officer," which meant that, per the latest brainstorm out of City Hall, she'd not only patrol the streets but also attend neighborhood watch meetings, respond to community needs, and carry out quality-of-life directives from the mayor's office and the chief of police. She had been married twelve days earlier, and this was her first day back and in the swing of things.

Bodamer had received complaints about homeless people in her district lying on doorsteps and urinating in people's yards; one such complaint had come in that night. She was wearing a bulletproof vest and carrying handcuffs, her radio, and a baton; she was armed, on her right side, with a Glock 17 9mm semiautomatic pistol with seventeen rounds in the magazine and one in the chamber.

A little before 7 P.M., Officer Bodamer, tired after her long holiday, decided to take a break. She backed her cruiser into a spot in an empty parking lot, a long thin rectangle that ran about 140 feet behind a salmon-colored office building on Platt Avenue, between Hyde Park and Plant Street. Plant was the street where Alan Houseman lived.

Bodamer intended to chill out for a bit and drink a diet Mountain Dew, the way cops do—car facing out, senses alert to the surroundings. The evening was dry and clear and mildly breezy; there were a couple of puddles in the lot from a rainstorm the day before. The winter light was thin and waning when she spotted a man, tall and skinny, in long pants and a shirt, crossing the lot. A median that ran lengthwise down the center of the deserted lot contained three mature trees, including a huge Florida live oak with sprawling branches that hung low from a massive trunk. The man stopped at the edge of the parking lot, perhaps seventy-five feet away from her and on the other side of the median, turned, and stood there. He was partially obscured by bushes but what he appeared to be doing was reaching for his zipper. He was, it seemed, peeing, and Bodamer thought, We're not going to have this, right in the middle of a parking lot in front of a police officer. This is unacceptable.

Alan Houseman had spent the previous week or more in a paranoid psychotic fog, his schizophrenia out of control. He was threatening people. He hadn't bathed, and he smelled. Thirty-six hours earlier, his brother David had filed paperwork in Hillsborough County Court asking a judge to approve his request to have Alan involuntarily hospitalized under the Baker Act. "Very upset and confused, will not take his mets [sic]," David had written. "He is very violent, to me and others." Alan had been unstable for much of the two years since he had been off Haldol. Nothing else seemed to keep him focused, to keep him together, and he had been hospitalized four times.

Alan was not aware of much, but at times like this he knew what was coming. He hated cops. Whenever uniformed officers came into the Hyde Park Market, where Alan bought coffee and cigarettes, he would drop his head and mumble animatedly, angrily. He had once seen a passing cop and told a neighbor, "He will hit you if you're not good."

On this night, as on many others, Alan had made the two-block walk to busy Platt Avenue to get some money from the ATM so he could buy cigarettes. He had cut through this parking lot hundreds of times on his way to and from home, a hundred or so strides away. The neighborhood he had lived in for forty-two years was gradually becoming more commercial. Big, old homes like his were being converted into lawyers' offices and other professional spaces, but it was still home, and Alan knew these environs, the brick roadway and shady sidewalks of Plant Avenue, as much as the people he shared them with knew him. In his pockets he had $3.86; three packs of unfiltered cigarettes, loose tobacco, and matches; a wallet containing his driver's license, Social Security card, and ATM card; and a piece of torn cellophane. He had on blue jeans; a red, blue, and aqua shirt that was unbuttoned, exposing his bare chest; and brown loafers.

When Bodamer saw Alan assume the stance men do to urinate, she set aside her Mountain Dew, put cruiser 331 into gear, and sidled up to him. Apparently trying not to be noticed, much less hassled, Alan began to walk away at a normal pace, much as Peter Nadir had. Officer Bodamer got out of the cruiser.

"Hey, come here, I need to talk to you for a minute," Bodamer ordered. Alan kept walking. Her plan was to get his ID and tell him he was not to do this in her zone anymore. She could not arrest him because she had not seen him pee. Again she called to Alan, "Come here, I need to see your ID." Alan heard this and turned around to face Bodamer. What she saw was a scared, sick, scary Alan Houseman, larger than life, beginning to move toward her. I have no name, he told her. "You're not a police officer," he said, advancing, "You're not a cop, you're not a police officer."

"Look, man, everything is cool," Bodamer assured Alan, who, at 6 feet, was roughly a head taller than she was. "I'm a cop," she said.

Bodamer realized that Alan was crazy and the thought crossed her mind that crazy people are unpredictable. She called for help.

7:01: "Get me a backup please," she announces into her radio, identifying herself by her number, 149, and giving her location as Hyde Park and Platt. She is calm.

7:02: Frank Five, a nearby cruiser, takes Bodamer's call for help and is on his way.

7:03: Bodamer gets back on her radio. No longer the calm officer of two minutes earlier, her voice signals panic, her pace has quickened.

"Would you get them 10-18!" she shouts, using the code to indicate an emergency.

Frank Five is told to "step it up," and he answers that he is coming. Sirens blare in the background.

7:03: "Get a unit 10-18!" Bodamer screams to the grainy, choppy beat of police static. Her desperation is clear. She is out of breath, panting, and sometimes unintelligible to the dispatcher.

At four minutes after seven, Bodamer reports: "I have one down. Give me an ambulance!" Then, twenty seconds later: "Man down! I'm behind 300 Platt. Man down—gunshot wound—I've been struck as well—with an asp," a police baton.

Multiple units are dispatched to the scene, and a supervisor is called. "Police shooting," goes out over the airwaves. "Minor injuries to the officer."

On March 8 at 7 P.M. Marc Dilieto was standing at his kitchen window finishing up his dinner chores. A fifty-six-year-old security guard who lived alone in an apartment at the back of Mary Arneaux's big white Victorian house on Hyde Park Avenue, Marc was a four-teen-year resident of the area. He knew Alan and Linda Houseman, had shared eggnog and cookies with them on the holidays, and on occasional evenings chatted amiably with them on the Houseman porch. Marc liked and admired Linda, a striking woman who wore white pants, pearls, and shoes that matched her purse, and had a small white poodle named Max. She was outgoing and kind. To Marc it was clear that Alan loved and respected his mother, and that she was good for him. When Linda knew that her cancer had recurred, about eight months before she died, she had talked to Marc. She had cried, for Alan. What would happen to him when she wasn't around? she asked. Would he take his medications, remain stable?

After Linda died, in November 1999, Marc had chronicled Alan's steady and sad degeneration, seen him grow disheveled and thin, and watched the Plant Avenue house go to ruin. Marc knew Alan had chased the boarder who lived with him with a hammer, and had threatened to kill a cat. Emotionally, he was like a powder keg waiting for a match, and Marc, fearing that he would blow, had written indignant letters to Alan's doctor and a local judge who handled Baker Act proceedings. Who, he asked, would take responsibility if this unkempt, uncontrolled, mentally ill man killed someone? How would they like it if he moved to their neighborhood? He got no response.

Marc Dilieto's kitchen window faced the parking lot and was about fifty yards from where Rebecca Bodamer had just confronted Alan. A tidy man, Marc had just finished the dishes, turned off the light, and returned to wipe the counter and sink when he heard what sounded like a machine gun—three, four, maybe five bursts of gunfire—and looked up. From behind a building to his left, which partially obscured the lot, a man ran into his field of vision. He was loping toward an empty corner of the lot when Marc heard more gunfire. The man ran twelve, maybe twenty feet, and stopped in his tracks, framed in Marc's window. Then he wheeled around toward the direction he had come from, and in the raw light of overhead security lamps, Marc saw him fall to the ground.

Moments later, when Frank Five finally arrived, he found a rattled Rebecca Bodamer bleeding from a wound on the left side of her head. Her gun was holstered and there were shell casings scattered about. In the corner of the parking lot, lying faceup with his eyes partially open was a white male who would later be identified as Alan Houseman. His mouth was closed, the officer wrote in his report, and with his hands drawn up on his chest he looked like a boxer ready to fight. "The subject's chest, hands and neck were smeared with fresh blood. There were two apparent gunshot wounds to the subject's upper left chest. Another apparent gunshot wound was located in the right side of the subject's lower abdomen. The subject's pants were partially down to his mid thigh, and his white brief-type underwear was exposed. A strong odor emanated from the subject's body as if he had not recently bathed. The man appeared to be homeless. There was an extended baton located under the subject's legs, which was spattered with blood. It was silver in color with a black handle."

Marc Dilieto made his way to the other side of the fence, having first called 911, and was immediately told to leave. "I think I know this man," he said, and a police officer and detective took his name. He was sure, as an eyewitness, he would be called immediately. Then Marc watched while police strung crime tape and inspected Alan's body, and news cameras arrived and rolled. He stared in disbelief. He thought of Linda Houseman. How would she have taken this? Her Alan, the boy his brother called Shimky, who called him Fig; the man who told his niece to study and stay away from drugs—shot four times by a police officer in fear for her life. Marc Dilieto did not sleep for weeks.

Everything that had brought Alan to this point—his illness, his brother's failed efforts to help, the mechanisms that under the guise of protecting his rights had set Alan adrift—had converged in a painful, tragic dénouement in a parking lot just steps from his front door.

CHAPTER NINE

Excusable Deaths in Florida

IN LIFE, PETER NADIR AND Alan Houseman never met and had little more in common than the fact of having mental illness. Peter was born in New York in 1971, eighteen years after Alan. His childhood was as tumultuous as Alan's was placid. Peter was slow and simple, and diagnosed with bipolar disorder. Alan was bright enough to get by with little work in school and yet win a full scholarship to the University of Tampa, interrupted as it was by schizophrenia.

In death, however, the two men found common ground. They died twenty-eight days and twenty miles apart in 2003, killed by police who meant well, who acted out of fear, and who stoked the fires of psychosis rather than quelling them. Alan, fifty, was shot; Peter, thirty-one, was suffocated. Both events could have been avoided. So many people with mental illness were killed by cops in Florida in 1998 that one study said their number accounted for 20 percent of the total nationwide.

In 2002, a California protection and advocacy organization studied the cases of seven people, who, like Peter Nadir, died of what is usually called positional or mechanical asphyxia, while being restrained. The scientific literature is rife with arguments over the role of other factors in such deaths—intoxication, health problems, and obesity, to name three—but the study concluded, as other papers have: "Individuals must never be placed in the prone position when restrained." A 2003 British review of the literature of restraint asphyxia similarly concluded: "The available evidence from this series shows that pressure exerted downwards on the chest in order to hold the person facedown must be categorically avoided." Keeping Peter on his back is likely all it would have taken to save his life.

Three years after Peter's death, on April 5, 2006, a thirty-four-year-old Tampa man, drunk and high after a long day of partying, became belligerent and engaged in a violent struggle with the Clearwater police. "Eventually, three officers were able to get handcuffs on [the man's] wrists, but he continued to fight and kick and roll, evading all attempts to defuse the violent situation," a department press release stated. He was shocked with a Taser stun gun four times, then subdued. Suddenly, the man, Thomas Tipton, went limp. The medical examiner ruled that Tipton died of asphyxia, caused when the officers compressed his chest while holding him facedown. Cocaine and alcohol intoxication was listed as a contributing factor; the Taser was not. Once again, although the department's own policy warned of the risk associated with facedown restraint, another person had died. As with Peter Nadir, both the internal police investigation and the state attorney's office exonerated the officers, each review citing the decedent's own culpability in resisting. The death of Peter Nadir three years earlier had precipitated no changes at the Clearwater Police Department and, it seemed, had taught the department nothing. The Clearwater Police

Department has not banned the practice of restraining people in the facedown position.

Rebecca Bodamer had been deeply shaken by her role in the shooting of a civilian. Driving down the interstate, she would see the specter of Alan Houseman's face. "I'll never forget that," she told a group of officers in a training session on mental illness in 2005. She had sleepless nights thinking about what her children would have done without a mother.

On March 13, 2003, and again on August 5, 2003, Bodamer was interviewed about the events of March 8, 2003. In the first interview, a homicide detective led the questioning, in the second, a detective in the department's internal affairs bureau. These were not like those tedious TV interrogations in which police parse answers and try to catch suspects in inconsistencies. There was no good cop or bad cop, and the officer was at times called Becky and Rebecca. The first interview took twenty-six minutes, the second, twenty minutes. Both times, Bodamer was asked to go through what had happened just once in sometimes leading questions. She was not pressed for any detail on such things as where she was standing as the encounter proceeded, how far she moved across the parking lot, or what direction she had moved in. In the first and more thorough of her two interviews, Bodamer recounted, somewhat disjointedly, what had occurred from the point at which a disheveled, agitated Alan first came toward her in the dusky parking lot, saying she was not a cop:

> *Bodamer:*   He starts raising his voice, he continuing [*sic*] to tell me I'm not a police officer. And at that point, um, I realize that this may not be a good situation, so I call for a backup 10-18. Um, he starts getting really, really aggressive with me and I—and I end

up pulling out my nightstick and call for backup now. Um, because I—I at that point was—was fearful that I was going to be hurt. Um, he—he kept coming at me and getting right in my face and getting—he never touched me physically, but he—he started aggressively lunging towards me, and so I pull out my nightstick and I strike him, um, on the left arm, two, maybe three times.

Questioner: Okay. When—when—after you displayed your nightstick, your asp baton, were you able to give any verbal commands or was his aggression so quick that you weren't able to do that ... prior to striking him?

Bodamer: I told him to just back off, calm down, back off. I think back off was—was I said mostly and several times. He is aggressively coming towards me and I'm walking backwards. ... I'm walking backwards because he's tall and skinny, but I'm short and skinny. And—and—and I felt that he could definitely overpower me. ... He's lunging at me again. I'd go to strike him again ... and he grabs my baton from the metal part, and he pulls it away. At that—at that time I'm walking backwards, walking backwards, and I pull out my gun at—at—at some point. And I'm like back off, back off, back off. Drop it. Back off. ... He's got that nightstick over his head. He is charging at me, he is coming at me. And, um, I don't recall if I shot at that point or if I shot after he struck me with the baton. ... I mean I—and he struck me with the baton on the left side of my head and knocked me down. He didn't knock me to the ground, I didn't touch the ground, but he knocked me down. Um, then he struck me again and I don't know if he struck me a third time.

Questioner:	Okay, so you're not sure if—if you fired prior to being struck.
Bodamer:	I do not recall.
Questioner:	But you are sure that you did not fire until he had already disarmed you and was in possession of your asp baton, correct?
Bodamer:	Yes, absolutely. . . . after I was struck, I go down. I get back up, cause he's charging at me still with the nights tick over his head. He's—he's going to hit me again, I just—I just knew it in my mind. I knew he was gonna hit me again. I go—I go to fire and I pulled the trigger twice and nothing happens. And, um, I realize ah that I had a jam. Um, I cleared the jam—
Questioner:	Okay, now the jam occurs after you fired approximately how many shots?
Bodamer:	Three . . . I remember bang, bang, bang.
Questioner:	Okay. Gun jams—
Bodamer:	Gun jams. I unjam it. . . . I didn't fire right away. I didn't fire. But then he's coming at me again. And—and—and—and I'm like back off, back off, back off. And he's not backing off, he's coming at me, and I fire what they tell me are five rounds.

After that, Alan falls. Bodamer tells the detective that Alan was to the east of her, perhaps ten to twenty feet away, when she shot him in the last round of bullets. He was charging toward her with the nightstick raised, which would have meant that he was moving east to west. Marc Dilieto, watching from his kitchen window about seventy yards away, said he saw Alan running in the opposite direction, west to east, then saw him fall.

After eagerly offering his name to a detective at the scene, Marc Dilieto, the eyewitness to Alan's death, waited eleven days before the Tampa Police Department came looking for him. And that was only after Marc had called David Houseman, who had called his attorney, who had called the state attorney, who had called the detective on the case.

Dilieto's interview, on March 24, took an hour and nineteen minutes, about four times as long as Bodamer's, and he faced far more probing questions than she had. Dilieto felt that his interrogators were trying to trip him up; it had the air of an inquisition. He was asked to describe the gunfire—bang-bang bang-bang, or bang-bang-bang-bang-bang-bang?—to estimate the time between volleys, to say which way Alan was facing. He was asked twice if he was suggesting that police had done anything that was inappropriate. He was made to repeat the story in full at least two times. It may have been possible to reconcile the differences between Bodamer's version—she'd been charged and hit by a madman and was understandably dazed—and Marc Dilieto's. But there was little attempt to do so, either in questions to her, or later in the formal findings of fact.

There were also two eyewitnesses to the first round of shots fired by Bodamer. Damien Lehfeldt and Stephen Hallenbeck, both sixteen and in a car together, had stopped at a traffic light on Plant Avenue, to the east of the parking lot, when they saw two figures engaged in a sort of pulling-pushing-grabbing wrestling match. Although the light was fading, Lehfeldt, in the passenger seat, noticed the cruiser and knew immediately that one was a cop. He saw the cop's baton go up, then saw the other figure grab it. Nearly simultaneously, the muzzle of the gun lit up, three or four times. Hallenbeck, who'd also seen the struggle and the shots fired, gassed his navy blue Acura and got out of there. Lehfeldt called 911 and was interviewed briefly on the phone that night by a detective. There was no follow-up, however, and Hallenbeck wasn't interviewed at all.

For official purposes, investigators needed only to know that Alan had assaulted a law enforcement officer who feared for her life. That was cause for the legitimate use of deadly force. Alan's autopsy indicated two wounds to the right chest, one of which pierced his lung and aorta, and one wound each in the abdomen and the right arm. The leg and abdominal bullets passed through him. If he was running away, as Marc Dilieto maintains, he was not shot in the back.

On March 31, 2003, just three weeks after Alan's death, the Hillsborough County State Attorney ruled that "the use of deadly force by Officer Rebecca Bodamer on March 8, 2003 was justifiable pursuant to Florida Statues 776.012 and 776.05." On October 8, 2003, the Tampa Police Department internal affairs bureau summed up the incident in three paragraphs that came down to: Alan lunging at the officer, taking her baton after she struck him, and refusing to back off when her gun was pulled. "At this time she fired her firearm a number of times at the subject, killing him and ending the threat to her safety." "NO VIOLATION OF POLICY," it concluded. No mention was made in the report of Alan's mental illness. No discussion ensued as to whether even a justifiable death could have been avoided. No changes were made in departmental procedure as a result of the shooting.

In 1998, after a Tampa police officer shot her son in the back, Carol Skipper decided not to sue. Instead, she started a campaign to better prepare officers to respond to people in psychiatric distress. A forty-hour course was offered to police agencies in the Tampa area, modeled on an approach in Memphis, Tennessee, called the Crisis Intervention Team. CIT seeks to change minds, hearts, and attitudes about mental illness. Police are taught how to defuse volatile people by developing a relationship of trust, avoiding false promises, staying positive. When police approach someone with schizophrenia it may mean something as simple as not banging on a door and shouting "Police!" Dispatchers and mental health workers assist police to ensure that the right people answer calls involving mental health issues. The program is most successful when embraced from the top and when officers enter it voluntarily and become designated specialists, a sort of SWAT mental health team. Memphis has seen a six-fold decline in officer injuries since the program's inception in 1988, as well as lower rates of arrest and jailing of people with mental illness.

By the time of Alan's death, about three hundred of Tampa's thousand officers had taken the CIT course. After an initial burst of enthusiasm, however, by 2006 the number of officers taking the training had dwindled to just ten to fifteen yearly. Advocates did not see much evidence that the approach had been embraced as anything but a quick fix to a complicated problem.

In 2003, when Rebecca Bodamer met up with Alan Houseman, she was not one of the Tampa officers who had gone through the CIT training. Nor, in the three dozen or so training courses Bodamer had taken since 1999, had there been anything related to mental illness, despite the fact that nearly one in four people in Florida's jails—all of them arrested by police officers—are mentally ill.

In her annual performance evaluation in May 2003, Bodamer received an excellent review, in part, for her performance under "stressful conditions." The review referred to an "incident" in which she was attacked by a "suspicious person" and was "forced to fire her handgun" and clear a jammed round. "Officer Bodamer maintained her composure during this stressful encounter from its inception to its conclusion," the review states. She was later promoted to sergeant.

Peter's autopsy report said he had multiple scrapes on his forehead, nose, cheeks, and chin, and cuts and bruises on his limbs. His wrists and ankles were marked from the handcuffs and hobble. There was no indication that he had been beaten. In fact, neighbors had commented on the restraint shown by the officers as they wrestled with the behemoth that was Peter. The cause of death was mechanical asphyxia with inhalation of Oleoresin Capsicum—

pepper spray—as a contributing condition. That meant that he had suffocated from the physical manner in which he was restrained and, secondarily, the chemical that was used to subdue him. The death was ruled a homicide, though not in the criminal sense.

Bernie McCabe, the state attorney for Pasco and Pinellas counties, concluded, on April 14, 2003, that the five officers "were in the performance of their legal duties when they attempted to apprehend and subdue Peter Gregory Nadir having established probable cause for domestic battery and battery on an elderly adult. . . . The actions and conduct of Peter Gregory Nadir constituted aggravated batteries on law enforcement Officers Alich and Koscielniak, and resisting arrest with violence on Officers Alich, Koscielniak, Wood, Rodgers, and Hailey. The actions of Mr. Nadir were such that [the officers] had every reason to be justifiably in fear for their safety.

"It is the conclusion of the State Attorney's Office that the death of Peter Gregory Nadir was accidental and excusable pursuant to Florida Statue 782.03."

Barbara Nadir could never get past the word "excusable" in connection with the death of her son. "They killed him," she told me more than once in interviews for this book. She wondered how such a thing could have happened or if she could have prevented it if she had stayed with Peter when police arrived. She blamed herself for asking a neighbor to call 911. "It's my fault he died," she told me. "It's on my conscience."

The Clearwater Police Department did a far more thorough job of investigating the death of Peter Nadir than Tampa did on Alan Houseman. Officers canvassed the neighborhood and spoke to at least seventeen neighbors, getting background on Peter's persona—often centering on his weird quirks and verbal bouts with Barbara—and eyewitness accounts of the incident. Many neighbors had a piece of the story to tell, from seeing Peter berate Barbara to watching the officers' struggle to subdue him.

The Clearwater Police Department has a policy, Number 103.92, relating to positional asphyxia. The policy warns of the potential for suffocation when, following a violent struggle, a suspect is placed facedown with his arms cuffed in back. Predisposing factors include obesity, substance abuse, enlarged heart, or having been exposed to Oleoresin Capsicum (OC) spray; officers are specifically warned that after a suspect has been sprayed they must not allow the suspect to remain prone with hands and feet bound together in back. Peter Nadir certainly met the bulk of these conditions: He was obese. He was on his stomach. He had been pepper-sprayed twice. He had engaged in a violent struggle. The medical examiner had ruled that the cause of death was mechanical asphyxia combined with exposure to OC spray.

The Clearwater Police Department's Office of Professional Standards, which performed the internal review of Peter's death, took an absolutist view of the policy. Whereas Peter was indeed on his stomach, his limbs were not bound together behind him, its report concluded. Nor was he kept prone "for an extended period of time after being sprayed with Oleoresin Capsicum spray," it said. "Mr. Nadir was not compliant and was continuing to actively resist the officers when he suddenly became docile and unresponsive in a matter of seconds." The report ignored the fact that Peter had been sprayed at the start of the encounter as well as just before he went onto his stomach, where he remained for more than "a matter of seconds." He had remained on his stomach long enough for Officer Hailey to shift from knee to foot and back, for officers to tell Peter again and again to relax, for Peter to ask them repeatedly to get off him.

In the end, the things that might have called into question what Clearwater's finest did on February 8 were shunted aside. The weight of evidence went against Peter, who was a suspect in a crime for which there was evidence and a victim—his mother. To boot, he was an uncooperative subject who complicated his lot by actively engaging in verbal, physical, and "aggravated" resistance. "The

SHAYNE EGGEN, "INDIAN PRINCESS"
B. AUGUST 13, 1963

School photo, age nine, 1972.

In Decorah, Iowa, undated.

Age forty-three, at the Mental Health Institute in 2007. *Credit: Gary F. Wilson/Art Thru Photography.*

Indian princess on a horse. *Credit: Shayne Eggen.*

LUKE ASHLEY—"MOOKIE"
JULY 12, 1979–DECEMBER 5, 2003

Age ten, at Whitewater Falls in
North Carolina, 1989.

Within days of his twenty-first birthday, Round Rock, Texas, 2000.

Peter Nadir—"Pete"
April 6, 1971–February 8, 2003

Peter, fourteen, and his sister Susan, seventeen, circa 1985.

Peter, twenty-six, and his mother, Barbara, circa 1997.

ALAN HOUSEMAN—"SHIMKY"
FEBRUARY 17, 1953–MARCH 8, 2003

Alan, right, and his brother David, at about ten and seven years old, Madeira Beach, Florida. *Credit: Houseman Family.*

Alan, about five, left, and his brother David, three, in Baltimore, 1958. *Credit: Houseman Family.*

Alan, thirty-six, Thanksgiving 1989. *Credit: Houseman Family.*

JESSICA ROGER—"JET"
MARCH 5, 1981–AUGUST 17, 2002

Second grade, Warring Elementary School, Poughkeepsie, age nine, 1989.

Jessica, right, and her sister Cora, about fifteen and sixteen years old, circa 1997.

Jessica, right, with her mother, Joan, at Bedford Hills Correctional Facility, circa 2002.

JOSEPH MALDONADO—"JOE-JOE"
OCTOBER 2, 1986–AUGUST 31, 2005

Age fifteen or sixteen, circa 2001.

On his eighteenth birthday at Preston Youth Correctional Facility, Ione, California, 2004.

officers used extraordinary restraint in defending themselves and subduing a man who fought them with an uncommon fury," Chief Sid Klein said when the review's results were announced.

The state attorney was equally eager to exonerate the police. Andrew Gaylord, the ride-along who had witnessed Peter's last moments, was interviewed for just eight minutes in a series of set-up questions such as:

> *Investigator*:   He never said anything at all in your presence about having any difficulty in breathing or having any kind of chest pain, or—
>
> *Gaylord*:   No. Not that I heard.

Gaylord's contention that Hailey was on Peter's back was dismissed in a similar fashion.

> *Investigator*:   And you couldn't tell if he was putting any weight on the victim or not?
>
> *Gaylord*:   He was definitely touching him, yes. But I don't know how much force he was touching him with.

Barbara Nadir played a key role in this tragedy as the victim of the crime that allowed police to detain Peter. Yet afterward, she was never asked if she had consented to press charges against Peter—she says she did not. In fact, after she was informed of Peter's death, she was never interviewed at all. Many neighbors were asked about Peter's behavior prior to February 8, particularly about arguments between mother and son. Why not Barbara?

In the end, Peter was to Clearwater police—as Alan was to their Tampa counterparts—an uncooperative suspect who threatened the safety of officers. As with Alan Houseman, Peter's own actions justified the manner and degree of force that was used against him. The question remains whether another approach could have worked, such as agreeing to take Peter to the hospital, as he repeatedly asked them to do, instead of to jail.

Peter Nadir was not the only victim of the tragic events of February 8, 2003. Tania Alich, the first female officer to respond to the call at the Nadir residence, had, in 2002, been named Clearwater's Officer of the Year after she had disarmed a man who was threatening suicide. She left the force after Peter's death, suffering, as her paperwork states, "psychological and physical issues." In the furious struggle to contain Peter, she had been robbed of her baton and struck. One result of the melee was a significant loss of her ability to move her neck, lower back, and left leg. In addition, in the curiously imprecise words of her application for a pension, the encounter left her with "an inability to be around others." She was granted a full disability pension due to permanent injuries.

Alich had received just three hours of mental health training since she'd joined the Clearwater police force five and a half years earlier. In the 790-hour training course to become a Clearwater police officer, candidates receive just twelve hours of mental health training, mostly a primer on the symptoms of mental illness and the law of involuntary commitment.

Clearwater has tried to change in response to the presence of mentally ill people in its community. Around 2000, its police department became one of the few in Florida to require its officers to take Memphis-style crisis training. In late 2003, the force also adopted the use of Taser stun guns, an alternative to the deadly force of firearms. These two measures, however, did not help Thomas Tipton, the out-of-control man suffocated by Taser-armed Clearwater police—one of them trained in crisis intervention—three years after Peter Nadir's death. Attitudes are likely the toughest thing to change. The *Tampa Tribune* found that after the introduction of Tasers, the Clearwater

Police Department's use of force grew by 58 percent; that means that police were using them in addition to, not instead of, other means. Nearly one in three Taser shots—each of which delivers fifty thousand volts of electricity—had been inflicted on people who were already handcuffed, the *Tribune* reported, as Peter Nadir had been pepper-sprayed after he was restrained. One of the Taser incidents involved a fourteen-year-old girl who had become unruly at school. She was jolted with a Taser in the back seat of a squad car because she was kicking at an officer as he tried to cuff her.

When the department's chief, Sid Klein, was asked about the case, he defended the officer, just as he had defended the officers who responded to Peter Nadir's resistance.

It was, he told the *Tribune*, "an extremely dangerous situation."

―――

Peter Nadir and Alan Houseman were among twenty-four people killed from 2000 to 2006 in confrontations with police officers in the Tampa Bay area. In two or three cases, police were the unfortunate tools of people who wanted to die and provoked police to kill them, but many more were killed while experiencing psychotic breaks that rendered them incapable of knowing how to behave in their own best interest; how, for example, to stop moving when ordered to do so. Ironically, the officers were similarly inept: their job training hadn't covered mental illness. They did not know how to properly restrain or negotiate with someone who was unhinged. They had not been prepared to fill a new role of twenty-first-century police: shoring up the tatters of an overwhelmed mental health system whose calls now went to 911. Florida is ranked forty-eighth in the nation in per capita spending on mental health care, leaving ninety-two thousand seriously ill adults without access to care. Many end up in jail or prison, the de facto mental hospitals to which police now take them when crisis units are full, insurance is lacking, or time is short.

Police have been asked to fill a hole in the social safety net. When their handling of people with mental illness leads to tragic results, they are usually forgiven. Of some three dozen officers involved in the twenty-four Tampa Bay cases, none were criticized for their actions, which, one after another, were deemed homicides that were "excusable" or "justifiable" or occurred after officers in understand-able fear for their safety employed the "appropriate" response. In the legal sense, the rulings may have been correct. The families of Peter, Alan, and others, however, believe there is something wrong. They do not understand how in the course of a few minutes cir-cumstances could have spun so utterly out of control. They do not understand why the police had to employ such destructive means on people with no criminal background or intent. They cling to the belief that with just a little more finesse and a little less force, the sit-uation could have ended differently.

On October 14, 1992, two Tampa police officers ordered a woman in the screened porch of her mobile home to drop a silver handgun she had earlier pointed at some children. When she refused, they shot her. Officer Ray Sheridan, thirty-nine, got off fourteen shots, and Officer Mark Fitzanko, twenty-four, got off one. Myrtle Phillips, fifty-six, died five days later. The aftermath of the shooting was horrific for both officers. The following May, a drunken Fitzanko, his blood-alcohol level more than twice the legal limit, was killed when he crashed into a palm tree. Sheridan, married twelve days after he shot Phillips, was soon charged with hitting his wife; he had a breakdown and was diagnosed with post-traumatic stress disorder. Then lightning struck again. On November 9, 1998, a mentally ill man named David Montgomery, thirty-nine, emerged from a Tampa apartment swinging the butt end of a barbecue fork. He struck Sheridan's new partner in the face and wheeled around just as Sheridan got off three bullets that hit Montgomery in the back. Two years later, an overwrought Sheridan, forty-six, broke into his estranged wife's home and threatened to kill her and her boyfriend. He'd already killed two people, he said.

Sheridan had attempted to come to terms with killing the woman on the porch. "In the strict sense, in the technical sense, no, I didn't do anything wrong," he told the *St. Petersburg Times* in 1993. "I can't get my own head to believe that." In the aftermath of shooting citizens, the challenge cops face is often whether they can forgive themselves—whether they can ultimately conclude that they made the right call and, equally significant, if they were properly prepared to make it. Ray Sheridan struggled on both counts. After the first shooting, he sued the police department, alleging that his partner wasn't properly trained. The suit was dismissed.

It was Montgomery's death that spurred his mother, Carol Skipper, to campaign for better training of Tampa police.

Investigations that follow police killings are narrowly focused on the moments of conflict just before the death and the laws pertaining to the proper use of deadly force. They are designed to assure the public that such deaths are taken seriously, that officers try to use the minimal amount of force necessary for the job. Police talk about how exhaustive the investigations are, how thorough. In the Nadir and Houseman cases, hundreds of pages of documents were generated. Formal depositions were taken and duly transcribed. Dispatch tapes were revisited. But the resulting probes had obvious, even glaring, omissions.

Peter Nadir and Alan Houseman had begun the day as unarmed, law-abiding people with mental illness; in the end they were suspects who disobeyed orders and racked up a litany of crimes such as resisting arrest, battery, and aggravated harassment, most of them at the provocation of police. The investigations by homicide and internal affairs divisions did not view Peter and Alan as sick; they viewed them as violent and dangerous individuals, which made the outcome of their probes a foregone conclusion. The benefit of any doubt went to the officer. Conflicting versions of events went

unresolved (in part, because there is no public proceeding in which
to resolve them). Independent state attorneys, using the same standard and evidence, came to identical conclusions.

Inquiries into the deaths of people with mental illness at the
hands of police rarely look at the bigger picture, such as why Alan
Houseman clashed with one police agency when another had been
assigned, and failed, to find him. They rarely question the tools that
the officer brought to the job: would a Taser have worked in place
of a gun? Was the officer trained for this specific encounter? Could
more conversation and less confrontation have saved the day? Tragically, the inquiries don't probe whether the death could have been
prevented, because such a conclusion could invite lawsuits.

The inquiries into the deaths of Alan Houseman and Peter Nadir
may ultimately have made the right call about the narrow issue of
the use of force in two brief windows of time. But they left many
questions unasked and unanswered—the kind of questions that may
have tormented Ray Sheridan. They torment the Nadir and
Houseman families. Nothing was done wrong, the investigations
concluded, so nothing needs to change.

When the G. Pierce Wood Memorial Hospital closed in February 2002, Alice Marsh was among the last ten patients to leave the
sprawling fifty-five-year-old facility, which in 1989 had 850 beds.
Marsh, a demure woman with green eyes and two long graying
braids resting on her shoulders, had been in a locked ward at the
hospital in Arcadia, Florida, for sixteen years. Suffering from severe
schizophrenia and believing that she owned the hospital, Alice was
dispatched to an unlocked room-and-board facility in New Port
Richey, a Gulf Coast town about forty-five minutes north of Tampa.
Within a month, she wandered away. One night on a garish, unforgiving, six-lane state highway nearby, a car struck and killed her. She

was sixty-nine at the time of her death. Alice Marsh, who could be seen in her early years wandering Key West, gesturing wildly, was another victim of the State of Florida's lack of care for people with mental illness. It's not that she should have been able to stay at Wood, where she likely had been kept too long; it's that the community she was sent to was thoroughly bereft of adequate alternatives for people like her.

G. Pierce Wood cost $42 million to operate, about $100,000 annually per patient. It was poorly run and had been sued over the deaths of several patients over the years. Located about ninety miles south of Tampa, it served sixteen counties in southwest Florida and was inaccessible for many families that wished to visit their loved ones. The hospital was the antithesis of the community-based mental health care ideal—expensive, impersonal, isolated. But with Wood's closing, and that of so many other hospitals nationwide, droves of former and would-be mental patients were scattered to the winds like the seeds of a woolly dandelion. Some, like Marsh, ended up in low-rent residential care facilities with little structure or security. Others ended up in jail, after committing crimes, taking up illicit drugs, or just tangling with police. Some joined the rolls of overburdened community mental health centers where they might be seen once a month—that is, if they showed up. The rest became homeless, or cycled through the psychiatric beds of general hospitals for brief stays, or died.

Charlotte County is a land of pretty Gulf Coast beaches, snowbirds, and citrus groves due south of Arcadia, the home of G. Pierce Wood Memorial Hospital. In 2001, just as the hospital was entering its final stages of closing, the county opened a new 528-bed jail. Within five years, the facility was overcrowded. As a growing number of mentally ill people filled its cells, the jail started to take on the aura of a mental institution: one in six inmates received mental health care or medication, up to a dozen on any given day were in solitary cells on suicide watch, and a psychiatrist and psychologist had been added to the staff. On October 20, 2005, the *Charlotte Sun-Herald* published an editorial with the headline, "Jail population swells because of state's neglect." It laid the blame for the inmate boom on the closing of G. Pierce Wood—a simplistic assessment but true in a much larger sense. Many things contributed to the closing of Wood and consequent influx of mental patients into jails. Societal views as well as laws have changed regarding the rights of people with mental illness to make choices for themselves and to live and be treated in the community. Medications have been developed that, while imperfect, have relieved the symptoms of serious psychiatric disorders. States have sought to save money by closing expensive, anachronistic hospitals. These factors have driven mentally ill people into the criminal justice system because the infrastructure into which the patients of Wood were tossed was a ragged, underfunded afterthought. Florida's spending on adult mental health care went up 10 percent in real dollars since 1997—about a third as much as the adult population. Charlotte's jail, and its burgeoning population, was not unique. Nearby Lee County, home to Fort Myers, also ran out of jail space in 2004 as more people with mental illness, patients from Wood among them, joined the ranks of inmates. "The fact of the matter," Commissioner Bob Janes told a reporter at the time, "is there is just no place to put these people." According to a report by a mental health advocacy group called Florida Partners in Crisis, 23 percent of inmates in Florida jails had a mental illness in 2002, three times the 1992 figure. More than ten thousand jail inmates statewide had severe mental illness—five times the population of the state's psychiatric hospitals. "Florida replaced state psychiatric hospitals with state and local correctional institutions," the report concluded. "We have made mental illness a crime."

Law enforcement officials have unwittingly assumed the role of caretakers and custodians of people with mental illness. In 2004, police in Florida consigned more than fifty-two thousand people to hospitals under the provisions of the involuntary commitment law known as the Baker Act, nearly as many as the almost fifty-six thousand they arrested for driving under the influence. The number of people examined for involuntary commitment soared by 69 percent from 1997 to 2004, while the state's population grew just 17 percent. These developments have changed the face, though not necessarily the nature, of police work. Police are trained to take control, to arrest. They answer to the rules of evidence and probable cause, not to the exigencies of illness.

Police need more than better training and attitude adjustments. They need the larger society to care about people with mental illness. With better housing and community care, fewer sick people would tangle with police. With more alternatives to jail, police would have somewhere to take sick people. Florida is trying to deal with the problem by avoiding unfortunate clashes between police and people with mental illness. Funds from the closing of G. Pierce Wood underwrote a new program called Florida Assertive Community Treatment. Each of thirty FACT teams around the state was assigned to care for one hundred seriously mentally ill people living in the community. These were the sickest and poorest—half had been in mental hospitals and 60 percent qualified for Medicaid. The mandate of the teams was to help mentally ill people find housing, visit them frequently to make sure they had access to and had taken their medications, counsel them, and otherwise manage their lives outside institutions. Team members would be a bulwark for the vulnerable. For the concept to work, however, the teams needed resources behind them, especially decent housing and mental health care. Those components are still missing in Florida.

In 2005, the FACT program served about 3,100 people. The results were dismal: 3,047 hospitalizations, 413 incarcerations in either jail or prison, and—most astonishing—forty deaths. This was a group of people who were receiving the highest level of community care that the system had to offer. Imagine what happens to those who don't receive such attention. In beautiful St. Petersburg,

a Gulf Coast city of pastel condominiums and palm-lined boulevards, one thousand of the city's homeless are considered to have a
disabling mental health condition.

The Florida budget may not include money for mental health
care, but it does for other things. In 1987, Florida had 32,764
inmates in its state prisons. By 1997, the figure was 63,763 inmates.
By 2005, the number had leaped to 84,901—this during a thirty-
year drop in the state's violent crime rate. From 1995 to 2004, the
state prison budget grew by $500 million, to $1.9 billion. Is it any
wonder that mentally ill people, who have trouble conforming and
often clash with authority, end up where the beds are?

EPILOGUE
for Part Three

The families of Alan Houseman and Peter Nadir did not sue the Tampa or Clearwater police departments. Alan's family looked into it, but because of statutes that limit the liability of police, the odds were long for a case of negligence. As for Peter's death, Barbara could not bring herself to go through the anguish of rehashing in a public proceeding what had happened to her son. She clings to what she has left. Memories of sightseeing in Las Vegas and climbing a Mayan ruin in Mexico, taking a cruise to Alaska and snorkeling off a catamaran in Key West. She cherishes Peter's old report cards, his signed glossy photographs of sci-fi stars, his soccer and graduation portraits, and the black string necklace with the gold dolphin charm that he loved and was wearing when he died.

David Houseman, meanwhile, sees his brother every day in sunny, downtown Tampa, in the faces of the tattered people who frequent the area near his office. Some 1,750 homeless mentally ill people wander the leafy byways of Tampa's Hillsborough County. Some are people who have been released from mental hospitals that were closed to save the state money. Many more came of age long past the time when psychiatric beds were plentiful. All know the limits of society's tolerance for them. They are people without decent homes and too little mental health care, people who cannot fend for themselves, people who are expendable in a society that's good at locking people up but not so good at setting them free.

PART FOUR

JESSICA

—⊶⊷—

Jessica Roger had always been obsessive about the things in her room, neatly lining up her jewelry and stuffed animals, her cassette tapes and photographs. A tall, heavyset girl with dark blond hair, a widow's peak, and adolescent acne, she was diagnosed at one point with obsessive-compulsive disorder, so strong was the link between her emotional well-being and the physical things around her. In March 1997, less than four weeks after her twenty-first release from a psychiatric hospital, Jessica checked her possessions as she often did and found them out of place. She accused her father. As she later told it, he pushed her and she punched him. Her dark-haired older sister, Cora, a large girl like Jessica, jumped in. In the melee that ensued, common in the turbulent Roger household, Kevin and Cora were attempting to restrain Jessica on the floor when she turned and bit her sister in the right forearm, drawing blood.

It was four days after her sixteenth birthday, and Jessica, now legally an adult, was arrested for assault. The real trouble started the next day, when, in one of a hundred fits of frustration she'd had during a confined and medicated adolescence, Jessica kicked a female jail guard, a peace officer under the law.

The door to the criminal justice system had been opened, and this troubled, mentally ill teenager had just walked through it.

CHAPTER TEN

There Ought to Be a Place

Jessica Roger's story begins in 1978, three years before her birth, in Poughkeepsie, New York, an old whaling town north of Manhattan on the railroad line that runs along the Hudson River. Kevin Roger, a lean and good-looking twenty-year-old with a generous head of hair, asked Joan Briggs, a round, petite girl with long, dark blond hair, if she would consider dating a cab driver. Joan, also twenty, was one of seven surviving children of a divorced housekeeper who had worked long, hard days to provide for them. Kevin, a serious young man, had been on his own since his early teens.

"If you're looking for a one-night stand," Joan had answered, "keep looking." Kevin apparently liked Joan's directness and said that was not what he wanted. Joan remembers the date and time, September 28, 1978, at 8 P.M., as if he had proposed marriage; that came later, very much an afterthought. Both were school dropouts of modest means so theirs wasn't the kind of courtship that came with dinner and dancing. They would go down to the Hudson River where it was wide and pretty, and catch catfish, eels, and suckerfish off a ledge in the shadow of the gunmetal Mid-Hudson Bridge. They would walk the ragtag streets of Poughkeepsie's north side, through neighborhoods forgotten by urban renewal. Even then, Joan was heavy, and she warmed to Kevin when he didn't seem embarrassed to be with her.

Within months of meeting Kevin, Joan became pregnant. She gave birth to Cora in August 1979, and in March 1981, to Jessica, another unplanned addition to the family. Joan and Kevin's life together, like their courtship, just happened. Kevin did body work or fixed car engines. Joan, who had only gotten as far as middle school, worked occasionally as a hotel maid and went on and off public assistance. The couple lived together intermittently in a series of tired old apartment houses as they went through spasms of harmony and warfare. They did not marry until 1987. Joan, like her mother, was a screamer. She told the girls, among other things, that she should have aborted them, and she would rail and rage at Kevin and accuse him of cheating on her. The girls came to know Joan's spells as Mom's "mood swings." When something set her off, there was no way back. During one fight, she went for Kevin with a knife that would have fulfilled its destiny had he not taken it away from her and broken it in two.

Separated by nineteen months, Jessica and Cora endured a loud, messy, and uneasy childhood. Cora, a firecracker of a kid with brown hair and eyes and an early air of confidence, somehow got through it, though hardly unscathed. Jessica was different. A little girl with hazel eyes and straight blond hair with bangs, she was sensitive and eager to please. Teachers wrote "very good" on her sentences. Her perfectly shaped C's merited a 90 in penmanship. She earned an award for not missing a day of third grade. Jessica was the little girl who climbed on her mother's chest to watch television, sucking her thumb and fingering the corner of a favorite pillow. She was the younger child who at night would cry on her big sister's shoulder when she heard Mommy and Daddy roaring at each other in the living room. She was sure they were going to kill each other.

Joan had gone from 185 pounds when she met Kevin to over 300, and it was taking a toll on her body. She had been taking medication for the pain of three compressed vertebrae in her back. In December 1991, it was clear that she had become addicted to it. The pain, the lack of money, the tension with Kevin, the stress of caring for the two girls—it all became too much for her. She had a breakdown, and left Jessica and Cora in Kevin's care. Jessica was ten years old.

> *The day you left me I wanted to die. But then I could not find a place to hide. I thought you were my mom, but before you walked out that door you said this is the end. . . . When you were gone the tears were back it was like rain pouring down my face.*
>
> —Jessica, several years after her mother left

After Joan moved out, Jessica seemed to drop out of life. She became withdrawn and angry. She began to make small incisions in her arms and legs. Her temper tantrums grew so extreme that she would scream and bang her head against the wall. When she didn't like what she heard, she would put her fist through a window, several times sustaining deep cuts in her hands. The little girl who, two years before, had dutifully done her schoolwork stopped participating in everything having to do with school. "During national testing Jessica simply sat and stared at her paper," a teacher wrote. "It has been a very sorry state of affairs for a long time. This school has done all it could to help. Jessica has responded to nothing."

Jessica was hospitalized for the first time in June 1992; she was eleven and in the fifth grade, the last grade she would complete. Sixth grade was aborted when she threw a rock at the school principal.

Jessica's life became a series of hospital stays until she was fifteen: three months at Four Winds Hospital in late 1993, seven months at Craig House in 1994, the bulk of 1995 and 1996 in Rockland Children's Psychiatric Center. The periods between these stays were punctuated by calamity. After one discharge home when she twelve, the Rogers had gotten together to have a yard sale at Joan's house. Suddenly, Joan heard Kevin scream for her to come to the bedroom; Jessica, who had said she wanted to nap, had taken all the doses of her medications. Kevin frantically attempted to rouse her while Joan dialed 911, and Jessica was rushed to the hospital. They pumped her stomach, then Joan kept vigil for three days and three nights. From the hospital Jessica was sent to a group home, where she kicked a staff member, smashed a window, and ran in front of a car that managed to swerve around her—all in the space of a day. She was sent back to the hospital.

While other girls her age were having sleepovers and going to gym class, at thirteen, Jessica was bonding with her roommate at a psychiatric facility. Tina, a skinny girl from Yonkers with straight brown hair and brown eyes, suffered from depression and had a mother who was addicted to drugs and alcohol. The two girls giggled, traded secrets, and came to understand each other as few of the hospital staff members did. When Jessica got out of control, hospital aides called Tina to calm her down. Jessica returned the favor, teaching Tina the perverse pleasure of the eraser burn, using the pink tip of a No. 2 pencil to engrave a mark on Tina's arm that would last for years. Best friends, the girls wove a fantasy that someday when they were older and better they would get an apartment together in New York City, and get jobs and have parties. It would be far from hospitals and, for Jessica, far from the pain of an imperfect family life. Tina heard Jessica's phone calls home quickly turn into screaming matches that echoed through the facility. She saw Jessica return to the hospital from weekend visits to her family all roiled up, and sometimes bruised. Jessica's life, it seemed, was a futile quest for familial peace and personal acceptance. Home was where she wanted most to be but she could never stay there very long.

In 1994, when Jessica was hospitalized at a treatment center in Beacon, New York, Kevin had observed that she was groggy and unresponsive. Both he and Joan hated to see her in a medicated stupor, a "guinea pig to science," Joan had often called her—on an ever-changing assortment of strong but, it seemed, ineffective drugs. This time, Kevin drew the line; he told hospital officials that if they did not discontinue Jessica's psychiatric medications he would remove her from the facility. Hospital officials refused to do so. Kevin tried to take her. They then reported him to authorities on an allegation of medical neglect. After this confrontation, officials contended, Jessica became destructive toward herself and the facility's staff; it is unclear whether her behavior was a direct result of Kevin's attempt to remove her, since that was her pattern anyway. What is clear is that the Rogers were watching Jessica's caretakers founder in their attempt to treat their difficult and depressed daughter, in much the same way that they had. The system the Rogers were challenging, however, had something that they did not—power. Based on the hospital's report, Jessica was made a ward of the state, a court-declared victim of parental medical neglect. Her care was now in the court's hands.

As a ward of the State of New York, Jessica was assigned a plethora of descriptions and diagnoses—she was, variously, depressed, "oppositional," compulsive, and manic. She was given a slew of medications, including Prozac, Clonidine, Depakote, Thorazine, Ativan, and Vistaril. She so overwhelmed the system's ability to care for her that in the final months of 1995, when she was fourteen, she was moved ten times, from hospital to group home, from boarding school to treatment facility. Twice, she lasted just twenty-four hours in the places she was taken to. The Rogers had lost all control over the fate of their daughter to a government that thought it could do better. When it came to Jessica, control could not have been more elusive.

After Joan left, Jessica's pattern of behavior continued: she rejected everything. She summarily left Rockland Children's Psychiatric Center in late 1996 when she was fifteen, but she was typically unsettled and unhappy at home. The county child welfare department found a place for her in a foster home in a rural Dutchess County town, but she refused to consider it. When a tutor arrived to home-school her, she was angry and uncooperative. She hit Cora over the head with a toilet plunger and then put her own hand through yet another window. In early 1997, she was again hospitalized at Rockland. Jessica had been caught in this cycle for a very long time; as her caseworkers put it, she had become "very comfortable in the psychiatric hospital environment."

In January 1997, Jessica's case managers wrote to the family court judge who had handled her neglect case. They detailed Jessica's litany of recalcitrance, her refusal to abide by their well-made plans. The Department of Social Services, they told the judge, "cannot be responsible" for her decisions any longer. It had done all it could. Jessica, then one month shy of her sixteenth birthday, had reached the limit of the bureaucracy's tolerance. Things were about to change.

> *A strikingly beautiful girl in 1992, Jessica is now an enormous 233 pound girl with severe facial acne. . . . When it was pointed out she has been withdrawn for several years, she did not know how many years, did not know if she wanted to remember when it started, or if she wished to emerge from*

it. "Eventually I'll change, if I want to." . . . So sad she can't
stand it.

—From a psychological assessment of Jessica, age
fifteen, February 1997

On March 5, 1997, Jessica turned sixteen, a milestone that her overseers in the child welfare department were clearly anticipating. Now, when she acted up, she would be somebody else's problem. When, just a few days later, Jessica bit her sister and kicked an officer in a fit of pique, she entered a new kind of arena—the criminal justice system.

After her arrest, Jessica was sent back to Rockland for a court-ordered evaluation of her sanity. Maybe the system would do right by her; maybe it would recognize that her actions were less criminal than pathological. A therapist wrote out a list of her strengths and weaknesses: She was verbal, insightful, caring, and likable. She loved to be praised and to care for animals. She was of average intelligence, motivated, and did not use alcohol or drugs. There was a lot here to work with. On the negative side were the words *impulsive, poor judgment, aggressive/assaultive, oppositional/defiant.* She had grown up in an atmosphere of turmoil, in which she and her sister had been encouraged to settle their scores with their fists, and their mother was a model of explosive instability. To survive, Jessica had to unlearn the patterns she had grown up with. Whether she could was the question.

In a few rare and peaceful moments, when she had hope, Jessica tried. While she was hospitalized, she filled out a "therapeutic contract," a sort of plan of attack for her self-identified issues. She wrote:

Issue 1: *Depression.*
Solution: 1. Talk to more people. 2. Adress why I am feeling this way. 3. Also take my meds.

Issue 2: *Mood swings.*
Solution: Stay away from other people when I am like
that so I don't hurt them.

Issue 3: *My court issues.*
Solution: 1. Stay out of trouble. 2. Don't use my mouth,
hands, or feet on other people.

These constructive moments inevitably gave way to stronger, all-
consuming forces, to a grief that was a million miles deep. When she
was given a pad of loose-leaf paper so she could keep a journal, Jessica wrote page after page, a few words on each, in what became a
horrific exercise in self-loathing. "Jessica Roger is really no good,"
she wrote in large red wavy letters on one page. "Please send me to
hell with the devil. I am just like him," she wrote on another. She
drew the outline of her hand with her wrist neatly colored with the
angry dark strokes of a red marker and the delicate outline of a vein
sprouting toward her palm. "Feel it," she wrote across the top. On a
picture of a curved gravestone bearing her name she inscribed the
words: "Dies painfully but now is in peace and quiet."

At the hospital, Jessica was asked to place check marks next to the
words that described her feelings. She checked the words angry, sad,
lonely, afraid, disgusted, ashamed, and worried. She added the word
"depressed" at the bottom.

In a session with a psychiatrist a month after her arrest, Jessica
analyzed her adolescent self. She had not accepted that she wasn't
nurtured and parented and never would accept it, she said. She carried her anger with her, kept it bottled up. She looked for trouble
and attention and was terrified of authority figures. Sometimes her
thoughts of hurting herself scared her, she told the doctor, and
sometimes they made her feel ridiculous. She realized that if she
didn't get help, she would have no future. And then, there was this:
"I feel safer when I'm locked behind doors. No one can get to me."

No one could disappoint or reject her in the hospital, no one could crush the little girl that was Jessica. Jessica had become a creature of the institution.

Later, when Jessica and her former roommate Tina were apart, Jessica wrote letters from hospitals and jail telling Tina to keep her act together and stay off drugs. "You better not be hurting yourself," she warned her. "If you do, I'll kick your ass from here to China." This, from the girl who had been driven to pain with a single-minded focus, using plastic utensils, paper clips—whatever was available—to cut and slash her skin. The girls never met again but they corresponded for five years. "Jessica + Tina—Sisters 4 life," Jessica wrote on the cover of her journal in 1997, a tribute to a girl she had loved, and who had loved her back. Their time together was what would pass, in Jessica's life, for stolen moments of adolescent bliss.

In July 1997, Rockland declared that Jessica was "not a danger to herself or others." Another place would have to be found for her while she awaited trial on charges of assaulting both her sister and a corrections officer. There was really only one alternative: a squat stone-and-wire building in a depressed neighborhood of Poughkeepsie known as the Dutchess County Jail.

Only sixteen years old, Jessica proved more challenging as an inmate than the jail's toughest con. She could barely adhere to the rules of society at large; the military-like strictures of a jail, with its demands of obedience and conformity, were guaranteed to add to her trauma and exacerbate her illness. In all, Jessica spent twelve months in the Dutchess County Jail, interrupted twice by stays at psychiatric hospitals. While she was there, she took apart plumbing, repeatedly flooding her cell, and attempted suicide. She wrote "666" in blood on the wall, refused orders, and kicked officers. Once, when she spat blood on guards from a wound in her mouth, she got the full-throttle treatment: helmet-clad officers shot her twice with a stun gun, forced her onto her bunk, and placed a "spit hood" over her head. Another time, two officers with stun guns and shields held the struggling Jessica facedown on her bunk and stripped her to her panties—a practice that recalls rape for many jailed women—ostensibly as a suicide precaution. She banged her head against the wall and repeatedly goaded the guards, telling one to "come in and get me," and another to "suck this." She was brought up on charges numerous times, and punished as a result—but by then, none of it mattered. "I don't care what happens anymore," she told her jailers after one incident. "Do what you want to me." Indeed, she'd received so many sentences to the jail's segregation unit that there wasn't enough time to serve them.

The judge tried hard to avoid sending Jessica Roger to prison. He cajoled prosecutors, wrote letters, and tapped friends in the state legislature, all in hopes of coming up with some other place to put this mentally ill young woman, this peg, as he would call her, without a hole. A home with counselors and intensive therapy and locked doors would have been nice, a place where she could have learned to trust people, to manage her emotions, and maybe even to like herself. A place where she would be treated instead of punished. Jessica was now eighteen, but the crime for which she was being sentenced in his Poughkeepsie courtroom had occurred when she was sixteen. More precisely, it had occurred five days past her sixteenth birthday, which is the defining moment under New York State law when children cease to be children, when in the blink of an eye the antics of adolescence go from family court to criminal court. It did not matter that Jessica had been in mental institutions twenty-four times in the preceding five years, or that, the law aside, she was still very much a little girl.

Judge George Marlow was a serious but kindly judge, short and round, with wiry hair, and thirty-two years in the system. He had been on the bench for seven years in a conservative county ninety miles north of New York City, where IBM and the Republican Party were dominant and judges were expected to be tough. Marlow did his part in that regard. But he did not like the turn that the system had taken in recent years, when more and more people with mental illness were appearing on his docket with fewer and fewer places to send them. He was not happy that a young girl with bipolar disorder and who-knows-what, a girl who had first tried to kill herself at the age of twelve, would have to go to prison. Sentencing her was not going to be easy.

Judge Marlow called the court to order, and Jessica shuffled from the holding area on the side of the courtroom, her dark blond ponytail swaying, her handcuffed wrists secured in front of her with a chain that was wrapped around her waist. She wore the quiet, chastened demeanor of the expectant defendant.

The *People v. Jessica Roger* had begun with a fight, one of many between Jessica and her older sister, Cora. The two girls mixed it up so often and so loudly that the Roger household was a regular stop on the domestic-strife circuit of the Poughkeepsie police. This time, when Jessica bit Cora, the police, on their second stop of the day at the Roger place, had issued Cora an ultimatum: press charges or we will. The case might easily have been disposed of had the situation not escalated. Jessica was volatile and she was big, with thick thighs, a bulging middle, and the facile flexibility of youth. While she was being processed for assaulting her sister, her wrists slipped from her handcuffs and a female officer attempted to put them back on. Jessica, who did not like to be touched, reacted violently, flailing and screaming. The SWAT team was called to contain her, and the female officer took a kick to her left breast. Assault of a peace officer, a felony offense, was added to her tally of charges.

Judge Marlow ticked off, for the record, all that everybody had done to help Jessica. He made a point of calling her a girl because, he said, that was what she was: a kid. He had spent more time on her case than on twenty-five other cases put together. He had met with her public defender and the county prosecutor, with mental health and probation officials. He had personally appealed to a state senator and an assemblyman to help find a place for her. And he had at last found a facility that would take her. It was a matter of waiting, and waiting, for a bed to become available in a system long on demand and short on supply.

Jessica could not wait. When she set fire to her bed in the psychiatric hospital where she was being held, she narrowed her future to one, and only one, option: she was guilty of crimes that had endangered people, and society needed protection. There was no other place for her but prison, and the time had come.

Jessica positioned herself before a robed and somber Judge Marlow. At her side was her public defender, a tall, angular Quaker named Thomas Angell who had made a career of representing the poor, the downcast, and the ill of Dutchess County, a man who at this moment felt as defeated as the judge. On a hard wooden bench in the second row sat Joan and Kevin Roger.

"I feel and I felt all along," the judge said, "that the system just doesn't have the capacity now to deal with this kind of problem in an appropriate way. When someone has a documented history of mental illness, as this defendant does, there ought to be a place where there could be both isolation and treatment. That is the only humane response to a young person like this to a crime like this." He did not have that place to offer, especially with arson on the list of grievances. "It's very sad for me to have to sentence her as I'm going to, but I have to."

"We tried every possible avenue," the judge told Jessica. "We all tried our best."

And so, on May 17, 1999, Jessica Lee Roger was sentenced to three and a half to seven years in the New York State prison system.

When Marlow asked her if she had anything to say, she shook her head. She had retreated, shut down, as she often did, at least for the moment. Her mother made a simple appeal to the judge in her gravelly but respectful voice: Please send Jessica to some other place.

"I know she is not going to make it in prison," she told him.

Jessica left the Dutchess County Jail in May 1999 the way she had arrived—with a bang. She had four major incidents in the nine days before going to the Bedford Hills Correctional Facility. She trashed the jail's dayroom and threw things around her cell; guards twice had to subdue and cuff her.

Jessica went to state prison with many marks against her: She was big, angry, and mentally ill; she had a record of jail calamities; she was going to prison for assaulting a guard.

CHAPTER ELEVEN

The Box

BEDFORD HILLS CORRECTIONAL FACILITY IS a complex of fifty brick-and-block buildings encased in silvery razor-wire. It is cradled incongruously in a wooded hollow amid the pricey real estate of Westchester County, forty miles north of New York City. The prison began in 1901 as the New York State Reformatory for Women at Bedford for 238 prostitutes and other such miscreants, and in the 1970s morphed into a maximum security facility for more than 850 inmates. On Jessica's arrival in 1999, more than half of these women were, like her, mentally ill, making Bedford part psychiatric facility, part prison. It was a pair of dueling missions that, as Jessica would learn, often worked at cross-purposes.

During Jessica's formative years, from 1991 to 2002, the ranks of mentally ill inmates in New York's prisons rose by 71 percent. Some of these people went to prison because of punitive drug laws, others by virtue of tougher laws for repeat felons or because of a new and unforgiving attitude toward parole violators and crime in general. Jessica, who had been released from Rockland Children's Psychiatric Center just three weeks before the fight with her sister, went to prison because she had reached the age of responsibility and because there was nowhere else to send her.

A Harvard social psychologist, Angela Browne, who studied the women of Bedford, found that 70 percent of them had been subjected to severe physical violence in childhood, and nearly 60 percent had been sexually abused. These factors were not so much the cause as the incubators of a plague that afflicted the women of Bedford, a plague of mental illness.

Jessica Roger fit into Bedford like a hand in a well-worn glove. She had had her share of childhood trauma; she knew the blight of mental illness. It was a toss-up as to which was worse. She had lived a narcotized adolescence in an ever-changing series of hospitals and homes. She had been tied down, drugged up, and had suffered the prompting and probing of an army of psycho-staff. She also had known the pain of abandonment, the grief of a family in turmoil. "To me," Jessica told a psychiatrist when she was seventeen, "my life has been nothing but hell." At age eighteen, when Jessica arrived at Bedford, she thought she knew the ropes. But there would be another dimension added to her life experience, another indignity to her repertory. Here, at the behest of New York State, Jessica would be punished both for her crime and for her illness.

As Jessica was moving toward her sixteenth birthday in 1997, New York prison officials began to believe that they needed another weapon in their arsenal of inmate-control techniques. The prison population had increased by fourteen thousand, some 26 percent, since 1990, and the ranks of the mentally ill were growing at three times that rate. While assaults on staff were dropping, the rate of inmate-to-inmate assault was rising. Many of the new "cookie-cutter" prisons that had been built in the '80s and '90s were dormitory-style housing that lacked individual cells in which inmates could be locked when they became unruly. In other, more traditional prisons, tensions were high as a flood of new inmates had to double up in bathroom-sized cells built for one inmate. The system, its overseers decided, needed a tool to contain troublemakers and send a message to the rest of the population. It needed more "special housing units."

From 1998 to 2000, nine additions and one new stand-alone facility were constructed in New York State, all around the same theme: sensory and human deprivation. Three thousand inmates in these "special" units would remain in cells with solid doors and little natural light virtually around the clock. They would eat, sleep, shower, eliminate, and exist in these closed worlds, leaving them for one hour a day of court-mandated recreation—and even that was often in a barren kennel attached to the back of the cell. When they were moved, it was with their hands padlocked to chains around their waists, as if they were wild beasts that had been let out of their cages. Inmates were allowed few personal photographs or possessions, no television, and limited reading material. Food was delivered through a small slot in the door; medical and mental health checks were conducted with patient and staff on opposite sides of a steel door, their conversations sounding muffled to each other but echoing through the hallways. This was a type of imprisonment, called supermax in some states, that defined those in it as subhuman and contemptible—most especially to themselves. It was also the modern-day equivalent of solitary confinement, the replication of conditions that were known to cause human beings, over time, to hear and see things, to lose their connection with reality, to unravel and break down. It had, for some at least, an even more cruel twist. Two men, men who might be violent or mentally ill or both, shared this space for weeks, months, and sometimes years at a time. At 8 feet by 14 feet, or 120 square feet, it was a space so small that only one of them could stand and move about in it at a time.

New York's prisons had long had a supply of about fifteen hundred special housing unit cells, many as small as fifty square feet, where inmates were known to have suffered prolonged and torturous confinement. Inmates had their own name for this place: they called it "the Box." What changed in the late 1990s was the scale on which this method of control became employed. By 2000, New York had more people, both in number and proportion, in punitive confinement than any other state in the country, about fifty-five hundred, or 8 percent of the prison population. Moreover, by default or perhaps by design, one in four of these people were mentally ill; in maximum-security facilities, more than three in five were. Decades after the back wards of state hospitals had been emptied, special housing units came to take their place. But unlike the hospital wards, the Box was a place of punishment, lockups within lockups. The units were noisy, smelly, dimly lit dungeons where men, and sometimes women, cowered behind locked doors, threw feces at staff, and set themselves on fire. Some inmates screamed and banged at all hours of the day and night. Others rambled nonsensically or believed their food was poisoned. Some tried, and a few succeeded, in killing themselves. From 1998 to 2003, nearly half of the suicides in New York State prisons occurred in New York's twenty-three-hour confinement blocks.

These units were a sign of the times, an outgrowth of the tougher, more unforgiving places prisons had become. In 1991, more than a thousand inmates had earned college degrees in the state's prisons; by 1999, thanks to program cuts, the number had dropped to seventy. In the latter half of the decade, the number of inmates enrolled in drug programs dropped by 30 percent, and those allowed to work toward release in the community dropped by 60 percent. From 1994 to 1999, inmates paroled after serving their sentences for violent crimes dropped by 48 percent, and for drug crimes by 9 percent. About the only good news was that more inmates had signed up for high school equivalency programs—but the ratio of teachers to pupils was cut, from 1:15, to 1:25.

On Thursday May 20, 1999, Jessica Roger arrived at Bedford
Hills, along with three other inmates. The other women, all white,
were nineteen, twenty, and twenty-one years old, and had been convicted of, respectively, possessing stolen property, possessing drugs,
and selling drugs. Jessica was fingerprinted, showered, issued a state
uniform—dark green cotton shirt and matching trousers—and
assigned a number, 99G0633. In the photograph taken for her ID
card, Jessica's brows are furrowed above deep-set eyes, her lips are
pursed in a round face. Her shoulder-length hair, tucked behind her
ears, looks as if she had just gotten out of a top-down convertible
rather than a prison transport. She was nonetheless described as
"cooperative and appeared to be adjusting satisfactorily," trying, no
doubt, to be good. She weighed in at 230 pounds, and was listed as
"depressed—on mental meds" in her mental health assessment.
When she finished her admission process, she became one of 70,000
people, including 3,400 women, in New York State prisons. More
specifically, she was now one of 400 women with mental illness at
Bedford, about 240 of them with schizophrenia, impulse-control disorders, or depression, in roughly equal proportions. She was at the
best facility in New York State for people like her, where there were
nearly thirty mental health staff members, a special psychiatric unit,
and an enlightened superintendent. In the end, however, the key
question would be: Was Jessica a patient or a prisoner? Was she, in
prison parlance, mad or merely bad? The answer would play a pivotal
role in the fate of inmate 99G0633.

8/26/86 Michelle Burris star[t]ed a fire.

*8/31/86 Carolyn Langley had plastic bag tied over her head
and fastened around her neck.*

*9/5/86 Faye Santiago threw urine in CO's [corrections
officer's] eyes.*

9/7/86 Rhonda Walker started fire in cell.
    —Logbook from Bedford Hills special housing unit,
                                                    1986

When Jessica arrived at Bedford Hills, she was determined to be good. "I really am sorry for what I did," she wrote to an aunt a few weeks later. "I did not mean to kick the officer. But I don't know what Jessica you are dealing with because one minute I am the tearful I'm sorry victim and the next minute I am the hard ass person. I don't even know who the real me is anymore." She wanted her aunt to know that she was doing well, however. She went on to say, with a touch of pride, that a guard had told her she hadn't given anybody any trouble and had added, "Let's keep it that way." "I said I planned on it," Jessica wrote.

At Bedford, Jessica was a presence—not unpretty with her hazel eyes and widow's peak, but large, with acne and the invisible scars of dysfunction. She was a bright and emotionally needy girl who, during her mother's visits in the prison's cavernous visiting room, would cling to her, her ponytailed head on Joan's shoulder, her thick arms wrapped around her. She would even take to sucking her thumb on occasion, a carryover from childhood. She seemed to lack something, to need something intangible. After an older inmate who was training a guide dog once let Jessica pet it, for months afterward whenever Jessica saw the inmate she would invariably ask, "Where's Mathilda?"

When she was happy, Jessica was engaging, articulate, and sassy. When asked to identify herself, she would announce in rapid fire, "Jessica Roger, 99G0633," rolling her tongue on the two thuh-REEs. Once, when an officer asked her why she had not replied to a question, she politely explained, "Because I was upset. There's a right time and a wrong time for me to speak when I'm upset." When she was sad, it was written all over her. She would talk in a barely audible voice. She would sigh. Sometimes she would say that she wanted to hurt herself.

Andy DeMers was among a small number of officers who befriended Jessica, a practice among guards that was not encouraged. At Bedford, the role of officers was to control rather than connect with inmates. It was a mind-set that led to many confrontations—as when Jessica's shirt wasn't tucked in and she got twenty days locked in her cell for refusing orders to tuck it in—and also to failed opportunities. DeMers believed in connecting. He had seen the difficulty Jessica had with authority figures, had listened when she spoke about her love for her father, had been jarred by the eraser burns on her leg that spelled "daddy." He wanted to help her. Every morning, when she wasn't locked up, Jessica would visit DeMers and put her head, puppylike, on the high counter he manned. It was a ritual they shared: He would "tune" her nose, that is, make a noise as he tweaked it. Then she'd be on her way.

From the day Jessica arrived at Bedford, except for a few minor infractions, she managed to stay under control for eleven months, no small feat for a teenager who had so tested the resources of the Dutchess County Jail. She was within five months of a parole hearing and release—counting time she had served before Bedford—when, on April 14, 2000, the long spell of relative peace officially ended.

Jessica had periodically had trouble containing her anxiety and agitation, a hallmark of her illness and her persona. These emotions would become so intense at times that she was driven to be destructive, to trash her room or to break things. She would say that she tried to control her emotions but the effort of it was overwhelming. Twice in two weeks she had had angry outbursts, once refusing a work assignment, and the other time calling an officer a "fucking asshole." She'd claimed that the officer first called her a "fucking juvenile delinquent," but she had been written up nevertheless. The incidents had been run-of-the-mill exercises in mouthing off to authority, but while she was in a prison dayroom waiting to see a doctor, her anger boiled over. She flipped tables and chairs and attempted to break a bookshelf by standing on it. She threw a pail and refused orders to stop. In an administrative hearing, Jessica was found guilty of creating a disturbance, refusing three orders, violent conduct, harassment, and property damage. She was sentenced to one hundred days in the special housing unit—the Box—the place with screaming women, stark encroaching walls, and unbroken solitude. She lasted twelve days before self-destruction and self-loathing took her on a trip to the dark side. She made her first suicide attempt, which apparently wasn't considered serious. Then, on May 5, officers found her lying on the floor of her cell, a sheet tied tightly around her neck. She had attempted to strangle herself. She was alive but unresponsive and her eyes had begun to hemorrhage. Nearby was a note with the outline of her hand spattered with blood. "This is how I feel," she wrote.

Jessica had been diagnosed as suffering a host of maladies: bipolar disorder, depression, mood disorder, and adjustment disorder among them. The most consistent label affixed to her at Bedford, however, had been borderline personality disorder. It was a diagnosis that in prison marked inmates as willful, ill-tempered and, incorrectly, all but untreatable. Borderlines were impulsive, emotionally unstable, and prone to angry outbursts. They could not maintain personal relationships and had little sense of self-worth. They were self-destructive and had intense fears of abandonment. They were not easy cases. They were also especially prone to unravel in the Box, so that Jessica's suicide attempt may have been a predictable, almost normal, response to the stresses of solitary confinement. In a landmark 1990s case against the California prison system, an expert witness, Joel Dvoskin, had testified that there were some people who "can't handle" twenty-three-hour confinement. "Typically, those are people who have a pre-existing disorder that is called borderline personality disorder."

After her suicide attempt, Jessica was admitted to Central New York Psychiatric Center, a mental hospital for prison inmates about two hundred miles northwest of Bedford in the small Oneida County city of Marcy. For psychotic inmates, the facility was a godsend—a humane hospital where inmates abruptly became patients and where they received a rich array of therapy, life-skills training, and recreation. Although there was security, there were no bars or cells, even for those inmates, like Jessica, who had come from the dehumanizing, high-security confines of the Box. Amazingly, there were also relatively few violent incidents there.

But Marcy, for the sick, was like a mirage. The hospital had just 189 beds to serve about seventy-five hundred mentally ill inmates and had not been expanded since it opened in 1981. Since then, the state had added thirty-eight prisons to the system, and the prison population had tripled. This meant that it was exceedingly difficult to get into Marcy, and for those who did, stays were of necessity brief. Consequently, two-thirds of patients relapsed after they went back to prison and had to return to Marcy within a year. Elaine Lord, Bedford's superintendent, gave a name to the system's incessant movement of sick inmates—from mental health units to the Box to the hospital and back. She called it "Ping-Ponging," but there was little she could do about it.

On admission to Marcy, Jessica was described as a nineteen-year-old white female with a mood disorder history and two dozen hospitalizations. About six months before, a clinician noted, she had begun to see "orange & purple monkeys swinging from lights," and over the years she had been given seven different diagnoses. "She has tried to kill herself 6x to include 2 recent attempted hangings. . . . She states she would like for us to help her not feel like harming/killing herself."

By June 13, 2000, after thirty-two days in the hospital, Jessica had recovered sufficiently from her suicide attempt to be sent back to Bedford Hills. There, officials did something quite amazing and incomprehensible. They returned her to the Box to finish her sentence.

Jessica's attempt to strangle herself, her caretakers believed, was rooted in her refusal to accept punishment for her prison crimes. They identified her as a "malingerer," someone whose suicidal overture was for a purpose other than dying. "Does not want to do her SHU [special housing unit] time," the prison staff had reported when she was sent to Marcy.

After a few days in the Box, Jessica again attempted suicide, and by June 26, she was back at Marcy, another ping–pong ball in the prison mental health system.

> *Patient states that she wants to die. There is nobody in this world for her. Appears determined to do self harm. This AM tightened strip of blanket around neck and knotted it so tightly that it only came off with difficulty—faced turned blue . . . was quiet, business like and determined. . . . Her young age, her severe depression and her determination make her a threat to self. Requires higher degree of treatment.*
> —6/26/2000, on Jessica's second admission to the
> prison psychiatric hospital at Marcy

Jessica's infraction and her hundred-day sentence in the Bedford special housing unit had prompted back-to-back suicide attempts and two hospitalizations, and it had another serious repercussion. On September 14, 2000, the state parole board ruled that releasing Jessica—a "seriously and persistently mentally ill" inmate—was "not in the best interests of society." A month after her release from Marcy, Jessica learned that her parole had been denied and she would spend at least another two years in prison. Just a week earlier, she had seemed to be making progress. A prison counselor had written in a logbook that she had "willingly admitted" her destructive impulses—a litany that included suicide attempts dating back to early adolescence, wrist cuttings, hair pulling, and even sewing her fingers together. She was tired. She had told the counselor she

wanted to stop, but she had said that before, and then her best inten-
tions would be blown away like a feather in a tornado. Other forces,
both those within Jessica and those without, were simply too strong.

Shortly after Jessica's parole denial, Bedford was shaken by the
simultaneous suicide attempts of three inmates. One of the women,
Iris Rodriguez, a forty-two-year-old Bronx convict, successfully
hanged herself while locked in her cell, using a sheet strung from the
cross-bars of her cell door.

A few days after Rodriguez's death, Jessica's counselor asked her
how she felt about it, how she was doing. She said she was okay.
Officers on her unit, however, reported that she was "oppositional."
In truth, she was on a slow but steady slide, like Iris Rodriguez, a
prisoner of a time that was short on tolerance, long on punishment.

> *To: Mommy,*
> *I'm trying to hold my head as high as I can but it is kind of*
> *hard to when you are locked up and locked in at the same time.*
> *Another words I am still locked until July 1, 2001. One more*
> *month of this stupid shit. I can't deal with it anymore. I am so*
> *fed up with these people it is not even funny anymore . . .*
> *Mommy I don't drink and these people make some one want to*
> *pick up a bottle and gulp it down. I'm sick of the system. I've*
> *been in it since the age of 11 years old. That's 9 years all*
> *together. Mommy I just want to come home and be finished*
> *with all of this in and out of places. Why can't I just be a*
> *normal person like the rest of the family. I know I have prob-*
> *lems but everybody does in there lives . . . Mommy these people*
> *are stressing me out again. They took my sheets, my blankets*
> *and my mattress out of my cell because I keep hiding under the*
> *bed and covering myself so they can't see me. . . . Mommy I*
> *really feel like hurting myself but I am afraid to tell these*
> *people because I don't want them to put me in a cold ass cell*
> *with nothing but a thin mat and a gown. . . . Mommy the*

feeling of hurting myself is getting stronger. Why won't these
feelings just stay out of my head forever? I can't deal with
them anymore. My thoughts about hurting myself are racing
now they are going faster than before.
        —June 2001 letter signed "Jessica Lee, your brat"

When Jessica wrote to her mother in June 2001, she was serving
two thirty-day sentences in "keeplock," an alternative to the special
housing unit in which inmates were locked in their cells for all but
an hour a day of recreation. She had earned this punishment for setting fire to a book, yelling during the inmate count, refusing a direct
order to put out a cigarette, and cursing at the staff—typical,
obstreperous Jessica. The excuse she gave to an officer was that she
was "not doing well." Keeplock was a grueling, boring test of
endurance but one that was appreciably better than the Box. At least
she could talk to inmates in the hall as they passed by. If the duty
officer was kind, she could even play Yahtzee or cards through the bars
with an older group that had taken it upon itself to keep the teary,
depressed young Jessica in check. It gave them pleasure to see her
laugh and enjoy the company of others. When she wasn't wallowing
in her despair, they thought, she was a good kid who could be fun
and engaging. She needed to know that.

Earlier that spring, Jessica had spent another month at Marcy
after she had hoarded medications in hopes of overdosing. She had
also sewn the letter "J" into her abdomen with a needle and thread
in her insatiable quest to feel pain. You're a young girl, the women
would tell her to lift her spirits. You'll be getting out. Jessica's
appearance did not help matters. She weighed nearly 300 pounds by
this point, and her self-image was miserable. She cried often. She
hated herself and believed she had shamed her family, her father in
particular, by going to prison.

One of the group, Betty Guzzardi, was a pert, brown-haired
fiftyish woman who was doing time for a minor drug sale and had a

daughter Jessica's age. Guzzardi had once been in a tutoring session in a dayroom when Jessica suddenly ripped an electrical plate off the wall, broke it in pieces, and slashed at her wrist, drawing blood. The incident had shocked both Jessica's tutor and Guzzardi, who was appalled at how prison authorities responded to Jessica's outbursts; it seemed the girl was perpetually locked in her cell or the Box, which only made matters worse.

In theory, the prison's disciplinary process had provisions for inmates who were mentally ill. Under regulations, mental health personnel could advocate for diminished punishment when they believed that inmates had committed infractions because of their illness—an attempt to strike a balance between mad and bad. But at Bedford and other prisons, the scales invariably tipped toward the bad. An ounce of compassion given was seen as a pound of control lost.

Mental health professionals repeatedly failed Jessica. In the following exchange, a psychologist, testifying at a hearing at which Jessica faced a charge of setting a book on fire, was offered the opportunity three times to advocate on behalf of her patient. She declined repeatedly, even after describing Jessica as anxious, upset, and depressed.

> *Hearing Officer:* Do you feel that her misbehavior, if you can characterize it as that, was caused by her mental state, her emotional state?
>
> *Psychologist:* I am not in a position to say that it was caused. I was not there.
>
> *Hearing Officer:* Do you think there is any role for punishment in her life?
>
> *Psychologist:* I am not in a position to comment on what decision you make.
>
> *Hearing Officer:* What I'm concerned about is the imposition of a penalty that is merely punitive to me is not enough.

> If it had some redeeming value, some virtue in it in terms of her future behavior . . .
>
> *Psychologist:* That's a very difficult question to answer as well and kind of goes beyond in terms of what my speculation can be with regard to a disciplinary hearing. She did something that she knows she should not have done.

In that case, the hearing officer gave Jessica just a week's confinement in her cell. In another case, she wasn't so lucky, even though the evidence of her illness was far more compelling.

On November 24, 2001, Jessica had a meltdown. Crying ceaselessly and banging her head, she was placed in the prison's observation unit. It was the place she had described in her letter as a "cold ass cell" because inmates were stripped of their clothing and placed in suicide-proof gowns. She tried to kill herself twice there. She was then sent to the psychiatric hospital at Marcy again, where she told a counselor that she felt helpless and worthless and had seen the shadow of someone threatening her family. She remained hospitalized for sixty days, the longest of her four hospitalizations so far.

On February 7, 2002, just seven days after her return to Bedford Hills, Jessica refused to go into her cell and spat in an officer's face three times; she also tied a sheet around her neck. She was put back in the prison observation unit for a week. On her release, she faced a charge of committing an "unhygienic act" for having spat on the officer, intolerable even if it had occurred when she was suicidal. In the following exchange, the prison psychologist notes Jessica's dangerous history of attempting suicide but again sits on the sidelines as Jessica is sentenced to the Box.

> *Hearing Officer:* In your view is this likely to have been an isolated incident or is this a part of her pattern of behavior over time?

Psychologist: Miss Roger suffers from emotional disregulation [*sic*]. She becomes frustrated and angry very easily. She often engages in self-harming behavior— rather serious and has made some *extremely* [speaker's emphasis] significant . . . and serious attempts to hurt herself, one of them occurring in SHU where she almost successfully hanged herself.

The hearing officer then asks if the psychologist believes Jessica knew that what she was doing was "assaultive," in effect whether she knew it was wrong.

Psychologist: She would be doing this because she was very angry at the officer.

Hearing Officer: You caught me on a day when anger is not to be rewarded.

Psychologist: That's good.

The hearing officer then sentenced Jessica to sixty days in the special housing unit, the place reserved, in the words of the prison commissioner, for "the worst of the worst." It apparently made no difference that she had made an "extremely significant" suicide attempt during her previous stay there. The purpose of the punishment, the officer wrote in his finding, was "to impress upon this inmate that this type of behavior will not be tolerated at this facility. Unhygienic acts are considered serious and spitting on staff even worst [*sic*]." The purpose may have been to teach Jessica a lesson. The result was another serious suicide attempt and another trip to Marcy.

As Jessica walked to the prison van, she spotted Andy DeMers, the officer who had been kind to her, with whom she had shared a silly morning ritual. "Who's gonna tweak my nose?" she asked.

On April 16, 2002, fifty-five days into her second stint in the Box, Jessica had a date in Dutchess County Court. Frustrated and angry, she had written a threatening letter to the jail corrections officer whose assault when she was sixteen had landed her in prison; for this, on her release from prison, she would be facing six additional months in the Dutchess County Jail. Jessica's prison time had been an unmitigated disaster—she was looking at serving her entire seven-year term and more time after that. This was typical of seriously mentally ill inmates, who were routinely denied parole because of extensive disciplinary records, and whose additional crimes often added to their terms in prison. Complicating matters, Jessica had been in the Box a week earlier and received another disciplinary sentence when she had refused to go back into her cell and, again, spat in a guard's face. This time it was sixty days in keeplock.

On her way back from court, sitting in the back of a green state corrections van, Jessica became unhinged. She began kicking at the windows as two officers struggled to restrain her nearly three-hundred-pound bulk, and when the rocking van stopped in an empty parking lot and the door opened, she tumbled out onto the ground. On her back, she spat and kicked as three frantic officers dodged and weaved and finally got her back in the van. Her stay in the special housing unit may have been intended to improve Jessica's behavior and deter future incidents, but there was little evidence that it had. The next day, Jessica was taken back to Marcy, the result, a report would later note, of an "attempted hanging and head trauma in the Bedford Hills CF Special Housing Unit." This was her fifth visit to the prison psychiatric hospital in two years.

At Marcy, Jessica was given the following goal: "Ms. Roger will be free from suicidal/homicidal ideation and/or behaviors by the time of discharge." A month later, having met the standard for release, she was sent back to Bedford to face two months of twenty-three-hour days in her cell as part of her keeplock sentence. She may have been psychotic when she committed the infraction and it may have led to a month-long stay at the prison hospital, but she had spat on an officer, and she would again face consequences.

Jessica made the most of her time in keeplock, studying for her high school equivalency degree, urging family members to visit, and in long letters, contemplating her life. "You know what I realized I have made alot of mistakes in my life and I wish I could go back and change all the wrong I have done from the age of ten up until now," she wrote to her mother two weeks into her sentence. "Mommy how can I make my life more easier? I am tired of living a rough life all the time." She asked for a baby picture so she could hang it up and see "the angel I used to be," not the devil she was. But she had some good news, too. She told her mother about a friend she had met in a recent stay at Marcy, a twenty-eight-year-old male inmate who was doing two to four years for larceny. It was against regulations to write to each other so she would write letters in care of his family, who would then send them on to him and vice versa. "When we both get out we are going to try to meet up with each other," she told Joan. "Don't worry there won't be anything going on between us. When he left he tried to come back just to spend more time with me why I don't know."

Six days after Jessica was released from keeplock, Betty Guzzardi heard a disturbing report: Jessica had been returned to the Box. She had had another one of her scenes—she had lit a cigarette in view of an officer, apparently refused orders to put it out, and by the time the incident was over, had spat at the officer and thrown a chair. She was charged with disobeying an order, unhygienic act, threats, damaging property, and tampering with an electrical outlet. (Inmates often lit cigarettes by drawing sparks from electric sockets to set toilet paper ablaze.) She was sent to the Box.

Guzzardi and the other women in Jessica's unit were appalled. "Are you crazy?" Guzzardi said to an officer when she heard the news. "She's too depressed." Earlier that week, Jessica had been sent to the prison's inpatient mental health unit, where she had tried to hurt herself, and told staff she felt like banging her head against the wall. In light of her prior suicide attempts, returning her to the Box was unthinkable. Not in the view of her custodians.

During two chaotic days in the Box, Jessica tied a sheet around her neck, and for a time was moved to an observation cell, but her keepers weren't convinced that she was serious. They fell back on the profile they had long ago developed for Jessica: she was being manipulative; she was trying to get out of the Box. They sent her back there.

When Corrections Officer Aubrey Lewis arrived for his morning shift on Saturday, August 17, 2002, other officers gave him a piece of advice about Jessica Roger: "Just keep an eye out," they told him. "She has a history of trying to kill herself." Other than that informal word, even though Jessica had just come out of suicide observation, there were no directives to take special precautions from either the mental health unit or the prison administrators.

At 12:15 P.M., Lewis was making his round of the twenty-four-cell unit. Inmates often covered the slit in the solid door when they were on the toilet, so Lewis would knock in order to ascertain whether they were alive. He got to Jessica's cell, which had been checked twenty-four minutes earlier, and found her window covered. He tapped on it. There was no response. He returned to the control area, notified the officer on duty, and called a nurse and his sergeant.

When the door of cell number 8 was opened, two officers found Jessica lying facedown on the floor. She had fastened a bed sheet to her neck and pulled it so tight that officers had to cut it off with a knife. It was the method she'd tried many times before. Officers administered CPR while they waited for an ambulance, but it was too late.

Word of Jessica's suicide spread quickly through Bedford Hills that sultry August weekend. Two corrections officers, including Andy DeMers, cried at the news. Many inmates were furious. Why had a woman with such clearly self-destructive impulses been put in the most difficult environment the prison had to offer? Meanwhile, among mental health workers there was a steadfast belief that Jessica had not intended to do what she did, that an attention-getting gesture of self-harm—typical of "borderlines"—had inadvertently turned into a successful suicide. "This was an accident and she had not intended to die," insisted an internal prison memo. But did Jessica's intention matter? Should prison officials have played the odds that her history might backfire on them? Should she have been in the Box at all?

At the time of Jessica's suicide, Elaine Lord, the prison superintendent, had been away for a few days' vacation. Before she left, she had given instructions: Don't put Jessica Roger in the Box. She had not, however, put the dictate in writing.

> *The whole facility was like "How could they do this knowing how she was?" It was very upsetting to us that a young girl like that took her life, and more than that, the facility helped her take her life.*
> —Betty Guzzardi, inmate at Bedford Hills

Jessica left no note this time. A state police investigator concluded, "Deceased had a history of violent and aggressive behavior with prior threats and attempts of [*sic*] harm herself. . . . Examination of the scene revealed nothing unusual or suspicious." No one faced any criminal or disciplinary charges in Jessica's death. It was the system, and not any particular individual, that had failed her. Jessica weighed 280 pounds when autopsied and was found to have pulmonary edema. The autopsy mentioned a "red abrasion measuring 1 by 1/2 inch" on her forehead as well as multiple purplish spots from ruptured blood vessels in her face. The cause of death was listed as "Asphyxia due to self-strangulation (with sheet). Suicide."

CHAPTER TWELVE

New York: A System Overwhelmed

THE NEW YORK STATE COMMISSION of Correction was harshly critical of prison protocol in the events that led to Jessica Roger's death. Its investigation concluded that she should not have been returned to the Box from the observation unit just before her death, particularly after making an overture of self-harm. Further, it said that after five admissions to Marcy, she should have been considered for long-term care there. The commission did not, however, criticize the system for its policy of putting severely mentally ill people into solitary confinement in the first place. Nor did it suggest that perhaps such people do not belong in prison at all, that something is wrong in a society that imprisons sick people on this scale. That would have been beyond its mission, which is merely to investigate these deaths and make recommendations for change, which aren't binding and often go ignored. Prison officials sloughed off the critical report on Jessica. She didn't need long-term care, they told the commission, and she'd shown no signs of suicide on the day of her death. The commission's work does serve an important purpose, nonetheless. It reveals a system in trouble.

Elaine Lord became the superintendent of Bedford Hills in 1984, and over the years she earned a reputation as a fair administrator who cared about her charges. She was respected by inmates within her prison and by other administrators in the Department of Correctional Services, not an easy sell. A round, motherly-looking woman with square glasses, pink cheeks, and curly reddish hair, Lord was known to advocate for mentally ill inmates who had misbehaved because they were sick, and to fight for more staff and better resources for her prison.

In the sixteen years before Jessica's arrival, Lord had seen the floodgates open to a new and difficult population. To be sure, Bedford had always had its share of "defectives," as they were called. In 1916, a "Psychopathic Hospital" was opened at the reformatory for especially problematic inmates; it had even led to a scandal as prisoners were flogged, shackled to their beds for days, and handcuffed to walls so their toes barely touched the floor. This modern population of mentally ill inmates was different, however; it was more extensive—one of every two inmates—and more troublesome, accounting for eight in ten serious incidents in the facility. The problems of this population were beyond the ken of prisons. Some inmates routinely cut themselves—alone or in groups—with whatever was available, from pieces of metal or floor tile to even the foil packets of skin cream. Others inserted screws under their skin, burned themselves with cigarettes, or swallowed safety pins, light bulbs, or bits of glass. One serial swallower chewed up a mercury thermometer, another gulped down a pair of scissors. More routinely, these inmates saw things that weren't there, had intractable fears, screamed inappropriately, and could not comply with prison routines, like stopping for several daily counts, standing on line for commissary or medications, and answering questions from staff.

"I remember an earlier time as superintendent," Lord wrote in 2002, "when it was unusual to admit a woman to Bedford Hills who was so seriously mentally ill that the intake process had to be halted. Then it became a monthly occurrence, and finally it became and continues to be a daily part of normal operations." Some inmates even arrive with twenty-four-hour guards to prevent their suicide.

In 1984, the same year that Lord became superintendent, two gutsy young lawyers named Elizabeth Koob and Joan Magoolaghan decided to take on the Department of Correctional Services for its treatment of mentally ill women at Bedford Hills Correctional Facility. Bedford's solitary confinement—or special housing—unit, their lawsuit contended, was little more than a twelve-cell mad-house where psychotic women were locked for months and years in a downward spiral of deprivation. The pair chronicled some four hundred incidents in the Box at Bedford from 1981 to 1987: women who cut themselves with glass, spread feces on walls, flooded the unit with sewage, and punched officers in an atmosphere of asylum-era mayhem. They obtained the testimony of five psychiatrists who studied Bedford's mentally ill women and concluded that solitary confinement was tantamount to torture. (They also asserted that the prison's chief psychologist had faked his credentials, and the state declined to defend him.) In 1989, a judge upheld the long-running lawsuit, which had nearly bankrupted the pair of lawyers. He found that the inmates' constitutional protection against cruel and unusual punishment had been violated by "the systemic lack of access to and provision of mental health care" and "the noise and squalor in which plaintiffs were confined."

By the late 1990s, *Langley v. Coughlin* had significantly improved care in the Bedford special housing unit. More mental health staff was hired and guards were trained to work with mentally ill inmates. Inmates were monitored and given thirty minutes of therapy at least twice monthly. They were offered daily recreation with each other rather than alone. There was much, however, that Langley did not accomplish. Seriously mentally ill inmates were still placed in the Box when they misbehaved, even by virtue of their illness. Mental health officials had only an advisory role in whether and, most important, how long they were placed there. And the litigation did not affect the rest of New York's prison system, which was increasingly coming to rely on twenty-three-hour confinement, the most extreme form of lockup in New York and, for that matter, America. From 1995 to 1999, the number of inmates sentenced to six months to a year in the Box—considered an unconscionable term by many experts—grew by 70 percent systemwide, while the prison population grew by 7 percent.

Koob and Magoolaghan weren't the first to point out the harsh realities of solitary confinement to New York's prison overseers. In 1823, the warden at the state's first penitentiary at Auburn reported that inmates relegated to solitary had become psychotic. One leaped from a gallery when his door was opened; another beat his head against a wall, taking out an eye. "A degree of mental anguish and distress may be necessary to humble and reform the offender," Warden Gershom Powers wrote, "but carry it too far and he will become either a savage in his temper and feelings, or he will sink in despair." In 1980, prisoner advocates sued the system over abominable conditions for people with mental illness in the special housing unit at Attica prison, a facility made infamous by a 1971 uprising in which forty-three people died. It took the state eighteen years to settle the suit, but the resulting changes were cosmetic and insignificant. In 2003, the advocates again filed suit, this time against the entire system.

Jessica Roger was on their list of reasons for the suit.

Prisons simply cannot keep up with the onslaught of seriously ill inmates. In 2001, the state commission investigated two deaths six months apart in which severely mentally ill inmates at separate prisons died from "decreased intake of food and water"—they starved, in other words. One had even announced that he was going on a hunger strike, and the other, ironically, was on a suicide watch at the time of his death. No one noticed the inevitable lethargy and withdrawal that precedes a starvation death, perhaps because such behavior was typical.

It seems plausible that the correctional system would be facing potentially huge judgments or settlements in lawsuits growing out of inmate suicides. This has occurred, but rarely. Inmate families tend to be disorganized and unconnected; they don't know how to go about pressing a case. Moreover, the lives of prison inmates are cheap, both figuratively and literally. Many prisoners have little work history or potential earning power on which families can stake a claim. In one New York case, attorney John D. B. Lewis fought for eight years before a state judge found the prison system "fully responsible for the systemic medical malpractice" in the death of a twenty-seven-year-old inmate. The inmate had ingested an entire bottle of pills that he should not have had. Two hours elapsed before an ambulance was called, and the family was not notified of the event for thirteen days while the inmate lay dying. The family was awarded $350,000 for the inmate's "conscious pain and suffering" and $25,000 for his mother's emotional trauma. It is a sum that does not encourage lawyers to press such risky, lengthy, and research-intensive lawsuits. Chances of success are even slimmer in federal court, where plaintiffs must prove "deliberate indifference"— that prison overseers were not merely negligent but that they were aware of the risk of death and consciously failed to act on it.

Jessica Roger was born on the cusp of an era in which colliding, and sometimes cruel, social forces would change the face and nature of prisons. In 1973, Governor Nelson Rockefeller presaged this rev-olution with a proposal to deter drug crime by locking up users and traffickers for long—sometimes lifelong—prison terms. By the 1980s, the Rockefeller drug laws were having an effect that had not been wholly predicted: While doing little to curb the drug trade, it was filling prisons with thousands of low-level offenders, many of them addicts, women, and small-time sellers. Iris Rodriguez, the inmate who hung herself during Jessica's time at Bedford, was a typical example of the system's overzealous prosecution of drug offenders, which captured addicts and mentally ill people like her more often than drug traffickers. Diagnosed with schizoaffective disorder, Iris had spent almost the entire four years before this prison stint in mental hospitals—three years at Bronx State Hospital, and for suicide attempts, eight months in two other hospitals. During her first prison sentence, in the early 1990s, she had been hospitalized at Marcy four times. Yet when she was arrested in 1999 for selling three small envelopes of heroin to an undercover officer, her history apparently made little difference. She got two and a half to five years.

At Bedford, Rodriguez was a disciplinary problem whose emotional state swung wildly and who had often refused to take her prescribed medication. During the months before her death she had heard voices, stabbed herself, repeatedly set her hair on fire, and hidden strips of cloth in her vagina that she could use to hang herself. Incredibly, self-mutilation and suicide attempts were violations of prison regulations, and she had been punished three times at another prison for the crime of "self-harm," once with a forty-five-day sentence to her cell. It did not deter Rodriguez. She saw her chance, on September 22, 2000, when two other inmates, twenty-six and thirty years old, had slashed their wrists and necks in a bloody, ugly expression of inmate despair, and the attention of officers was momentarily diverted. Rodriguez was blue and without a pulse by the time anyone noticed.

A report by the State Commission of Correction concluded that Bedford Hills had done little to help Iris Rodriguez in her nine months in prison. It called her course of care "tumultuous" and "inadequate" and said that after her repeated acts of self-mutilation she should have been sent to the hospital at Marcy. Superintendent

Lord also had believed that Rodriguez needed r
therapy and less punishment, and had clashed wi
mental health staff over the issue before. They, however, w
a separate bureaucracy, the Office of Mental Health. OMH workers
often tended to downplay inmate symptoms, to view them as acts of
manipulation and malingering. It was a classic tug-of-war in an
overburdened system: the corrections side was supposed to take the
"bad" inmates and the mental health side was supposed to take the
"mad" ones, and there were always arguments as to who belonged
where. The corrections/mental health relationship was a quintes-
sentially dysfunctional one, and Iris Rodriguez was a prime example
of the outcome.

In 1982, the year after Jessica's birth, a two-decade-long prison
construction boom was in progress unlike anything New York had
ever seen. That year, six prisons were opened for forty-two hundred inmates. In the following two years, seven more prisons
opened for sixty-two hundred inmates, and in the two years after
that, five more for forty-six hundred inmates. Between 1976 and
2000, when the peak finally hit, the state had built forty-nine more
prisons and seventeen additions. The new capacity for forty-five
thousand inmates brought New York's total inmate population to
seventy thousand.

Nearly half of everyone sentenced to prison in New York in the
1990s had been convicted of drug crimes.

Politicians soon learned how popular this new punishment ethic
could be, and they began finding other ways to keep prisons full,
from longer sentences to cracking down on a host of social ills to
reduced opportunities for parole.

Other changes were brewing, too. In the 1950s, New York State
had ninety thousand psychiatric beds spread out across dozens of
campuses statewide. Had Jessica come of age in the 1950s or 1960s,
she would likely have bypassed the criminal justice system altogether
when she assaulted her sister, and gone straight to a mental hospital.

By the time Jessica entered Bedford Hills, the number of psychiatric beds in New York had been reduced to about four thousand.
The idea behind this move was to treat people in their home communities, a reality that had been made possible by new drug therapies and that had been fostered by a body of pro-patient civil
rights law. But hospital closings had the same effect in New York
as elsewhere in the United States. When the back wards of hospitals were closed, former and would-be mental patients instead
became homeless; they overwhelmed ill-prepared and cash-starved
community programs; they tangled with police, racking up records
of petty crimes and drug offenses that often led them to jails and
prisons.

> *WJ appeared a broken man. Inmates on either side of him
> reported that he is "totally gone" and refuses to leave his cell
> for recreation or showers. Decomposing orange peels rotted on
> the floor under his bed. This and his poor hygiene left a nox-
> ious stench in his cell. The first day we met him, WJ was
> curled on his bed under a blanket. He didn't move or speak
> to us when we attempted to engage him. When we returned
> the second day, WJ was sitting on his bed, motionless and
> staring into space. He would not lift his head, make eye con-
> tact or speak. After several minutes, he muttered: "I want to
> speak to mental health." When we communicated this to a
> deputy superintendent, he reported that WJ had just
> returned from an evaluation with an outside psychologist,
> who considered him a malingerer and not in need of services."*
> —Description of a long-term inmate in the Wende
> special housing unit. The Correctional Association of
> New York, 2004

Jennifer Wynn was a lively advocate for inmate rights who was
in her thirties, had brown eyes, brown highlighted hair, and a sharp

eye for injustice. She worked for the Correctional Association of New York, a 160-year-old not-for-profit organization that had been given legislative authority to enter the state's prisons and report on their functioning. The association, funded by private foundations and community largesse, took its mission seriously, routinely visiting lockups and releasing an annual "State of the Prisons" report. The Department of Correctional Services had long resented the association's meddling and had taken every opportunity to label it a bunch of bleeding-heart prisoner-lovers without a clue about the realities of prison operation. It was a tactic designed to change the subject rather than deal with it, used by a bureaucracy that much preferred to operate in secret. From 1998 to 2003, the association made forty-nine visits to twenty-six special housing units and produced a special report on the Box, written by Wynn, in 2003. It was a well-researched, meticulously documented study, with inmate surveys and interviews, and it was harsh indictment of the system's use of twenty-three-hour confinement.

Wynn had been horrified by what she and other association visitors had seen in New York State's special housing units. "On nearly every site visit," she wrote, "we encountered individuals in states of extreme desperation—men weeping in their cells; men who had smeared feces on their bodies or lit their cells on fire; prisoners who cut their own flesh in a form of self-directed violence known as self-mutilation; inmates who rambled incoherently and paced about their cells like caged animals; individuals with paranoid delusions—'The COs are poisoning my food,' or 'The prison psychologist is drugging me.'" One inmate said objects talked to him, another that officers raped him at night, another that people spied on him. Many feared for their sanity. The association surveyed 258 inmates and found that the average sentence, including consecutive terms, was thirty-six months, a far cry from the department's claim of 130 days in time served.

The department's response was to issue a press release that attacked Wynn not for the content of the report but for her unrelated correspondence with an inmate in long-term solitary confinement, for whom she had felt sorry.

Wynn's experience of the Box is captured in its essence in a story about an inmate named Al Kirby. Kirby, a Rastafarian with long dreadlocks, had been sentenced to the special housing unit at Attica on an array of charges, including an attack on guards. He suffered from schizophrenia and had bounced between the Box at Attica and the prison hospital at Marcy seven times. It was a nonsensical cycle of psychosis induced by isolation, followed by a period of treatment and wellness, followed by a return to isolation, and so on. The last time Wynn saw Kirby, he was bone-thin because his jailers had taken to feeding him the "loaf," a fortified bread-like concoction served with raw cabbage and water to inmates who were particularly recalcitrant. (New York regularly used food as a punishment, even though the accrediting American Correctional Association advises against it.) Kirby was soaked in urine and had scabs and open sores. There were flies all over because of the feces he had spread on the wall. He had been on a waiting list for six months to go to the prison hospital. Seven months after Wynn's visit, after another hospitalization and a return to the Box, Kirby strangled himself with a torn strip of sheet. He was among six suicides in the Box in 2003, 40 percent of the total systemwide.

The association's report gave the lie to any rationale for New York's wholesale use of special housing.

In the years since the department had added three thousand beds to special housing units, incidents of self-harm among inmates—such as cutting or burning skin or head banging—had gone up by 66 percent. Half of the inmates in isolation units had been punished with additional measures, such as loss of showers, recreation, and food, a sign that this most extreme measure of control was having the opposite effect. About 40 percent of the inmates in the Box had been put there for nonviolent offenses, belying the assertion that these prisoners were the system's most unmanageable prisoners.

Finally, and most significant, a hugely disproportionate share of inmate suicides were occurring in special housing units. The department's press release never mentioned the word *suicide*.

> *This absolute solitude, if nothing interrupts it, is beyond the strength of man; it destroys the criminal without intermission and without pity; it does not reform, it kills. The unfortunates, on whom this experiment was made, fell into a state of depression so manifest that their keepers were struck with it; their lives seemed in danger. . . .*
> —Gustave de Beaumont and Alexis de Toqueville,
> commenting on the use of isolated confinement
> in New York State's Auburn prison, 1833

> *Special housing units are "the most severe, psychologically painful, difficult-to-serve environment in the prison system— for healthy people. Mentally ill people cannot be expected to survive and not deteriorate in that kind of an environment."*
> —Craig Haney, prison expert

> *We have no doubt that supermaxes regularly hold psychotic and seriously mentally ill prisoners. We suspect that many in supermaxes are getting worse, more dangerous, and more psychologically disturbed. It seems clear that many prisoners in supermaxes are deprived of adequate mental health care. We doubt that any state prison system can be rendered safer by building a supermax. And, finally, it is clear to us that many supermax prisons have been built for political reasons rather than to meet correctional needs, the initiative often coming from the legislature rather than the department of corrections.*
> —Michael H. Tonry and Norval Morris, eds., *Crime and Justice: An Annual Review of Research*, 2001

Inmates place themselves in disciplinary housing based upon
their own conduct. It is really as simple as that.
                    —Glenn Goord, Commissioner, New York State
                              Department of Correctional Services

---

Elsie Butler is a tall, dignified black woman with straight, cropped black hair, a gold cross around her neck, and a master's degree in social work. On this early spring day in New York, her hand runs gently over the contours of the granite headstone of her son, James, in a cemetery that she often visits five times a day.

James W. Butler Jr. was thirty when he hanged himself in June 2000 after spending six months in a special housing unit in a New York state prison. Butler, who like Jessica Roger came from Poughkeepsie, was a cocaine addict who had a long history of petty theft and one assault conviction. He had been sentenced to four to eight years in 1996 for a $20 drug sale to an undercover officer. It was an offense that would have drawn a fraction of that time before Nelson Rockefeller's calamitous war on drugs, and, at $32,500 per year to imprison him, it likely would have been more cost-effective to treat his addiction. Butler had also battled other demons: he had been hospitalized twice for bipolar disorder and had attempted suicide, once threatening to jump from a bridge.

In late 1999, when Butler was within a year of parole, he failed to return from a prison work-release program and assaulted an ex-girlfriend. For his infraction, he was returned to prison and sentenced to twelve months in Fishkill's special housing unit. The SHU was one of nine new additions that had been built statewide, each holding two hundred inmates in sterile, sometimes stifling, two-man cells, to which small cages had been attached for recreation. Elsie knew in short order that James was in trouble. He had been sleeping day and night and told her about people who were out to get him and to destroy his family. He warned his mother not to visit, fearing for her safety. He said he heard threatening voices. On May 1, 2000, Elsie sent a certified letter to the prison warden. "We're at your mercy sir," she wrote. "I'm begging you to please, please, please transfer my son to another facility to avoid termination of his life. I love my child, and I don't want any harm to come to him while he's incarcerated."

On June 3, 2000, the six-foot, 240-pound Butler hung himself from a ceiling vent in his special housing unit cell. It was the first of two suicides in the unit that year. No one at the prison had asked about Butler's history of psychiatric care or suicide attempts when he was put into the SHU. Later, after he was diagnosed as depressed, suffering from insomnia, and hearing voices, no one made any attempt to remove him from the SHU. A notation showed that Butler had told his keepers, "It's too stressful to be in the Box."

When James Butler died, New York was one of more than thirty states that operated twenty-three-hour confinement units and prisons. Many of these supermax facilities were built in the 1990s in a frenzy of construction that by 2004 imprisoned at least twenty-five thousand Americans nationwide. That compares to about fifty inmates similarly housed in prisons in England. The difference between these new prisons and the nineteenth-century design that proved so toxic to Auburn's inmates was mainly the technology: electronic doors, surveillance cameras monitored by guards in security "bubbles," in-cell plumbing with outside controls, intercoms and other high-tech communication, and weaponry. Every detail served to inhibit contact between staff and inmates—and inmates themselves—the bells and whistles somehow indicating that this was progress. When blood was drawn for medical reasons, it was with the inmate thrusting his arm through a slot in the door used for the delivery of food. Mental health care, what there was of it, was rendered with counselor and patient on opposite sides of a steel door.

When inmates received visitors, it was behind Plexiglas, through mesh wire, and sometimes via video monitor.

Some inmates were put into a supermax as an administrative decision; others, as in New York, were put there because they had violated prison rules. But the basic idea was the same: isolation, sensory deprivation, and enforced, unrelenting idleness.

The resurgence of solitary confinement dates to a single day in October 1983, when two guards were murdered in separate incidents at the simmering federal penitentiary at Marion, Illinois. The violence-riddled facility was put on total "lockdown"—inmates neither came nor went but stayed confined behind bars—and the level of mayhem declined. For guards, it was a dream come true. The irony was that Marion was the initial salvo in a war that was largely of the system's making. America's prison population was on its way to quadrupling from 1980 to 2000. Prisons crowded with gang members, the drug-addicted, and the mentally ill—16 percent of jails and prisons nationwide—presented a daunting management challenge. The notion that prisons could or should rehabilitate inmates was a distant memory, as gymnasiums gave way to dormitories and teachers to guards. Supermax was an easy answer to the tensions of overcrowding and idleness. It was one that sold well in an era when politicians made their names by being tough on crime.

In November 2000, Glenn Goord, the head of New York's prison system, attempted to justify the state's wholesale return to solitary confinement. In a position paper, he listed ten inmates who were serving long sentences in the Box. One had punched and stabbed an officer with a pen; another had stabbed an inmate to death; a third had cut an officer with a razor. On his list was Al Kirby, who had attacked officers with a shank. Goord did not mention that Kirby was schizophrenic and had been hospitalized numerous times. He did not know, obviously, that Kirby would commit suicide three years later in a cell covered with feces. Kirby no doubt needed containment. The question was where. Moreover, the suggestion that the 3,451 inmates then in New York's special housing units were all in a league with those ten men didn't hold up. Goord's numbers showed that just 15 percent did time for assaults. Nineteen percent were in for drug use or possession, and 28 percent, the largest number, had been sentenced for "creating a disturbance/demonstration"—a favorite, often trumped-up, charge, which had been leveled against Jessica Roger for her fits of resistance.

Indeed, the numbers showed something else entirely. New York's confinement units weren't filled with hard-core toughs. Instead, they were snagging the people who could least cope in the tense, strenuous world of prison: the mentally ill.

Three years after her son's death, Elsie Butler had an opportunity to tell a panel of lawmakers in New York what had happened to James. She sat at a table in a building in Manhattan, a microphone in front of her, her daughter Tammy behind her. She began: James was "my pumpkin, my only son. He was a big sweet kid at heart." She stopped, unable to go on. She was told to take her time. A friendly hand rubbed her back. Audience members gently urged her on.

Then, over the next ten minutes, Elsie told the tale—the mental illness, the Box, the paranoia, the appeals for help, the suicide. "My son was crying out for help and no one listened," she said. "He died a horrible death that I think could have been avoided."

⸺

Jeffrey Brody, who practices personal injury law in Kingston, New York, across the Hudson River from where Jessica Roger grew up, is representing the Roger family in a lawsuit against the New York State prison system. Fit, slightly balding, and looking younger than his sixty-one years, Brody is an angry man. He believes that Jessica suffered long before she went into the Box for the last time on August 15, 2002, that she experienced pain every day she was in the special housing unit and every time she attempted suicide there. "It was all a slow process that led to her death," he said.

I visited Brody in the spring of 2006 when he was preparing for the wrongful-death suit on behalf of a nineteen-year-old youth who had been killed in the backseat of a car that had been broadsided. By coincidence, I knew the boy; he'd been a friend of my daughter's. Brody's conference table was heaped with file folders and documents for the impending trial. Off to the side were four large photographs of Gerald, a handsome African-American kid, one in a cap and gown, flashing a winning smile. Brody was angry, too, that Gerald had died. He had so much potential, he kept saying. A sensitive man who gave up divorce law—"Divorce makes good people bad and bad people evil," he said—Brody seemed to be grieving for Gerald, a boy he'd never known, in the way a biographer does. He wanted to change the outcome of the story.

In her thirty-nine months in prison, Jessica Roger was charged with seventy-six infractions of prison rules and found guilty of sixty-five of them. She was locked in either the Box or in keeplock for more than a third of her time in prison and constantly lost privileges to go to the commissary, receive packages, and make phone calls. There's little doubt that Jessica Roger was a difficult inmate. The question is how much accountability could have been expected of a mentally ill young woman who had grown up in institutions and shown every sign that her self-harming overtures were anything but insincere. As a psychiatrist who looked into her case put it, "Just because behavior is, in part, manipulative does not mean it will not lead to death by suicide." Yet the prison system would hold Jessica accountable, even if doing so fed the very thing it was meant to curtail and, in turn, worsened her tenuous mental health.

On August 20, 2002, Jessica's counselor closed out her file. He noted that she had gotten off keeplock a week earlier and that he had encouraged her to go out for recreation. He had given her a poster and colored markers—"a reward for inmate's appropriate behavior while on keeplock status." They discussed her pending disciplinary charges.

> *This writer would ask inmate if she had decided if she wanted to get a new ticket yet [misbehavior report] and inmate would laugh and say she wasn't going to get locked. Writer would then ask if she knew why she wouldn't get locked. Inmate would answer that she wasn't going to do anything to get locked and that is why . . .*

Before long, however, the inevitable happened.

"Inmate acted out after hours and was sent to SHU," the counselor wrote. "Writer was informed of her death yesterday morning on 8/19/02. She will be missed."

EPILOGUE
for Part Four

I first visited Joan Roger in 2004 when I was writing an article on Jessica for the *New York Times Magazine*, which was published, on October 31, 2004, with the title "A Death in the Box."

Joan was forty-six at the time but she looked and felt much older. Like her daughter, she was grossly overweight. Her sweatshirt was faded and stained and she wore stretch pants that hugged the rolls in her legs. Wisps of gray-streaked hair fell from a small tight knot and across her ruddy face. Every now and again she would rise with great effort from a chair at her green Formica-top table to retrieve a box of this, a scrapbook of that. She had a store of Jessica memorabilia: report cards, stuffed animals, and letters—lots of them—from the places in which Jessica was so often confined.

Jessica was in every cranny of her tightly cluttered, tidy three-room apartment, where she lived, divorced from Kevin, on a disability check from the government. The white walls charted the stages of Jessica's life: Jessica at eleven months clutching a teddy bear; Jessica at four, beaming and bright-eyed in matching red-and-white print short sets with six-year-old Cora; Jessica as a chubby teenager with acne, posing with her mother and grandmother in the parking lot of a psychiatric hospital. Like the chapters in a book, these pictures reached a culmination—closure, if it could be called that—in a frame above Joan's bed. There was Jessica in her casket wearing blue jeans and a lavender T-shirt with a depiction of the Tasmanian Devil cartoon character across her chest. She had liked that T-shirt. Her hands, clutching a navy blue bandana, were folded on her stomach. On her forehead was the bruise mentioned in her autopsy, small but clear, and it added to her mother's questions.

In the course of our interviews, Joan offered herself up as a sacrificial lamb in a story of family dysfunction, accepting blame—maybe too much—for what happened to Jessica, her "Jet." Jessica's father, Kevin, a thin, intense man with brown eyes and loosely combed-back salt-and-pepper hair, would not go to the places that Joan did, would not let the people from family court and Child Protective Services define him. This was a story, he insisted, about them, not him, about their failures, not his.

In July 2006, I went back to Poughkeepsie to visit Joan. It had been two years since I had seen her, and in the interim she had had gastric bypass surgery and had pared down from 430 pounds to just under 200—from size 50 pants to size 14. She looked terrific, her ears adorned with four silver earrings each, her arms in silver bracelets. She wore jeans instead of stretch pants, and a V-neck shirt with maroon and gray stripes. Her hair was pulled back in a pony tail, revealing a widow's peak just like Jessica's.

She had moved since our last meeting and was living in a few rooms on the first floor of an old Victorian house in Poughkeepsie that had been carved up into apartments. The apartment was bright and clean, and filled, like her last place, with photographs and knick-knacks. Cora's daughter Andrea, four, played quietly with a Barbie doll nearby.

Seeing her in this place, where she was warm and well, made me think that some things in American society do work. Joan is disabled from her spinal problems; the government paid for her surgery, and it supports her modest life in this apartment.

Joan believes that she has not found out all there is to know about the path that led to Jessica's death. She hopes that the lawsuit against the state will reveal the nefarious ways in which she believes the state overtly or by default contributed to the events of August

17, 2002. Moreover, she hopes that telling Jessica's story may prevent parents from having to hear the news she heard that day, the news that her mentally ill daughter had strangled herself in the Box at Bedford Hills.

Joan has sorrow and she has regrets. If she could do it all over again, she would not leave Jessica as she did when her daughter was ten.

She has built a shrine to her younger daughter in an alcove in her bedroom. Jessica's ashes are in a cardboard box on a table in the center, awaiting the day that Joan can afford a proper urn with Jessica's name engraved on it. All about, there are statues of angels that Joan has bought at yard sales and in stores.

Behind Jessica's ashes, in a place of prominence, is a small replica of a plaster Pietà, a dead Jesus in the arms of his devastated mother. Joan painted it blue and white years ago, and when it went crashing to the floor, she painstakingly pasted it back together. You can't see the cracks, not even a hint of them, she points out, and of this she is proud.

Andy DeMers, meanwhile, left the Department of Correctional Services.

Betty Guzzardi was released from prison.

Elaine Lord, who cried at the inquiry into Jessica Roger's death, retired as superintendent of Bedford Hills.

The lawsuit filed on behalf of New York's mentally ill inmates went to trial in 2006 and was in settlement discussions as this book was going to press. Lord testified in a deposition taken for the lawsuit.

"We need to stop arguing about whether people are mad or bad," she said, "and design some effective interventions."

PART FIVE

JOSEPH

Wire mesh cages. The overuse of Mace and physical restraints. Over-medication of juvenile offenders. No rehabilitation. No education. No prevention. Recent reports on the California Youth Authority are scathing and shocking, sounding more like a description of a jail from another century—and another country. Indeed, one juvenile crime expert said he was haunted by his review of the California system.
　　　　　—Editorial, *Oakland Tribune*, March 2, 2004

I think I'm going crazy being in this cell all this time.
　　　　　—Letter from Joseph to his girlfriend, Angela,
　　　　August 8, 2005, after thirty-two days in lockdown

CHAPTER THIRTEEN

Child of the Streets

SABRINA IS THE MOTHER OF five children, eleven to twenty-three years old, the offspring of four fathers. She lives with none of the children nor any of the men. She is thirty-eight, which is not old, but her years have been heavy ones and she carries them—in her swollen belly, which she grasps when she moves, in her mouth, which is missing teeth, in her eyes, which hide behind long brown wisps of hair that she leaves where they have fallen.

Two of the children, a boy named Rafael, eleven, and a girl, Desiree, fifteen, live with other families in the Sacramento area. The boy has been a foster child since infancy, while the girl was adopted when she was four, a couple of years after an unfortunate incident in which she was burned. Two other daughters, Renee, twenty-three, and Selena, twelve, live together in a two-bedroom apartment a mile or so from Sabrina. The elder daughter fills in as mother to the younger one, something she learned to do, of necessity, at a very early age.

Sabrina's other child was Joseph. Joey. Joe-Joe. Little Rat, as an uncle called him, the Flea, as an aunt did. The small, quiet one, wiry and quick, with a full mop of straight black hair and a pointy nose, Joseph. Joseph liked to box at his Uncle Angelo's gym in the Del Paso Heights area of Sacramento, an air-conditioned escape amid the litter and seediness of Del Paso Boulevard, its ring a simple, spare vision under long fluorescent lights. He would ride his ten-speed bike along the rail line after his day at the middle school—that is, if he'd gone at all—taking lessons or sparring with a speed bag along a mirrored wall, working the staccato din of muscled fighters.

Angelo was the kind of uncle that kids in neighborhoods like Joseph's had aplenty—his half-sister's dead father's brother—a tortured connection and not really his uncle at all, but a real enough relationship nonetheless. Angelo was a middleweight fighter who had gone up against the world middleweight champion Oscar de la Hoya, and he owned the Prime Time Boxing Gym on the boulevard. He was the son—one of thirteen—who had made it, while three brothers went to prison and two were shot to death. Joseph had lived in Angelo's home for nearly five years as a youngster, one of many stops in his fitful childhood.

Sabrina gave birth to Renee, her oldest, when she was just fifteen and in the ninth grade. Robert, Angelo's brother, a ruggedly handsome Latino with combed-back brown hair and lean, muscled biceps, was her first boyfriend, and Renee's father. Joseph, Sabrina's second child, came when she was eighteen and several months into both an addiction to heroin and a relationship with a fellow addict named Daniel, Joseph's father.

Oak Park was a community of clapboard bungalows and tired Victorians, surrounded by chain-link fences and littered with broken sofas and beat-up cars. Around the time of Sabrina's birth in the late 1960s, it became a place of crime and prostitution, an era ushered in by the inevitable march of progress. First, Highway 99 was built on its western fringe, lopping it off from nearby neighborhoods.

Then the city tore down a cluster of low-rent projects along the Sacramento River, sealing Oak Park's destiny as the place to which the unfortunates fled. The neighborhood was about five miles and a world away from the blinding white dome of California's colonnaded State Capitol, a gleaming counterpoint to the forgotten enclave and people of Oak Park.

Sabrina tried to keep Joseph off Oak Park's tattered streets, with their gangs and guns, their routine shootings, their illegal drug and legal liquor trade on every corner. The trouble was that she didn't just reside in Oak Park, she breathed it in, was a part of it, lived it. Her kids covered for her—fought off the sheriff with the eviction notice, fed the dogs, and put out the trash—while she was off doing her thing.

Sabrina had been beautiful once, a petite Latina with rich, long hair that fell below her breasts and feathered off her face, and taut olive skin. She liked to wear makeup and creased pants. She had a dazzling smile. Drugs changed her looks, ruined her teeth and her shape. The demands of her addiction were bad enough when she was on heroin but hardly better with methadone. Heroin made her steal, and methadone made her sluggish and sick. She would wake up nauseous and shaky, and if she didn't get to the clinic every day, weekends and holidays included, she'd feel as if she had the flu. She lived the life for twenty years: the hitched rides to the clinic, the kids left with each other or a friend, the street drugs that got her through the day and sent her friends to early graves. But now, today, Sabrina has finally put all of that into the past. Joseph is a part of that past, too. In 2005 he left Sabrina with a one-sentence note saying that he loved her.

Joseph was born on October 2, 1986, into the hands of Debbie Jordan, an older single mother who had taken Sabrina in during her pregnancy and who herself had given birth to a son just two months earlier. Debbie, thirty-two, was a big-hearted aunt to Joseph's father, Daniel Maldonado, twenty-two, who at the time was working his way through a two-year sentence for narcotics possession. She was also something of a mother to Sabrina, who needed one. At birth, Joseph was a delicate wisp of an infant who did not cry until prompted but had what Debbie swore was a tiny smile on his thin, dark lips. Sabrina saw it, too, and, there in the UC Davis Medical Center delivery room, after a labor in which Sabrina had screamed and pulled Debbie's hair, both of them cried.

Joseph immediately went into withdrawal from the methadone that Sabrina had been on since her fourth month of pregnancy. Sabrina had known that she risked having the child taken away from her if she stayed on heroin, so had opted for the lesser, and legal, choice of evils. As it was, her daughter Renee, almost four years old, was being raised in a blue-and-white house on Poplar Street by the little girl's paternal grandfather, Robert Nuñez. Robert knew the kind of life Sabrina was leading; he had seen the signs before. When some money was missing after a visit from Sabrina and her new boyfriend, he decreed that Renee would stay with him. Sabrina, who was perhaps sixteen at the time, did not argue.

In the first weeks after Joseph's birth, when Sabrina unwrapped him from his thin baby blanket, his fragile legs would fly forward, twitching and jerking in the tremors of withdrawal. Once, after she left the hospital, Sabrina feared that Joseph's breathing was labored and took him back to the hospital for reassurance. Whatever had gone into Sabrina's body, the nurse had explained to her, had also gone into Joseph's. Whatever Sabrina had been addicted to, now, so was he. She was told to keep Joseph tightly wrapped in the two to three weeks that it would take for the drugs to leave his body. Sabrina went home to Debbie's townhouse, where she slept in the living room with Joseph nearby and babysat for her baby and Debbie's while Debbie was at work. Sabrina had sworn a hundred times during her pregnancy that she would never do heroin again. For

now, there was harmony and hope in an arrangement that worked
for both mothers.

Throughout these first unsettled and difficult weeks, Sabrina's
mother did not come to visit, although she lived nearby. Marian,
forty, had kids and troubles of her own. Her twin boys, the fourth
and fifth of her children, were two years old. Perhaps inauspiciously,
the babies had been conceived on a conjugal prison visit. Marian's
husband—Sabrina's father, Jaime Perez—was in prison for burglary,
robbery, and possession of a weapon and narcotics. It was a trying
time for Marian—her husband locked up, her stomach in sutures
from a Caesarian section, her babies wailing. When it got to be too
much, she turned to her own demon drug, first "crank," or methamphetamine, which lifted her mood and gave her pep, then heroin.
She was soon hooked, and many things began to fall by the wayside.

When Joseph was still an infant, Debbie came home one day to
find people in the house; Sabrina had returned to the drug life. She
asked Sabrina to leave, which pained her, but that had been the
deal—she could stay as long as she was clean. Sometime later,
Debbie received a call from Marian, who was then caring for Joseph
along with her own babies. Come and pick up Joseph, Marian
demanded, or she was calling child protective services to come and
take him. When Debbie arrived at Marian's, she found that Joseph
was naked and had lice. He had no clothes for Debbie to take with
them. There did not seem to be enough food, and there certainly
was not enough money.

This, then, was the kind of life Sabrina Ruby Perez had been born
into, the reason some people shake their heads when they talk about
what became of Joseph, why they say neither one of them had a
chance. Sabrina had a father who went to state prison thirteen times
from 1981 to 2002, bedeviled, as was his daughter, by the seductive
lure of heroin. She had a mother who herself dabbled in the drug
life, when there were young mouths to feed and bottoms to wipe.
She lived in a milieu in which boyfriends and fathers and brothers

existed on a conveyor belt that stopped at the police station, the courthouse, the jail, and the state pen, with brief interludes for family and briefer ones for work. She grew up in a community where drugs were traded on street corners in the pursuit of pleasure and income, and in a society in which addiction was something to punish rather than treat.

But Jaime and Marian, now fifty-seven and sixty, deserve some credit. They have been married for thirty-nine years, from the day they slipped off to Reno—he, a seventeen-year-old with dreams of becoming a lawyer, she six-months pregnant and just shy of her twentieth birthday. Jaime, an intensely serious man with a reddish-gray crew cut and a solid build, has worked for the past five years as a window installer and has been promoted to a supervisory position. He has been clean for a decade. He was within months of college graduation when he was first arrested, a stupid mistake he paid for dearly. He does not dispute that he lived the misbegotten so-what-if-the-electricity's-been-cut-off, drug-hunting, stealing, partying life of a heroin addict. He takes responsibility. So does Marian, who quit drugs on her own after a couple of years. Under their roof today live four of their five children: Jaime Jr., thirty-nine, who was disabled from a gang member's bullet to the head fifteen years ago; Sabrina, recently detoxed; and the twins, Albion and Fabian, twenty-one, who both suffer from mental illness. They live in a Mediterranean-style duplex with a lawn and tiled roof in the Northgate section of Sacramento, a house chosen for a special reason. On the other side of it lives their daughter Sonia, twenty-eight, with her seven children, ranging in age from one to thirteen. Her first child was born, as was Sabrina's, when she was just fifteen. Jaime pays the rent on both places.

If the marriage that produced Joseph's mother was an enduring union of survivors, the one that produced his father, Daniel, was a fleeting clash of cultures. Rene Maldonado, twenty-three, had married his pregnant girlfriend Marsha, nineteen, in 1964 and moved her into his parents' home. His Mexican mother did not speak English, and Marsha did not speak Spanish. She left before her baby was born and never went back. As a career civil servant with the welfare office, Marsha was able to provide a good home for Daniel, a lively boy with dark hair and eyes who made her laugh. She adored Daniel, looked after his every need, and as a single mother of one will do, spoiled him. When he became a teenager and began to talk back and get into trouble, she did not know how to make this untamed young stallion behave, and his father was not around a lot to help out. When Daniel was eighteen months old, Rene had volunteered to go to Vietnam, in part to escape the crushing obligations of three children by two women. At the time, he didn't much care if he got killed; he survived his stint as a military policeman, and when he got home, the demands of child support were waiting. A union longshoreman on the Sacramento docks, he saw his son infrequently.

Daniel, who was twenty-two at the time of Joseph's birth, was, like Sabrina's father in the early years, a man overly fond of heroin who spent as much time within the walls of California's prisons as he did outside. In Joseph's first eight years of life, Daniel was sent to prison thirteen times, mostly on drug possession charges. Whenever he was paroled, he'd last two months, three months, at most nine months, on the streets before being sent back for parole violations. Each time, he'd go into prison skinny and strung out and emerge buff and ready for action.

At the age of two, Joseph went to live with Robert Nuñez, Renee's rotund, five-foot-tall Mexican grandfather. As he had with his granddaughter, Renee, Robert took it upon himself to assume the care of Joseph, even though this child of Sabrina's was not even a blood relative. Raising children was what he did; seven of the thirteen sons he fathered lived with him as well. Robert did not like what he had seen of Joseph's care any more than he had of Renee's. The boy's parents were a rootless pair with four children and two drug habits between them.

When Robert insisted that Joseph stay with him, Sabrina was in no condition to refuse. She had recently been arrested twice, for possessing a hypodermic needle and for petty theft, and was sentenced to fifteen days. She had tried to stay away from heroin, but she hated what methadone, the legal substitute, did to her, how it made her feel. Occasionally, she'd fall back on the needle, then retreat. Sometimes she'd mix methadone with methamphetamines for a boost, until she'd get caught in a urine test at the clinic, which would threaten to cut her off. Robert would give her a twenty-dollar bill every now and again, a small kindness and a way to ensure that little Joseph stayed with him.

Joseph joined his sister Renee and stayed with Robert for almost five years, in a home that was nothing if not always filled with people. Robert Nuñez had been injured in a construction accident in 1969 and his wife had moved out in 1977, leaving the boys. With his mother and so many of his son's girlfriends around, Robert liked to say that he'd never had to change a single diaper. A former prizefighter, however, he was not averse to a different form of child care. He beat his own children with his hands and with sticks, and the kids knew when grandpa had taken some of his prednisone pills for chronic asthma because he'd just about go crazy, chasing after whoever crossed him with arms flying, mouth going. One day, when Renee had gotten into a fight with a boy in first grade, Robert wrapped her hands like a miniature bantamweight's and made her hit a punching bag until she was exhausted. The little girl was left wondering whether she was being taught how to fight or being punished for it. He once raged at Joseph for failing to oil his hair. He had a board inscribed with the names of his grandchildren that one of them spirited out of the house one day and burned.

Joseph was the runt of the large Nuñez litter, a kid who soon became scared of his own shadow. If you moved too quickly, he flinched. When he was challenged by Robert or the neighborhood kids, he'd begin a slow, painful stutter. He was the kid in the classroom whose emotional baggage was hidden behind a quiet façade. Surrounded by a sea of Nuñez males, Joseph nonetheless longed for a father, someone to call his own. Daniel was usually incarcerated or at points unknown, making him the fantasy dad of an orphan boy's imagination. When Joseph was seven, he got what he had longed for, after a fashion.

Renee's father, Robert Jr., had followed in his father's footsteps and been a professional prizefighter who, as a teenager, had scored a novice Golden Gloves title in San Francisco and went on to win ten consecutive fights. He had given up the fighting life in 1990 after a sixth-round loss to a former world lightweight champion and turned to something more reliable, house painting. In 1993, he came home and announced that he had a new girlfriend and an apartment, and after ten years, he wanted his little girl to live with him. Renee, who had an independent streak that would serve her well in future years, refused to move from her grandfather's home without her brother. She and Joseph were a unit, siblings in a world of far flung relations. They had played tag and hide-and-seek together, slept out in the garage on overnights, and shared a loving if flawed grandfather. Robert Jr. agreed to the terms, and sister and brother moved in with him.

The new arrangement lasted a year, until Robert Jr. and his girlfriend broke up. Joseph went to live with Sabrina, and Renee went to Sabrina's parents.

On October 10, 1994, Joseph's father, Daniel, was shot five times by his wife's nineteen-year-old son, who was attempting to protect her from what had been a series of abusive attacks.

On October 31, Robert Jr. was gunned down in a Sacramento park, apparently over an affair with another man's wife. In a weird symmetry reflective of the world in which they lived, both Robert Jr. and Daniel were murdered, in separate incidents, three weeks apart. No charges were pressed in either case. Both men were thirty years old.

Joseph was not told of his father's death until Renee's father was

killed. His sister cried but he was uncertain how to react. He was
supposed to have seen Daniel the weekend of his death, but Daniel
had not shown up. Joseph sat clutching a photograph of his father, a
man he knew as a shadow at the periphery of his life, searching for
an emotion. He was eight years old, a child who was learning that
the strongest relationships in life were the most profoundly
ephemeral. In a single moment, he had lost not one but two fathers.

After the deaths of their fathers in October 1994, Renee and
Joseph, eleven and eight, embarked together on the risky business of
living with their mother. Sabrina, now twenty-six, had been arrested
twice in the previous sixteenth months, once for selling marijuana,
which was dismissed, and the other time for reckless driving, to which
she pleaded no contest and was sentenced to eight days in the county
jail. She had also given birth the previous April to a fourth child, a
girl she named Selena, and whom Joe-Joe and Renee affectionately
called Nina. By this point, Sabrina had given up her hopes of
regaining custody of her daughter Desiree, who had been taken from
her in 1991 at fifteen months. Desiree had been severely scalded
while being bathed by Sabrina's fourteen-year-old sister Sonia, with
whom Sabrina often left her. They did not seek medical attention for
the scalding until the next day, and Child Protective Services got
involved after hospital officials questioned their story. Sabrina went
to parenting classes, but she eventually stopped visiting Desiree. In
October 1992, the little girl became someone else's child.

Over the next few years, Sabrina, Renee, Joseph, and Selena, a
family of four with four different surnames, lived on public assistance
at a series of Oak Park addresses. Joseph got an all-black pit bull that
he named Hennessy, for the cognac, and Renee got one that she
called Alizayh. Sabrina went to the clinic every day for her
methadone and tried to make do, and she was still involved with

Selena's father. In June 1995, she was arrested for drug possession, to which she pleaded no contest, and in May 1996, she gave birth, a month early, to a fifth child, a boy she named Rafael. Like Joseph, Desiree, and Selena before him, Rafael was born addicted to drugs. He was immediately taken away by the authorities. From July 1997 to March 1999, nine referrals were made to Child Protective Services for the children of Sabrina Perez, including allegations of severe neglect and caretaker absence. She eventually lost Rafael as well.

Renee, a feisty girl with full lips, exotic, almond-shaped eyes, and thin, raised brows, often clashed with her long-absent mother and decided, at the tender age of thirteen, to move out. From then until she graduated from high school—an event that no one but she took any particular interest in—Renee, the independent survivor who would make it on her own, moved seventeen times in five years. She stayed with relatives or friends or occasionally with Sabrina, and usually landed on her feet. When she left, Joseph was a scrawny slip of a boy, about ten, with small hands and feet, dark eyebrows and lashes and combed-back black hair. In Renee's absence, he would be the devoted son, the child who held things together, who obeyed. He took out the trash and washed the dishes; he followed his mother's curfews. He was the man of the house who got Selena ready for school—even curled her pony tail—and gave her his windbreaker when it began to rain at the bus stop. After years of waiting for a father who never came, of being the odd child out amid the Nuñez legions, Joseph finally had a home. He had a fierce instinct to be with his mother and to protect her.

When Miguel Martin, Desiree's adoptive father, visited in hopes of uniting his daughter with her siblings, Joseph barely spoke and refused to look Martin in the eye. He seemed suspicious of Martin, a soft-spoken man who only wanted to help. Joseph's only association with outsiders had been with the official kind, harbingers of strife and of the attrition in his dwindling family.

Joseph mourned his absent father for years and often questioned why he had died. He told friends that the thing he wanted most was to be with his dad. Now he was devoted to his family, including his mother, however flawed and unstable.

In 1998, Joseph, eleven, and a friend were hanging out in Joseph's room when there was a knock at the door. When they ignored it, the sheriff let himself in. He told them to pack up. They were being evicted. Sabrina had spent thirty days in jail for possessing drug paraphernalia and the rent had gone unpaid. Ahead lay three home-less shelters, another eviction, and the start, more or less, of a new life for Joseph—on his own. He stayed with his grandparents for a while and with friends. He'd walk across the bridge over the freeway and disappear for a couple of days at a time. At one point he moved in with a man who had sold heroin with his father, and who regaled him with stories of his five years in prison in solitary confinement. Joseph grew his hair into a sculpted pony tail, called a Mongolian, that was associated with gang membership, and had red rags—his gang color—dangling from the pocket of his baggy pants. Once, his grandmother was called to the middle school to explain why Joseph had been late and truant, why he had been talking back to teachers. "It's not me," Joseph told Marian. "It's the teachers." When Sabrina was stable, Joseph would eagerly move back in with her to live in sparsely furnished flats in marginal neighborhoods. Miguel Martin stopped by once a day or two before Christmas when Joseph was home alone. He seemed dejected to Martin. There were no decora-tions on the tree and no presents under it. There was no food in the house. His mother was out, Joseph had said.

In February 2002, when he was fifteen, Joseph stuck the handle of a fork into the ignition of a 1985 Toyota Camry and took it for a ride. Twenty minutes later, he was arrested. Had he not stolen another car two months later, this time using a knife, the system might have cut him some slack. In June, Joseph's two counts of mis-demeanor auto theft were sustained, and he was sent to a county juvenile facility on twin sentences of a year—effectively eight months. Before he went away, Sabrina had expressed her dismay about his sentence and told him she would not visit him or take his phone calls while he was incarcerated. If he got into trouble, she said, she would not be there for him. At the facility, he picked a fight within days, kicking another resident's chair and hitting him in the face and back. "I cannot believe how much he has changed," Sabrina told a probation officer. She was homeless again, living with relatives and waiting for a subsidized apartment to become available.

"Getting in touch with her may be difficult," the officer wrote in her report.

In the beginning Joseph tried to make a go of juvenile hall. He got A's and B's in school and had no behavioral infractions. He wrote letters to Renee in crafted cursive swirls or meticulous printing and told her he was "doing real good" and that time was flying. He thanked her for being there for him, while he wondered when Sabrina would visit and why she had missed his birthday. Whether his mother's attention would have made a difference is an open question. But after a while, Joseph lost interest in being good.

When he got out of juvenile hall, his grandfather Jaime, a no-nonsense man who, unlike Marian, could talk to the boy, was waiting. Jaime Perez had been sentenced over the years to upward of twenty years in prison and had learned his lessons well, if late. He feared the life that Joseph was making. He sat the boy down in the small bathroom of the Perez home. "Is this where you want to be, in your cell staring at the moon?" he asked Joseph. "Is that where you want to be?" Joseph, now a small, tough sixteen-year-old who weighed barely over 100 pounds, cried and said he wouldn't steal again. "I'm sorry, Grandpa," he said.

But Joseph's pattern had been set. A Nuñez uncle who had been close to Joseph when he was a youngster ran into him at the boxing gym, the place where Joe had spent joyful, sweaty middle-school afternoons. Happy to see him, the uncle asked what he was up to, if he had a girlfriend. Joseph was reticent, withdrawn; he rebuffed the man's hug, offering only that he was staying with Sabrina's parents. Later, his uncle would recall a floundering, solitary kid, one who had only himself to rely on and had done so for too long.

After that, Joseph stole another car, then another, then yet another. Once he crashed a car during a police pursuit and fled through a field. Another time, drunk, he led police on a harrowing chase through eight red lights, several stop signs, and the wrong way down a one-way street. Still another time, he was forced from a car and ordered to the ground at gunpoint. When hearings were held in court, it was Renee who regularly showed up to vouch for Joseph, to say he'd have a place to live when he got out and someone to watch him. At an age when her mother had had two children and a drug habit, Renee had a full-time job and a car. Joseph's half-sister, who was nineteen when Joseph was first arrested, was considered the stable force in his life, the family member who could be counted on when a probation officer called.

Joseph was less trustworthy. He was released once to live with Renee but soon cut off the electronic ankle monitor that tethered him to home and took off. He was placed in a group home and left. He escaped from a Reno, Nevada, juvenile facility, running through desert sagebrush and dry lake beds to a casino parking lot, where he and three other youths stole a car and drove to Sacramento. From February 12, 2002, until January 29, 2004, a period of 716 days, Joseph was locked up in five different Sacramento County juvenile facilities, for a total of 533 days.

> *The only reason they were trying to send me to a group home [was] because mom never came to my court date and they think when your parents don't come to court they don't want you. . . .*
>
> *I made my honor and I can go home on my first home pass in two weeks. But I have to get a visit this Sunday so mom can meet my probation officer. . . . Mom's been telling me*

*that shes going to come visit me on Sunday ever sense I got
here and I have been doing everything I have to do getting
good grades in school staying out of trouble and not getting
into any fights so I can get threw this program in 105 days.*
—Letters from Joseph to Renee when he was at
Sacramento County Boys Ranch, September 2
and October 12, 2002

After Joseph's escape from Reno, Sacramento County authorities decided it had had enough of his antics. He was a kid with a "smart-aleck" attitude who had trouble with authority figures, especially female, a probation report stated. The system had tried again and again, but he had shown that he "had no intention of cooperating with the court's efforts to help him turn his life around." Moreover, he had been tagged, early on, as a member of Sacramento's Hispanic Norteño gang, and had been suspected, while in custody, of "undercover gang agitation." Although he had committed no violent offenses, he was considered a likely candidate to reoffend. It was therefore recommended, in February 2004, that this small, troublesome seventeen-year-old, just a few inches over five feet, be sent to a place that better suited him, and that place was deemed to be the California Youth Authority.

CHAPTER FOURTEEN

Lockdown

THE PRESTON YOUTH CORRECTIONAL FACILITY is a fenced compound of low brick buildings, cracked basketball courts, and asphalt paths in the yellow and green foothills of the Sierra Nevada, about thirty-five miles southeast of Sacramento. High on a hill overlooking the sixty-five-acre facility, ringed by a dense fringe of cedar, palm, and manzanita, is a 116-year-old redbrick building called the "Castle," replete with turrets and tower, squat stone arches, and wide staircases. The building is a shuttered but imposing reminder of the generations of young men that have passed through the place, beginning with the first seven boys—or "wards" as they were called—transferred to the Preston Industry School in 1894 from California's legendary prison at San Quentin. The facility was founded in the belief that youthful miscreants should not be mixed with hardened adult criminals, that "training and good citizenship," according to a pocket history, were better teachers than "punishment and harsh discipline."

It is this place, which in 2006 housed 426 mostly minority youths with an average age of seventeen, that Allen Feaster would like to tear down. And for good reason.

Feaster is a tall, trim African-American man with close-cropped hair, a small stud in his left ear, and a knee covered in denim that jiggles when he talks. He has been around the block a few times, a man who was incarcerated, addicted to heroin, and thrown out of the military after a decade for alcoholism. Feaster, who has been sober for twenty-one years, commutes two hours from Modesto each day to shine shoes at the tony Westin St. Francis Hotel in San Francisco. That is how he makes his living. But at fifty-two, this one-time preacher has another passion, and that is the death and rebirth of the California Youth Authority—from an entity that imprisons children to one that sets them free. California's bureaucrats changed the name to the Division of Juvenile Justice in 2005, but that has not changed its identity as the worst juvenile system in the nation. In January 2004, Allen's adopted son Durrell, eighteen, was housed in cell number 27 in the Ironwood Lodge at Preston with a ward from Los Angeles named Deon Whitfield, seventeen. Durrell was a child of Cuban descent who came to Feaster as a foster placement when he was three and whom Allen adopted when he was around twelve. Once, after the fearless Durrell, four, had jumped into a swimming pool over his head, Allen had dived in, fully clothed, to rescue him. Of all the kids he'd cared for, Durrell was the one who had a place in his heart. When his foster kids were taken away on charges that Allen had hit them, it was Durrell, then six, he had fought to get back. A kid with thick eyebrows, a curly Afro, and a thin adolescent mustache, Durrell had been in the California Youth Authority since October 2001 for car theft. At Preston, he had learned landscaping and had acquired a teardrop tattoo under his right eye, which signified the gang he had joined for both camaraderie and protection. He had spoken to his father about getting out, about the two of them moving to New York and starting a gardening business. "Dad I need you to be there for me," he had written to his father. "Don't give up on me. You are the only thing or person I got to be happy to come home to."

Durrell and Deon were living in Ironwood on "23-and-1" status, which meant that they would stay in their cell for twenty-three hours a day. The other hour was reserved for "large-muscle recreation," and sometimes meant sitting in a cage and watching television. Ironwood was a squat brick building at the edge of the facility's grounds that existed solely to punish wards who had misbehaved within the confines of Preston. It comprised fifty cells on a long, dim corridor, twenty-five on opposing sides, with sliding doors that opened into an area about the size of a modest bathroom. For some two months, Deon and Durrell's world had been four walls and a steel door with a slot through which food was delivered. There was a set of bunks, a stainless steel combination toilet-sink, and two small windows—one six inches square in the door, the other a very narrow rectangle in the outside wall. While on 23-and-1, the boys did not attend school, religious services, or any other program. They did not do anything.

For Deon and Durrell, the message of Ironwood, delivered in a variety of ways, was that they and their compatriots were something less than human. They were creatures of violence who deserved no more than this minuscule space, people so dangerous that they had to be caged and cuffed during their brief moments of freedom. This was a sort-of kiddie version of—and, for some, preparation for— California's infamous solitary confinement prison at Pelican Bay. At units like Ironwood, which existed throughout the Youth Authority, staff often got what they expected from these angry youths—and sometimes returned it in kind. Reports had trickled out over the years of youths hog-tied and dragged naked from cells, sprayed with chemicals that burned their skin and their lungs, coerced to take psychiatric medications, and denied food as a means of control. Many of the reports proved to be correct.

Wards went to Ironwood if they engaged in fights or attacked staff or if they were identified as members of gangs that perpetrated such mayhem. Durrell had told his father he had been in a fight the previous November. He had also told Allen of being kept in his underwear around the clock in a "cold, clammy cell." He said he had been sprayed with Mace and then denied access to an inhaler that he needed for control of chronic asthma. He said he had been beaten.

On January 19, 2004, Deon and Durrell decided that they had had enough. Just after lunch on what was a breezy, cool, northern California winter day, they took two pieces of bedsheet, fastened them to the upper bunk of their 6-by-8-foot cell, and in a joint, dramatic expression of wretchedness, hung themselves. A correctional counselor named Virginia Kegg found them on a routine check, clothed in their white boxer shorts and white socks, their arms hanging limply at their sides. She pushed the panic button on her body alarm and ran for help. By the time they were cut down, the youths were dead. The boys had left a dual suicide note: "PleASe tell ARe FIAMALY We LOVe them." Another note, passed to two other wards at lunch, said "Acus ME and StonEy caNt TAKE this Shit no more. Staff KEEp on Fuccing with us."

In 2001 the state's inspector general found that 16 percent of youths in the custody of the California Youth Authority were housed in twenty-three-hour confinement, some for periods of up to a year. The reasons were often poorly documented or overblown. "The potential adverse impact of the 23 and 1 program upon the wards' physical and psychological well being," the report had warned, "is profound." This was exhibit number one.

In August 2004, seven months after the youths' twin suicides, the new director of the California Youth Authority sat before state legislators in a Sacramento hearing room and announced that the authority had ended its practice of locking up youths around the clock. "As of today . . . it is over," said Walter Allen, a fifty-four-year-old former mayor of Covina with a twenty-eight-year career in law-enforcement. "We are going to change our way of doing business."

Six weeks later, the state's inspector general placed unannounced visits to five Youth Authority facilities. He found nearly one in ten youths still confined to their rooms for twenty-three hours, some for as long as two hundred days, and others let out only to shower. Walter Allen's well-intentioned promise to change the business of round-the-clock confinement proved far easier to make than to keep. It would make all the difference for a small skinny kid from Sacramento named Joseph Maldonado.

Beginning in January 2004, Sacramento County officials drastically cut back on the number of troubled youths that it transferred to the California Youth Authority. Critics of the system had spearheaded a statewide boycott of the agency after a series of government reports verified the horrific reports of violence and abuse that had long been kicking around. Some counties stopped sending youths altogether. Sacramento merely became more discerning. Joseph Daniel Maldonado was nonetheless committed to the state's care, arriving at the Preston Youth Correctional Facility on April 5, 2004, about three months after the deaths there of Deon Whitfield and Durrell Feaster.

Over the next eighteen months, Joseph would find a new family to call his own and become proficient in the use of his fists. He would experience up close the stuff of which damning reports on the California Youth Authority had already been made, and he, himself, would be fodder for studies yet to be written.

Joseph was screened for mental health problems and tested for his potential to commit suicide in a survey that asked such things as whether he had thought about or attempted suicide and if he had recently lost a loved one, felt depressed, or fallen out of contact with family. He was found to be a low risk for suicide. An assessment did note that Joseph's review yielded "high levels of concern under drug/alcohol use, impulsivity, and anger," but no effort was made to follow up.

Preston, one of the system's intake facilities and home to around four hundred fifty wards, was at the time coping with a serious increase in gang activity. In the month that Joseph arrived, there were sixty-four gang-related incidents, a 150 percent increase from the April before, and part of a yearlong trend. More than 80 percent of the Preston population had been identified as gang members, labels that divided youths into categories with such names as Crips, Bullfrogs, Sureños, Norteños, Asian Boys, and even one called Peckerwoods. The tags were sometimes easier to get than to shed, and they most certainly solidified within the confines of the California Youth Authority. The gang was a not just a reason to mix it up; it was a shield against attack. Just before coming to the Youth Authority, Joseph had rejected his past association with gangs. He had told an officer on his arrest in January that his Norteño days were over, and told friends that he wanted to remain "neutral."

Renee had never been concerned about Joe's gang associations. She saw his gang interest as little more than kids' stuff—a way to fit in, a style and not a hard-core commitment to the dark side of gang culture. He was a joy riding car thief and a rebellious, misbegotten kid, she believed, not some tatted agitator from the 'hood. He was too gentle, too small. Within a few months of arriving at Preston, however, Joseph had been recruited, schooled, and indoctrinated into the gang. In a letter that September, he told Renee that he was "Keeping my head up high toward the sky maintaining my status and learning more and more about the Northern"— Norteño—"history everyday." Soon he wore his commitment where everyone could see it. Beneath the outside corner of his left eye, above a soft and unblemished adolescent cheek, were four blue dots in a square pattern, the symbol of the Norteño life.

A little guy with quick arms who didn't waste words, Joseph developed a reputation at Preston as a fighter. He once solidly drubbed a kid who was a head taller, his head and arms craning upward in an awkward but effective attack. From May 3 until July

17, 2004, Joseph was involved in five fights and two group disturbances, after which he sought medical attention. His injuries were caused not by the fight but the oft-used method to break it up—Mace. At the time, the Youth Authority was on its way to settling a lawsuit that alleged, among other things, that staff used excessive amounts of Mace in overzealous efforts to restrain youths.

It wasn't long before Joseph's fights kicked off a series of extended stays in Preston's Ironwood unit—the twenty-three-hour confinement block that had been the undoing of Deon Whitfield and Durrell Feaster. On August 9, Joseph wrote to Renee, "Im in lock up now for the group disturbance I was in last week," he wrote. "I got to be here for 90 days. . . . Its hella boring in lock up im in my cell all day and I only get up for one hour a day. And when I do get up for my hour up its in a cage." Neither the deaths of two wards nor critiques of the overused, poorly documented practice of twenty-three-hour confinement had significantly curbed its use. The only change at Ironwood was that youths no longer shared cells.

Solitary confinement was a mental test of endurance, and it was beginning to wear on Joseph. More than the sum of the four dots on his face, he was the guy who stole a furtive peak at his girlfriend's picture every night before going to bed, the one who shed the gang veneer for the facility minister, talking and smiling with him in a way that made him think Joseph was redeemable, the one who loved his mother more than anything, though he never saw her. Sabrina couldn't visit Joseph at Preston because she had blown off a ninety-day sentence for drunk driving. A warrant that had been issued for her arrest would have shown up on the background check done for all Preston visitors. In the fall of 2004, after six months at Preston, including a three-month sentence in Ironwood, Joseph was in distress. On October 7, he broke his hand in a fight and made the first of four requests for mental health help. "Im been stressing about family problems," he wrote in a note to the medical unit. "I need to talk to physic [sic]." On October 30, he wrote another request, and on November 4 was offered help, which he declined. On November 18 and December 6, he made two more written requests to talk to mental health workers—"I need to speak to psychologist," he wrote the last time, getting the spelling right. No one made any attempt to follow up on Joseph's initial refusal, as would be policy, or to answer any of his three other requests. It was a systemic problem.

Throughout the winter, Joseph continued the pattern he had established. He reinjured his hand in a brawl. He got a nosebleed in one fight, a cut on his cheek in another. He got Maced again. After he had racked up fifteen fights and group brawls, a line was drawn. On March 18, 2005, Joseph was transferred to the N. A. Chaderjian Youth Correctional Facility, which was located on a flat farming plain outside Stockton, California, about an hour south of Sacramento. Chad, as it was called, was the end-of-the-line juvie jail in California, the threat that frustrated staff hurled—among many others—at recalcitrant youths. Joseph had never attacked a staff member or used a weapon. He was deemed a follower in the gang hierarchy. He was small, just five-foot-five and 120 pounds. Still, he was considered dangerous enough to be sent to a place where 79 percent of wards were considered assaultive, 32 percent had committed sex crimes, and the average age of the population was nearly twenty, with some wards as old as twenty-four. For Joseph, the real test lay ahead.

—

When Joseph arrived at the N. A. Chaderjian Youth Correctional Facility, or Chad, in March 2005, it was the kind of facility where employees went to work each day and wondered if they would go home in one piece. Staff assaults were almost double those of the previous year and, as the overseeing Corrections Standards Authority would delicately put it in the summer of 2005, "It appears that staff have lost the authority or ability to discipline wards in a meaningful manner."

Opened in 1991 and built for six hundred youths, Chad was in every way but name a maximum-security prison. Its six "halls" were cavernous monoliths with double tiers of steel-doored cells overseen by elevated glass control rooms. There were video cameras and endless strings of coiled barbed wire. There was an arsenal of weapons to which staff often resorted—37-millimeter gas guns, high-powered launchers for pepper balls or nonlethal pellets, and the usual handheld spray cans and canisters of Mace and tear gas. There were circus-style cages for high-risk youth—paradoxically called SPAs, for Special Program Areas—and shackles and spit masks for those who couldn't mind their manners.

Chad was a scandal in and of itself. In December 2003, a video camera showed a German shepherd, under the control of an officer, as the canine was allowed to bite a prone and unresisting twenty-year-old ward on the leg. The following month, a camera caught a Chad staff member as he landed twenty-eight punches to the head of a facedown and handcuffed ward who had earlier attacked him, an incident that led to the firing of six employees. Two wards had died in 2004 under unexplained circumstances, including one who ingested toxic chemicals. The situation had become so bad by June 2005 that an Oakland advocacy group called Books Not Bars had embarked on a campaign to shut the facility down.

At Chad, a siege mentality existed among a beleaguered staff, beaten down by years of official indifference and what one report called "benign neglect." Nine superintendents had come and gone in five years. Short-staffing had often led to forced overtime. Leaking pipes, rusted door frames, burned-out lights, rodents, roaches, and sweltering cell blocks were mere symptoms of a greater decay. One-third of classes were canceled on any given day, often when fearful teachers called in sick. Youth correctional counselors spent only one-tenth of their time actually counseling youths because of security concerns and lack of training. The tension at Chad was palpable and damaging to both staff and wards.

Joseph managed to stay out of trouble for his first two months at Chad, though at the end of June, he had two back-to-back fights. On July 6, 2005, three staff members were jumped, kicked, and punched by three Hispanic youths, a turning point for both Joseph and Chad. The entire facility was put on "lockdown"—a condition in which all wards were locked behind the steel doors of their cells. On July 20, much of Chad went off lockdown, but not the youths in Northern Hispanic units, including Joseph's. In the previous week, several of the youths had launched attacks—"gassing" a staff member by hurling liquids that sometimes included urine, slipping from hand-cuffs and battering a counselor, hurting an officer during a restraint. The Norteños, it was decided, would stay confined, forgoing even the hour of recreation granted in 23-and-1 confinement. Wards would leave their six-by-eight cells, which had been stripped of all personal possessions, only three times a week, to shower. There would be no exercise, television or family visits, and no schooling or mental health care—services to which wards were entitled by law.

Over the years, a San Francisco advocacy group called the Youth Law Center had waged frequent battles with Youth Authority offi-cials over Chad's prolonged and, in the group's view, inappropriate use of round-the-clock confinement. In 2001, more than one hun-dred members of two gangs, the Bullfrogs and the Norteños, had been locked in their cells for more than six months over fights that had involved a small number of youths. Essentially, entire blocks of youths were being denied treatment and education simply because of their race and home address, which was often all that was needed to tag a ward as a gang member. These standoffs were not an uncommon practice, and they persisted into 2005.

On August 8, thirty-two days into the lockdown, Joseph wrote to his girlfriend, Angela, a petite dark-haired girl from West Sacramento he'd hooked up with a couple of months before going to Preston. He told her that he was locked in a cell from which all his "shit" had been taken. "The only thing I have in my cell are tooth paste, tooth brush, my bed, boxers, sox and the two pictures you just sent me and writing material," he wrote. He asked her to send a magazine so that he would have something to read. He told Angela he was "hella stressing," and it was "hella boring." Joseph's world was four white cinderblock walls, a thin rectangular window that looked onto Chad's grassy fringes, a combination toilet-sink, and a yellow door scuffed with graffiti on which was painted, outside, a large number "4."

A standoff, a battle of wills, was under way in Pajaro Hall that would not formally end for fourteen weeks. Youths were given two choices: either renounce gang activities or stay in lockdown. For Joseph, a puny blip in the Hispanic gang culture and an acknowledged follower, this was a Hobson's choice in the take-no-prisoners world of prison gangs. He had committed to the gang at Preston, cemented it with the four blue dots that had been tattooed on his face. At Chad, the Norteños were headed by a powerful ward—a "shot caller," in the parlance—who had already done time in an adult prison. (Wards who committed crimes in the Youth Authority could be sentenced to adult prisons and then returned to complete their juvenile sentences.) The shot caller had been the number two man among Norteños at Pleasant Valley State Prison, an overcrowded institution in Coalinga, and he was a considerable and fearsome force at Chad. If Joseph renounced the gang, he would be severely beaten at the behest of the shot caller, whose job it was to oversee gang discipline. If he did not renounce the Norteños, he would suffer the torment of confinement, which had proved so difficult at Preston. "I think Im going crazy being in this cell all this time only leaving when I take a shower," he wrote to Angela.

On July 26, in a coordinated action with other wards, Joseph jammed his door and placed paper over the window. He was "fogged" out of his cell with chemicals, a practice that an oversight report years earlier had warned could lead to asphyxiation. For five days, from July 29 to August 2, he refused meals until he became so weak that he required treatment at the facility infirmary. Despite this, and despite his prior requests for mental health care, Joseph was not offered counseling or assessed for his potential to commit suicide.

A dozen years earlier, when Joseph was five or six, he had climbed into an old broken dryer that was parked in the driveway of Robert Nuñez's house—a perfect hiding place for a compact little boy, until the air and the light closed behind him. An aunt heard a tiny voice— "Let me out. I don't want to die," it was saying—and freed the shaken Joseph. This time his pleas for help would not be heard.

On August 31, the boy reached his limit. He had been in cell number 4 for eight weeks. He penned a note, which he passed, in the resourceful ways of the incarcerated, to the cell next door. "Tell the homie I love them"—a reference to his homeboy buddies—"and call my mom and tell her I love her." He instructed his neighbor not to read it until later that evening.

At 6:15 P.M., a staff member on routine thirty-minute rounds saw that the window in Joseph's door was covered with a towel. The officer tapped with keys and got no response. He then knocked forcefully and asked Joseph if he was okay. Joseph still did not respond. Although a policy required reporting such situations immediately, the Pajaro Hall supervisor wasn't told for fifteen minutes. The supervisor, in turn, delayed calling the required four-member "search and escort team" to open the door. Youths on lockdown sometimes lay in wait behind doors to attack staff; the team was a protective measure. By the time the door was opened, thirty-eight minutes had elapsed. Inside the cell, officers found Joseph in a partially seated position on the floor at the edge of the lower bunk. A sheet was fixed at one end to the frame of the upper bunk and at the other to his neck. His skin was blue and warm. He could not be revived.

The autopsy described the "well-developed, well-nourished body of a teenage Hispanic male appearing the stated age of 18 years. . . . The scalp hair is dark brown-black and up to approximately 5 inches in length. . . . There is a black mustache that is approximately 3/8-inch long with some facial hair in the beard area that is up to

approximately 1/2-inch in maximum length." The description concluded, "There is a tattoo forming a square of a dot at each corner
located on the lower lateral left orbital region."

Death was caused by asphyxia due to hanging.

Juvenile Justice Staff:

*There was a tragic incident last night A young man at N.
A. Chaderjian Youth Correctional Facility took his life. These
incidents tell us how difficult the world is for the young men
and women we work with. But it also shows us how, in spite of
sometimes overwhelming conditions, our staff are uncondition-
ally dedicated to their work.*

*I had a chance to talk with youth correctional officers after
they worked tirelessly to try to breath life into this young man.
I saw facility managers work as a team to maintain facility
order and coordinate the investigation with local law enforcement and Internal Affairs. I talked to facility staff who had
an impressive grasp on the current living conditions of the
living unit. Then there were the partnerships within the
agency: Office of Victims staff providing crisis support and
Parole staff members working hard to track down family
members.*

*A mother lost her son. In the face of this tragedy, I was
inspired by the professionalism, dedication and commitment of
staff in Juvenile Justice. You are the unrecognized heroes.*

Thank you for all your work.

Bernie Warner

Chief Deputy Secretary

—E-mail, sent September 1, 2005, to the staff of the
Division of Juvenile Justice, formerly the California
Youth Authority

Renee, dressed in gray slacks and a black silk camisole with thin straps, sat in the front row at a graveside service for Joseph on September 7 at East Lawn Memorial Park in Sacramento. Her almond eyes were puffy and red, her cheeks streaked with tears. She was devastated by the loss of the brother she had tried to save, bereft, too, that he had said nothing to her in his brief parting note. He had mentioned his homeboys and expressed love for his mother but not for her. He likely thought she knew. "Your one of the reasons why Im doing so good," he had written her from juvenile hall in 2002. The people who passed the casket and hugged Renee certainly seemed to know all that she had meant to Joseph. After the service, the priest presented her with a brass crucifix and gave another to Sabrina, dressed in a T-shirt and jeans. She was not feeling well and had been upset that she had nothing to wear. She sat a few rows back during the service, with the assembled aunts, uncles, grandparents, and cousins of a boy with a large family.

In the aftermath of Joseph's death, the state's inspector general issued one more in a long line of scathing reports on the California Youth Authority. This document was unprecedented, however. While others had dealt with the system as an amorphous whole, this so-called special report was on the death of a single ward, one among twenty-two suicides that had occurred over the previous fifteen years. In it, investigators examined the tenure of an unnamed but identifiable Hispanic youth who, at eighteen, had hung himself in a cell at Pajaro Hall on August 31, 2005. The report showed how Joseph Maldonado had been failed from the day he entered the Preston Youth Correctional Facility sixteen months earlier. At Preston, no one properly assessed his mental health or followed up on the anger and impulsivity he was noted to have, findings that should have raised a "red flag." Despite four written requests for mental health care, no one gave him any psychological help. At Chad, where he was a gang follower who had not been part of the fight before the lockdown, he was abandoned for eight weeks in a barren cell and given an untenable choice between his freedom and his gang. Even his five-day hunger strike did not prompt a response. Finally, the staff of Chad failed to open Joseph's door for thirty-eight crucial minutes on the day of his death, minutes that might have made the difference between life and death. "The eight weeks of isolation and the denial of mental health and other services may have contributed to the Ward's suicide," the report said.

At Preston, where Joseph still had friends, the word was that he had been ordered by the gang to rush—attack—a staff member and that he was not up to it, that he had caved in to the pressure. Some of his homies said that Joseph should have known, before getting involved with the gang, that this was the price of gang-banging. It was a mental game of control, and he had made a choice to be part of it. But had he? Or had the collective failures of a family, a system, and a society at last come down to this?

In 2003, researchers found that the levels of psychological distress among incarcerated youth were so high that they rivaled those of severely disturbed adolescents hospitalized in a psychiatric unit. There are perhaps few environments in America that are as challenging as the California Youth Authority, in particular to a youth like Joseph who had suffered a host of deprivations, including the murder of one parent, the dysfunction of the other, and the loss of two siblings.

Miguel Martin, the adoptive father of Sabrina's daughter Desiree, once took Joseph shopping for clothes. The boy had always had a cast-off kind of look, and Martin thought he'd like something stylish. As they walked through the aisles, Martin kept asking, do you like this shirt, these pants, those socks? Joseph just kept shrugging. Finally, Martin put a pair of tiny men's bikini underwear—men's thongs, actually—into the cart. "Okay, I'll decide," he said. With that, Joseph gingerly lifted the briefs from the cart and substituted a package of plaid boxer shorts. The ice was broken. When Martin dropped him off afterward, Joseph hugged him. "Thank you," he said. Few people spoke when invited to do so at Joseph's wake. Jaime Perez, Sabrina's father, thanked people for coming. An uncle read a passage from the Bible. Renee wanted to get up and speak but could not. Miguel Martin considered saying something, but stopped. He thought about how he should have done more for Joseph, how he should have tried to reach beyond the façade of the boy who, it seemed, tried so hard to be invisible. He imagined that others were feeling the same thing. He was sharing in a wave of collective, tangible guilt. Everyone had failed Joseph Daniel Maldonado, a fatherless boy from Sacramento, and now there was nothing that could be done about it.

CHAPTER FIFTEEN

Scandal in California

If I had a sledgehammer, I'd . . . take that sledgehammer and commence to beating the hell out of the walls and the barbed-wire fence. That would be the first thing I would want to do, because if they did it in Germany, the Berlin Wall, they need to get rid of those walls there.

    —Allen Feaster, father of Durrell Feaster, at a California State Senate hearing, September 2004

It is abundantly clear from the range of data that I collected for this review that the YA [Youth Authority] is a very dangerous place, and that neither staff nor wards feel safe in its facilities. One might easily conclude that an intense climate of fear permeates California's state youth corrections facilities.

    —Dr. Barry Krisberg, in a report to the court in *Farrell v. Allen*, December 23, 2003

*Not since the scandals within the houses of refuge have we wit-
nessed the total failure of juvenile prisons as in the case of the
California Youth Authority.*
        —Randall G. Shelden, in *Delinquency and Juvenile
                          Justice in American Society*, 2005

When Joseph entered the California Youth Authority in April 2004, it was in the throes of a full-blown scandal. The agency's mission was "to protect the public from criminal activity by providing education, training, and treatment services for youthful offenders." In the sixty-three years since it was founded, however, it had strayed about as far as it could get from reclaiming wayward youth. By 2004, the authority was, instead, a system of violent, abusive prisons over which no one—not administrators or corrections officers, not overseers or legislators, not even the quaintly titled wards themselves—had meaningful control. California taxpayers were paying $450 million a year for this corrupt bureaucracy, or about $115,000 per youth.

The years leading up to Joseph's incarceration had seen a slew of reports on Youth Authority abuses. All of them somehow rolled off the backs of California's leaders and bureaucrats, starting with a series by the Commonweal Research Institute in the 1980s. A 1982 report warned of overcrowding and stressful conditions and called facilities "among the worst in the country." A 1985 report called "Bodily Harm" told of wards who slept in large open rooms with one eye open and spent valuable school time "looking not at the blackboard in front of him, but over his shoulder in fear for his safety." A 1988 report said that authority facilities were "seriously overcrowded, offer minimal treatment value despite their high expense, and are ineffective in long-term protection of public safety."

In the 1980s and '90s, much of the problem had been due to overcrowding, with facilities sometimes holding 50 percent over their designed capacity. From 1980 to 1997, the population rose from five thousand to almost ten thousand, even though juvenile felony arrest rates had been more or less static throughout the period—a reflection of the punitive trend that was sweeping the country. After 1997, the Youth Authority's population began to drop markedly. Juvenile crime rates were sinking and, moreover, the state was asking counties to pay on a sliding scale for their incarcerated youth—the less serious the crime, the more they paid. Counties responded accordingly and stopped sending so many youths to state care. By 2004, the authority's population had dropped to four thousand. But while overcrowding eased, conditions did not improve. From 2000 to 2003, the state's inspector general issued nine audits showing that youths were not getting counseling or education, were being housed too long in isolation, and were being subjected to excessive use of force.

It was not until January 2004, however, that the case against the California Youth Authority was effectively sealed. The twin suicides at Preston were just part of the reason. A lawsuit had been filed against the state the year earlier on behalf of a mentally ill youth named Edward Jermaine Brown, who also had been a ward at Preston. Brown had been kept in solitary confinement for seven months in a cell spattered with blood and feces from previous tenants and where the toilet often did not work. Severely ill, the youth had been fed "blender meals" through a straw and coerced to take psychotropic medications with threats of longer stays in solitary. He was not allowed to watch television or listen to the radio; he was permitted one phone call a month. Five expert reports, released that month, showed that Edward Jermaine Brown was but the tip of a very large iceberg. A top-to-bottom, damning indictment of the agency and its operations, the reports also came with a special and singular imprimatur—they had been prepared by experts chosen jointly by the defendants and the plaintiffs in a move toward settlement. They were government admissions of incompetence and failure.

Barry Krisberg, longtime president of the National Council on Crime and Delinquency, wrote the lead report in sometimes breathtaking prose. The authority was a system of youth prisons in which there was "a stunning amount of violence," and "an intense climate of fear," he wrote. Facilities were "antiquated and in a general state of disrepair due to budget priorities," including some in which conditions were "deplorable," "filthy," and "vermin-infested." He said that staff members routinely demeaned the wards with comments about their families or sexual preferences, telling them they were "worthless and had no chance for rehabilitation." Wards were forced to sleep on cold cement slabs in their underwear or "to spend long periods of time on their knees (sometimes on sharp surfaces) with their hands bound behind them." He recounted the "dangerous and potentially fatal use of high powered weapons" that sprayed chemicals directly into wards' rooms, at the risk of asphyxiating them.

The report on mental health conditions in California's juvenile facilities was written by Raymond Patterson, a Washington, D.C., a forensic psychiatrist, and Eric Trupin, a child psychologist at the University of Washington in Seattle. It was equally unsettling. The experts, well known for their measured and fastidious research into conditions for Americans in custody, were unequivocal. "The vast majority of youths with mental health needs are made worse instead of improved by the correctional environment," they reported. Punishment was excessive and unsupervised, including twenty-three-hour lockup, placement in cages, and frequent dousing with chemicals. Psychotropic medications were administered liberally and without follow-up. There were too few mental health workers, inadequate substance abuse treatment, and poor employee training. The authors expressed "grave concerns relative to the competence of psychiatric staff."

As with its myriad other problems, the authority had plenty of notice that it was failing wards who were mentally ill. Over the years, as the authority's population in need of mental health care rose—to 45 percent of the male population in 2000 and 65 percent of females—California did the bare minimum to meet its needs. Psychotropic drugs were prescribed sloppily and without oversight.

Psychiatrists and their staff were overworked. Small, poorly run units were opened only for the most acutely ill.

In 2000, an investigation by the Youth and Adult Correctional Agency, which reviewed the Youth Authority's operations, found that the agency "lacks a systematic approach to delivering medical and mental health services to wards." In 2002, the state's inspector general reported, "The vast majority of wards needing mental health treatment . . . receive no mental health services at all," and the treatment of those who get it is "substandard." In 2003, a budget report concluded that the department's program "does not come close to meeting the diverse mental health needs of our population." The agency had one-fifth the necessary psychologists—seventy-two more were needed, along with nineteen additional psychiatrists. At one facility, the staff had revolted, issuing a memo that said the "imbalance" between mental health care needs and resources had "reached a near alarming level."

Joseph Maldonado and his mental health needs, whatever they were, were a small part of a much larger problem. The fights and the noise, the unpredictable outbursts, the anger, were not merely the manifestations of a depraved and indifferent populace; they were the symptoms of seriously disturbed and needy youths. In perhaps the most exhaustive look at the character of the authority's population, three Stanford University researchers concluded in 2001 that 71 percent of wards had three to five psychiatric diagnoses. Among these, 31 percent suffered anxiety disorder, 12 percent suffered from bipolar disorder or depression, and 4 percent exhibited psychosis—all rates several times higher than that in the general population. At Preston alone, nearly half—48 percent—of the population had disorders related to anxiety, depression, mania, borderline personality, or oppositional/defiant disorders.

The Youth Authority had not only failed to provide treatment to its charges. With its heavy reliance on 23-and-1 confinement, the agency had also created an environment in which mental illness could flower. Average stays ranged from 52 to 114 days, according to one expert report—"much longer than those encountered in virtually any other juvenile correctional system in the nation." The solitary confinement unit at Preston, where Joseph was sentenced to 90 days, was a place to which mentally ill youths were banished, "away from staff observation or interaction" and without any review by higher-ups, another report said. No research existed to suggest that such long punishments were in any way therapeutic, the agency's critics stated, while "most psychologists and mental health professionals would argue that this severe isolation is antithetical to sound treatment practices."

After Durrell Feaster's suicide, Allen Feaster learned something he had not known: While his son was being housed in the system's most mentally challenging form of housing, he was also being treated for mental illness. According to his autopsy report, Durrell's body harbored the SSRI (selective seratonin reuptake inhibitor) Prozac, and he had been prescribed three other medications as well—the mood stabilizer Depakote, the antipsychotic Zyprexa, and the antidepressant Trazodone. "[D]ecedent Feaster had a history of suicidal tendencies prior to arriving at Preston CYA," an investigator wrote in the coroner's final report, raising but not answering a key question. The sensory deprivation of Deon's and Durrell's confinement had long been known to be harmful to the human psyche—to make prison inmates hypersensitive to sounds, to bring on anxiety and panic attacks, to cause hallucinations and obsessive thinking. Why was a mentally ill youth with suicidal tendencies kept for two months in such a place? A Youth Authority chaplain in the Krisberg report is quoted as saying: "The YA has a serious problem with gangs, but their solution is demonic."

The system did not deny the accusations. "The observations of the state experts in these areas are substantially correct," Sarah Ludeman, a spokesperson for the authority, told the press, "and our department is reviewing each of these reports to develop a plan to correct the issues raised." If the promise was familiar, the admission had never been so clear.

Allen Feaster was offered one hundred thousand dollars to settle his lawsuit against the system. He declined. "This country can't make enough money," he likes to say, not needing to finish the sentence.

EPILOGUE

for Part Five

The state Personnel Board decided Tuesday to reinstate correctional officers caught on tape beating inmates in Stockton's N. A. Chaderjian Youth Correctional Facility. Six correctional officers were caught on surveillance cameras hitting two young wards in January 2004. The guards, supported by the correctional officers union, appealed the California Youth Authority's decision to fire them and received a judge's recommendation to get their jobs back.
—Oakland Tribune, September 2, 2005

Three youth prison staffers were suspended without pay [for two, five and 10 days] for not preventing a ward from hanging himself in his cell last year, state corrections officials said. Joseph Daniel Maldonado, 18, committed suicide at the N. A. Chaderjian Youth Correctional Facility on Aug. 31, 2005, after a hunger strike. His requests for counseling were ignored, according to the state's prison watchdog agency. "To me, that's nothing at all," said Maldonado's sister, Renee Nuñez. "Whoever put him on an eight-week lockdown, took away his schooling and didn't allow him to take showers, I feel that has a lot to do with what happened that day."
—Associated Press, August 31, 2006

An inmate at the N. A. Chaderjian Youth Correctional Facility tried to hang himself exactly one year after another young man committed suicide there, state corrections officials said. Staff members found the 19-year-old breathing and coherent after Thursday's suicide attempt.
—Associated Press, September 1, 2006

Adolescence and early adulthood are particularly vulnerable times of life for suicide. Youths in juvenile facilities, for all their fearsome toughness, are perhaps the most vulnerable. They come from dysfunctional families, have high rates of substance abuse, have suffered losses, and have been subjected to emotional, physical, and sexual abuse—all possible risk factors for suicide. Isolating such youths around the clock, in a place of sensory deprivation and in a milieu that tells them they are less than human, confirms their worst inclinations and magnifies their considerable anger.

In a study of 110 juvenile confinement suicides that occurred from 1995 to 1999, researchers learned what they had long known about suicides in adult prisons—that a disproportionate number occurs when people are locked away as Joseph Maldonado was. In the study, published in 2004, 50 percent of incarcerated youth who committed suicide were in isolation at the time; another 12 percent had been kept there prior to their deaths.

Eight months after Joseph's death, in April 2006, Sabrina weaned herself from the drugs that had sustained her for twenty years. She returned to live with her parents and reconnect with her family after a very long absence. She was weak and in pain for months but is slowly coming around and hopes one day to get her own place.

In the fall and winter of 2006-2007, Renee moved twice, settling in a two-bedroom townhouse in Roseville, a quiet Sacramento suburb, with her sister Selena, a pretty middle-schooler with long straight brown hair. Renee works as a processor in a mortgage company, but she has applied to become a corrections officer because she wants to make a difference in the system that claimed her brother. She has held several car washes in an attempt to raise money for a headstone for Joseph, whose grave, provided by his paternal grandmother Marsha Maldonado, is marked with a green plastic tag. She will hold more fund-raisers for the $1,500 stone when she has time.

Renee has filed a lawsuit against the State of California for its treatment of Joseph, alleging that his civil rights were violated. The battle will be long and difficult, but she has a good lawyer, Stewart Katz, who has waged such fights before. Renee's name is unlikely to remain on the lawsuit as plaintiff, since Sabrina has rightful standing under the law. Renee does not mind. Like Joseph, she loves her mother. She is proud that Sabrina has at last given up the drug life after a siege of many years. Her only hope is that something good comes of the death of her brother, whom she misses every day.

"I hope that my brother's voice and strength will lead me to open doors for others like him," Renee says.

A Prescription

THERE WERE MANY PEOPLE I could have profiled in this book, too many, in fact, which is the point. I didn't choose my stories because they were aberrations. I chose them because they were terribly, tragically typical. While their endings are often extreme—suicide, death at the hands of police, extreme self-mutilation—they represent what people with mental illness endure every day in their encounters with the criminal justice system. Shayne, Luke, Peter, Alan, Jessica, and Joseph are six among hundreds of thousands: people who are treated as suspects when they are psychotic. People who are jailed when they should be healed. People who are thrown into prison solitary confinement units when, and because, they are sick. In the journey that was this book, I came to know many others who suffered at the hands of American justice. They also need a voice, and they need our outrage.

One of the people I came to know was Jesse McCann, a mentally ill seventeen-year-old who was sentenced to a New York State prison for a crime he committed when he was sixteen. A sandy-haired adolescent who was five-foot-eight and 160 pounds, Jesse was a scared kid who did not belong in prison, not by a long shot. His road there was a series of missteps, a tragedy of errors that demonstrates how unforgiving a society we have become. Jesse wasn't blameless; he and his friends had broken into a house, and on the day he got probation, he lifted a wallet with $18 and credit cards in it from an unlocked car. Charged with grand larceny, Jesse was booked into the county jail, the quintessentially wrong place for him. There, this child who had never been able to control his emotions, who had been hospitalized for mental illness for the first time when he was ten, refused to leave his cell. When a phalanx of guards rushed him, as they are trained to do when they are disobeyed, he resisted violently and assaulted one of them.

Jesse went from jail to prison, not because he had stolen a wallet but because he had assaulted an officer at the jail. Like Jessica Roger, Jesse's very interaction with the criminal justice system is what led him to a prison term. His jailers not only failed to address his raging psyche, they coaxed him into committing a crime. It happens often. Had Peter Nadir not been suffocated during his ill-fated encounter with police, he would likely have gone to jail for assaulting them—an offense he committed while he was psychotic, during a botched restraint by poorly trained officers. This disastrous interplay between people with mental illness and the criminal justice system is part of why jails and prisons have become America's de facto mental institutions. Another is the lack of care in the community, which first drives people with mental illness into the arms of police.

The Ulster County Jail, where Jesse was incarcerated after his arrest, is the local lockup in the area where I live, in a bucolic county about a hundred miles north of New York City. It is run by good, well-intentioned people who follow the rules of the overseeing State

Commission of Correction, which establishes minimal standards of care. But it is typical of jails across this country: its mission is to confine and secure inmates, not to care for the mentally ill. When I visited the facility in 2005, about fifty of its 263 inmates, nearly a fifth of the population, were on psychotropic medications. I asked a social worker to describe the jail's mental health staff. "You're looking at it," she responded. Aside from her, a psychiatrist visited for eight hours weekly to prescribe medicine, the sole form of treatment. Like thousands of other jails in the United States, the facility was a veritable mental hospital except for the key fact that it provided little legitimate mental health care.

From the jail, Jesse went to Downstate Correctional Facility, a state prison, on a sentence of three to three and a half years. He wrote letters home that, kidlike, were punctuated with happy faces and requests for Twizzlers licorice. He also described the anxiety attacks and shortness of breath he suffered when he was locked in solitary confinement, where, unable to cope and chronically misbehaving, he had spent much of his jail time. Seven weeks after he arrived at the prison, Jesse had another of his outbursts. The official report of it reads:

> *At 9:20 A.M. on 3/16/01 while an officer was escorting 15 inmates to Complex One, inmate McCann became verbally abusive stating "f— all the doctors and officers." He was given a direct order to stop the language and then stated "you haven't seen my record." The officer instructed the inmate that he was going back to his cell and placed his hand on McCann's shoulder to direct him. The inmate pulled away and hit the officer in the ribs. The officer used a body hold to bring the inmate to the ground and then escorted him to ID for processing of the incident as it would result in SHU [special housing unit] placement.*

Jesse was stripped, searched, and placed in a solitary confinement cell. He was noted to have red eyes from crying. Jesse had been in prison only fifty days, and he had spent thirty of them locked in his cell around the clock. Just thirty-eight minutes later, he was found hanging from a bedsheet that he had attached to the cell window. He was the youngest suicide in a New York prison in at least ten years.

Nearly half of New York's prison suicides occur in isolated confinement, where many people like Jesse can be found, though just 7 or 8 percent of the prison population is housed there. In 2005, 69 percent of California's prison suicides took place in solitary confinement, where just 5 percent of the population was kept, according to a report in USA Today.

Jesse's death raises questions about the quality of care for mentally ill inmates. In jail and prison, he was managed by guards with little training in mental health who hurled orders and laid hands on him, exacerbating his condition and compounding his crimes. (Three years after his death, a female inmate at the Ulster jail assaulted officers after exhibiting "strange behavior," went to prison for it like Jessie, and committed suicide there in 2006.) He was put in closet-sized rooms for weeks on end when hospitalization or placement on a special unit would have been more appropriate.

The bottom line, however, is that Jesse should not have been in prison in the first place. Prison should be the domain of the truly deserving, those who rob banks, mug old women, and kill wantonly. Yet it is the place where there is always a bed, where another body and soul could be crammed in until, by 2005, nearly 2.2 million of us were behind bars. The sentencing judge in the Jessica Roger case tried to avoid sending her to prison, knowing that she had been hospitalized some two dozen times. There simply was nowhere else to place her.

Prisons have become a self-perpetuating industry in America. They have brought construction projects and jobs to small rural towns across the nation—an economic boost, though usually short-lived and small. Prisons bring political clout as well. Inmates are counted in federal census data for purposes of doling out federal aid and apportioning political representation. Inmates mean money for roads and education and seats for savvy legislators. And politicians have cashed in.

Some of us are paying the price for these trends.

Jesse loved to read—everything from Stephen King to Norman Mailer—and he was intensely bright. He had wanted to become a lawyer and had a strong sense of justice. His first fight, as a freckle-faced six-year-old, was in defense of a hearing-impaired youngster who was being teased by classmates. As a teenager, Jesse was outraged when he learned that a Florida boy had received a life sentence for the rough-housing death of a little girl when he was twelve, incredulous that an unintended death by a preteen would bring lifelong imprisonment. "What don't they understand?" he asked.

Indeed, what?

America's prison boom has given it the world's highest per capita incarceration rate: 714 per 100,000 people in 2005, followed at a distant second by Russia, Belarus, and Bermuda, which were tied at 532. We spent $60 billion in 2001 to run some five thousand state, local, and federal lockups. In America, it seems, there is always money for jails. On the day of my visit to the Ulster County Jail, the finishing touches were being put on a replacement facility next door, with room for 60 percent more inmates and twice the number of punitive segregation cells. Meanwhile, the jail's social worker, Karen Bitner, bemoaned the dismal lack of community housing and what it portended for barely functioning mentally ill inmates. "It's just a matter of time until they come back," she said.

The money to build and maintain all those prisons had to come from somewhere. Prison spending tripled in the last two decades of the twentieth century, while state spending on mental health care increased by only a fifth and per capita spending on higher education rose by a third.

More money spent on bricks and mortar also meant less to

rehabilitate the people inside. Lateef Islam, a former drug dealer who grew up on the gritty streets of the Bedford-Stuyvesant neighborhood of Brooklyn, took advantage of the schooling available to him during his eleven years in a New York prison and earned a bachelor's degree in criminal justice in 1984. Islam went on to direct a large social service program in the city of Poughkeepsie, led community efforts against racism, and before his death in 2005, inspired a generation of city children. In many states, if Islam went to prison today, he would be out of luck. From 1991 to 1997, the share of inmates receiving job training and educational instruction dropped by 16 and 20 percent, respectively—cuts that have only accelerated since. New York State awarded college degrees to forty-six hundred inmates in the 1990s—inmates who proved to be half as likely to return to prison as others. Nonetheless, New York eliminated the program in 1995 after the abolition of federal Pell Grants; many other states followed suit.

In America, perhaps one-third of prisoners receive job training or education. Only about one-fifth of inmates with drug problems are treated. A little more than one-tenth receive any preparation to be released.

America's lock-'em-up mentality is not for the purpose of protecting us from those who would do us harm. Those people were already being incarcerated. This new prison dogma has captured groups of people who in years past would not have gone to prison and whose crimes against society—a term to be applied loosely—could have been addressed in less expensive and more productive ways. In 1980, 57 percent of the people sent to prison in New York State had committed violent offenses; these were the people who presumably deserved to be segregated from the rest of us. By 2005, the share of violent commitments had dropped to 29 percent. Nationally, the trend was the same: Three-quarters of all prison inmates in 2002 had been convicted of nonviolent crimes.

Who are among the 2.2 million inmates who might not have been locked up a generation ago?

This mass of imprisoned humanity includes at least three hundred thirty thousand people with mental illness—7 percent of federal inmates and 16 percent of those in state and local lockups, perhaps one-third of whom may be actively psychotic—in other words, very sick. (A subsequent study based on inmate reporting found that more than 50 percent of inmates had mental health problems.) The prevalence of mental illness in correctional facilities is three times what it is in the community at large. Another half million mentally ill Americans are on probation. We have become so inured to the criminal justice alternative that there is a growing trend in mental hospitals to arrest patients who assault staff during psychotic episodes. Not too long ago, these people would not have been considered candidates for arrest, based—correctly—on the theory that they had little control over their actions. No more.

Drug addicts have also been swept up in America's prison boom. Luke Ashley, the twenty-four-year-old Texan who committed suicide in jail, was one of them. Luke's proclivity to self-medicate posed no threat to society; nevertheless, he was sent to jail, even though it would take four months, at a cost to the county of seventy-five dollars a day, for a drug treatment bed to open. In Texas, the number of people imprisoned for drug crimes grew by 420 percent from 1988 to 2002, about twice as fast as the population overall. Drug offenders accounted for 8 percent of state and federal inmates in 1980 and 23 percent in 1998. America's costly drug war has sapped money from treatment, and from education and jobs programs that are far more effective in deterring drug use and addressing addiction.

One of the best ways to ensure the destruction of the family in poor neighborhoods that have seen vast numbers of fathers and sons imprisoned is to incarcerate women. America did that, too. Eight times as many women were in prison in 2004 as in 1980, twice the increase of men. Of these women, one-quarter were mentally ill, three-quarters had been sexually or physically abused, two-thirds had minor children, and one-third were serving time for drug crimes. Under New York's harsh Rockefeller drug laws, women who were mere carriers of drugs for dealers went to prison when their babies were in diapers and emerged when those babies were young adults. The damage done to those families will cost society plenty.

Most tragically perhaps, the U.S. punishment agenda has captured children like Joseph Maldonado and marked them early and forever as delinquents and felons. As a teenager, Joseph stole several cars but committed no violent crime. Nonetheless, he was sent to the most violent, most troubled juvenile system in the country. There he easily fell under the control of a gang, and committed suicide after two months in a locked cell. From 1991 to 2003, there was a 23 percent increase in boys committed to juvenile facilities, and an 88 percent increase in girls. Meanwhile, the number of juveniles who, like Jesse McCann, were consigned to adult penal institutions in the United States tripled from 1990 through 2004. In 1998, Amnesty International reported that this country had more children in adult prisons than any other in the world, and five times as many as India. How can this be, especially when the rate of juvenile violent crime has been declining dramatically since 1994—to levels not seen since the 1970s?

Rob Wrighton, a tall, thin African-American man in his forties, pulled up his sleeve to show me a razor-thin scar on the soft inside of his wrist. "I had no choice," he told me. "That was the only way I could get anyone's attention." Wrighton suffers from schizophrenia. For three years, six months, and two days—by his account—he was confined around the clock in a small cell in the New York State prison system known to inmates as the Box. During that time, he was alone. He had nothing to do, no radio or television, and few possessions. What he did have was his paranoia and his voices. He floated in a colorless nether world, unaware of time and connected to reality only by a rectangular slot in his door through which food was passed. When he slit his wrists, he did it to be noticed, to get out. Wrighton is among the thousands of inmates nationwide who have experienced what many human rights and psychiatric experts have long considered a definition of torture. He is, in fact, a textbook case.

In 1979, Stuart Grassian, MD, a psychiatrist on the faculty of Harvard Medical School for twenty-five years, interviewed fourteen inmates who were housed in the small, windowless cells of a solitary confinement unit at the Massachusetts State Penitentiary in Walpole. He found that the inmates had descended into either a mental torpor—a fog in thinking and expression—or outright psychosis. One inmate could not recall the days just before and after he slashed his wrists. Another described feelings of panic and fear of suffocation. Many heard voices, were hypersensitive to sounds, or obsessed over thoughts of torture and revenge on guards. "I try to sleep sixteen hours a day, block out my thoughts," an inmate told Grassian. "I can't stop it." Such conditions, Grassian concluded, are intensely damaging to the healthy human psyche. Imagine their effect on people who are mentally ill.

In November 2004, a quarter century after Grassian's findings, I toured Walpole, a walled prison about twenty-five miles southwest of Boston with nine observation towers and capacity for eight hundred maximum-security inmates. Although the name had been changed at the behest of the residents of the town of Walpole—to Massachusetts Correctional Institution–Cedar Junction—not much else had. Five days before my arrival and a day before Thanksgiving, an inmate by the name of Richard A. Street, fifty-three, had hung himself in a prison segregation unit much like the one that had been the focus of research by Grassian.

Street was a wretched man who had indiscriminately shot two people one night in Boston in 1980 and then went on to exhaust the patience and resources of the Massachusetts prison system. Suffering from schizoaffective disorder and calling himself "Jesus Christ, Future King of the Vampires," Street would rant, self-mutilate, and perform naked pirouettes around a basketball in the prison yard. He spent years in solitary confinement in the system's departmental disciplinary unit, the only place where he could be controlled.

I obtained Street's medical records for a six-week period in the spring of 2004. In that time, he was twice found hanging in his cell; he repeatedly cut and gouged his skin; he swallowed an inch-and-a-half piece of metal, and was taken to a local emergency room six times. He smeared feces in his hair, complained that solitary confinement was making him hurt himself, and asked for—and was denied—contact with his lawyer. Photographs show Street displaying a gruesome array of wounds on his legs and forearms. Nonetheless, a prison clinician wrote in the midst of this: "Pt. [patient] is not depressed . . . nor at risk of harm due to mental illness." After his death, which went unreported in any newspaper, the sentiment among officers on a union Web site was that Richard Street had belonged not in a prison but in a mental hospital.

Massachusetts was the state where Dorothea Dix began her national crusade in the 1840s against the abuse of the incarcerated insane. "I proceed, Gentlemen," Dix wrote in her famous appeal to the Massachusetts state legislature, "to briefly call your attention to the present state of Insane Persons confined within this Commonwealth, in cages, stalls, pens! Chained, naked, beaten with rods, and lashed into obedience." In Richard Street, the state had come full circle. He was not alone. Solitary confinement is the treatment of choice for mentally ill inmates across America.

In 1890, the U.S. Supreme Court observed that prisoners in solitary confinement "fell, after even a short confinement, into a semi-fatuous condition, from which it was next to impossible to arouse them, and others became violently insane. . . ." That did not stop America from adding thousands of so-called "supermax" prison cells in the 1990s, constructing entire prisons around the theme of round-the-clock confinement and sensory deprivation. The idea was to heap punishment on punishment, to make prison so unpleasant that no one would want to return. "The supermax," said Governor Tommy Thompson of Wisconsin in 1996, "will be a criminal's worst nightmare." There was no research to bolster the view that this kind of confinement would make prisons safer or make inmates less likely to reoffend, but there was plenty, like Grassian's, to suggest otherwise.

Psychiatric experts say they can judge the quality of a prison system's mental health programs by a quick visit to their supermax facility or solitary confinement units. In many states, they are dumping places for the mentally ill, units where inmates cry and scream, vegetate and self-mutilate. In New York, which added isolation capacity for three thousand inmates in the late 1990s, nearly 20 percent of the inmates in isolation were mentally ill—as were 64 percent in maximum-security solitary confinement units. In other states as well, the share of mentally ill people in isolation is invariably much higher than in the general population: in Oregon, 28 percent; California, 32 percent; Washington, 29 percent; Massachusetts, 33 percent. In 1999, a federal court judge in Texas described these units as "virtual incubators of psychoses—seeding illness in otherwise healthy inmates and exacerbating illness in those already suffering from mental infirmities." In 1995, a California judge likened conditions for the mentally ill in such units to "the mental equivalent of putting an asthmatic in a place with little air to breathe." The average time that inmates are confined under these conditions is unfathomable—5.2 years in Texas, 4.2 years in Massachusetts, 3 years in New York.

In 2006, Human Rights Watch released a report on the use of dogs as tools of control in seven state prison systems in America. The report included a videotape from Massachusetts, posted on the Internet, of five officers in helmets and riot gear as they rushed into a cell to take down an inmate, a snarling, barking German shepherd in tow. The scene is one of pandemonium and screaming, the inmate telling the officers to kill him and get it over with, the officers thrusting him to the floor and ordering him again and again to put his hands behind his back. The inmate has no shirt on; his skin is flaming pink against the thick black coats worn by the officers. This exercise in control was launched because the inmate had refused repeated orders to relinquish a piece of Plexiglas. He had been locked in a solitary confinement cell, so the only person he could have hurt was himself. The effort to stop him was legitimate, but there was no negotiation, no talking with him, just repeated orders to drop the instrument.

The inmate was twenty-eight at the time of the incident in 2004; I corresponded with him in 2005 when he was at the Massachusetts prison at Walpole. He had a history of severe mental illness and attempted suicide. As a child, he had been beaten with broomsticks, extension cords, and belt buckles; needles had been driven through his fingers. Not surprisingly, he grew up to be hateful and violent. He committed murder. "I became what I hated to be, a monster," he wrote to me. He had spent sixteen months just prior to the incident in the prison system's mental hospital and, before that, nine years in solitary confinement. Like Richard Street, this inmate was one of too many mentally ill inmates in a system with too few resources. The scene with the barking dog and a herd of overwrought officers was but a small sliver of his experience.

Prisons resort to such tactics because they have been forced to accept a mentally-ill population they do not have the expertise to cope with. In 2006, the New York State Legislature passed a law that would exclude mentally ill inmates from twenty-three-hour confinement and that would build special units for their care. Governor George Pataki vetoed it. It would have cost too much, he said.

The cost of mental health care in prisons is admittedly high—$246 million in California in 2003, $84 million in Michigan, $24 million in New Jersey. This is what happens when mentally ill people are incarcerated, and on such a scale. But prisons also pay for their failure to provide appropriate care. Mentally ill inmates have poor disciplinary records—often because they have received poor treatment—hence they spend, on average, fifteen months longer in prison. Those *additional* fifteen months in 2005 cost state prisons alone at least $5.7 billion for the mentally ill inmates who were incarcerated. That is a conservative estimate, using an annual per-inmate rate of $22,650; mentally ill inmates usually cost far more, 75 percent more, for example, in Pennsylvania.

Then there are the incalculable costs that accrue when people are released from prison to the streets, sicker and more damaged than they were when they went in. Many states release inmates directly from solitary confinement—shackled one minute, free the next. These are people who are angry, disoriented, disconnected—and, sometimes, dangerous. Like Shayne Eggen, they are given a bus ticket and a small supply of medication; there is little effort made to line up housing, community services, or medical care for them. Shayne spent the last month of her incarceration in Iowa's "hole"; within six weeks of her release, she set a fire that caused four hundred thousand dollars in damage. She was one of many inmates who "max out" of prison, meaning they serve their entire sentence because they have poor disciplinary records, so they are released without the supervision of a parole officer. Yet Shayne was exactly the kind of person who needed supervision.

Litigation has forced prisons in at least sixteen states to improve mental health care; many of these lawsuits have stemmed from abusive conditions in solitary confinement. A few lawsuits—notably in Wisconsin, Connecticut, New Mexico, Indiana, and Ohio—have led to a ban on the placement of seriously mentally ill inmates in solitary confinement. The prohibition should extend nationwide.

Among these states, Connecticut has embarked on an intriguing experiment in the care of its mentally ill inmates. In settling a lawsuit over egregious conditions in its supermax prison, the state agreed in 2004 to consign its most seriously ill inmates to a single prison-turned-asylum called Garner Correctional Institution, in Fairfield County. There, units were established based on inmates' ability to function, and corrections officers were specially trained to work with mental health staff. When inmates acted out, counselors were called to defuse potentially violent confrontations and to avoid punishing behavior that was illness-related. This well-intentioned experiment has been far from successful, however. In the two years since the transition, one inmate hung himself and two were killed when restrained by officers.

In theory, all prisons should be moving in the direction of Connecticut's Garner. Mental health units should be established for seriously ill inmates. The limits of mentally ill inmates to conform in prison should be recognized. Officers should be trained in the manifestations and management of illness and the value of persuasion over force. Clinicians should play key roles in inmate management. At the same time, Connecticut's experience suggests that the inherently adversarial nature of keeper and kept may not square neatly with the goals of treatment. The problem is the irony of Garner itself: with six hundred inmates—or is it patients?—it is the state's largest mental institution. Yet, as a prison, it is ill suited to the role of hospital.

Few corrections officials understand the demands of mental health care. Aside from accrediting agencies that enforce minimum standards, prisons have no independent oversight of their mental health services, as a hospital would. Given the power dynamic inherent in prisons, inmates aren't trusted to report symptoms or side effects honestly, and their behavior is often labeled "malingering" and "manipulative." Prisons are also often located in rural areas where medical and mental health positions are difficult to fill. Their generally inferior salaries may attract people with checkered backgrounds. As staff turns over and inmates are shuttled from prison to prison for security reasons, and often without their medications, continuity of care is frequently compromised. More broadly, there is precious little public disclosure about what goes on in prisons, leading, invariably, to abuse. The ability of inmates to challenge conditions in court has been sharply curtailed by legislation and legal rulings. Finally, prisons are, first and foremost, places of punishment; they are tense, rigidly controlled environments that are exceedingly tough on sane people. Mentally ill people should be kept out of prisons—which means they must be provided decent care on the outside.

In 1960, there were four inpatient psychiatric beds for every one thousand Americans. By 1994, the figure had dropped by two-thirds to 1.3 beds per thousand. Lesser known is another, perhaps related, statistic. During a time when bed counts were dropping drastically, more people with mental illness were dying. The death rate among people with mental and substance-use disorders, which commonly overlap, nearly tripled in America, from 5.7 per one hundred thousand in 1979 to 15.5 per one hundred thousand in 1995. Death rates also went up in four European countries and in Australia, all of which saw huge declines in inpatient capacity. According to a study presented in Philadelphia at the 2000 Institute on Psychiatric Services of the American Psychiatric Association, the only country in which the rate of death declined among mentally ill and substance abusing people was Japan, a country that saw bed counts increase. Many factors might account for the trend, the study found, but it noted: "In the U.S. persons with serious mental illness often lead a marginal existence, with poor health habits, high rates of substance use, and little access to all forms of health care."

No one wants to return to the days when people with mental illness were summarily hospitalized for months and years at a time, often under brutal and dehumanizing conditions. But in 1955, when America had five hundred fifty-nine thousand people in mental hospitals, these were five hundred fifty-nine thousand people for whom states assumed some sort of responsibility. They accepted their role as the primary players in an imperfect system of care. Then, in 1953, came Thorazine, which allowed people with schizophrenia to live outside institutions. It was followed in 1963 by the Community Mental Health Centers Act, which mandated a community system that would take the place of hospitals. It was never fully implemented. These developments, along with legal rulings that defined the rights of mentally ill people to refuse treatment, allowed states to shed their responsibility to people with serious mental illness. And shed it they did.

The State of Iowa was typical. In 1955, it had 5,336 patients in public mental hospitals; by 2006, there were 287. The paucity of beds meant that hospitalization was an elusive and fleeting option when Karen Duncan slipped into a deep depression in early 2003 at the age of thirty-three. The mother of three sons, an eight-year-old and four-year-old twins, Karen was a striking woman of Mexican-American descent who threw joyous backyard birthday parties replete with piñatas and a cake for each of the twins. She and her husband, Chris, had recently opened a diner together with an elaborate playground Chris had built that attracted neighborhood kids. Then came Karen's suicide attempts: in an asphyxiation attempt, she took apart the furnace; she slit her wrists and ran in front of a speeding truck. She was hospitalized for depression four times in two months, but each time for only about seventy-two hours, and only for the purpose of stabilizing her on a growing list of medications. Karen's final stay at a state mental hospital ended in June 2003 when attendants dropped her off at the couple's house without any notice to her family. Two weeks later, Karen Duncan drove a pickup truck, with her children on board, into the Missouri River. Passersby could hear the children screaming as the vehicle plunged down a twenty-five-foot embankment. Everyone in the truck died. "I couldn't even begin to tell you what my life is like today," Chris Duncan told me two years later, after he had moved to Kansas to start over. "Everything in my entire life changed—mentally, physically, spiritually, emotionally—in every way, shape, or form."

America has a crisis in inpatient psychiatric care. From 1990 to 2000, the number of state psychiatric beds, which had already been drastically reduced, declined from ninety-eight thousand to fifty-nine thousand. Since then, thirty states have eliminated additional beds. What few state hospital beds exist are being filled with the growing overflow of the criminal justice system: people deemed incompetent to stand trial, not guilty by reason of insanity, or civilly committed, sometimes after their release from prison. In a 2001 survey, twenty-eight states reported increases in this so-called forensic population, which takes up one-third of state beds—beds on which 46 million uninsured Americans, like Luke Ashley, for example, must rely.

At the same time, the number of private psychiatric beds has also contracted sharply as general hospitals realize that, thanks to poor reimbursements, there's little money to be made in the provision of psychiatric treatment. From 1990 to 2000, private psychiatric beds declined from forty-five thousand nationally to twenty-seven thousand—a drop so dramatic that the share of private insurance spending on mental health and substance abuse disorders dropped by nearly a third from 1992 to 1999. All told, the nation has eliminated more than three hundred thousand beds since 1970, a 59 percent reduction at a time when the population increased by 38 percent.

One way to fix this bloodletting would be to pass strong insurance parity laws across the country, as some states have done, that mandate equivalent coverage for mental and physical illnesses. Unless insurance pays for the service, hospitals won't provide it. Another way would be to eliminate the provision of federal law that prohibits the expenditure of Medicaid dollars on "institutions for mental disease." This federal funding loophole has encouraged states to empty psychiatric institutions, for which they don't get Medicaid dollars, forcing patients into places that do, such as nursing homes. A third way would be for America, at long last, to face up to the problem of its uninsured with a universal health care system.

Beds are just a part of a much larger systemic problem in the delivery of mental health care, however. In 1999, the U.S. Surgeon General reported that two-thirds of people with mental illness in America received no treatment at all. In 2002, President Bush's New Freedom Commission on Mental Health declared, "America's mental health service delivery system is in shambles." In 2006, the National Alliance for the Mentally Ill gave the nation a D in a report card on mental health care. The inadequacies of the community system of mental health care are evident in myriad ways: Mentally ill people tangle with police on a regular basis, thousands are in jail, and thousands more are homeless. From 1992 to 2003, emergency rooms saw a 56 percent increase in people experiencing psychiatric crisis, people who were unable to access services that are invariably less expensive than the relapses that result from inadequate treatment.

Besides a paucity of short- and long-term hospital care, people with mental illness have trouble obtaining the most basic human needs, among these shelter. I once interviewed a forty-two-year-old woman named Deborah Grenald at a job training program in Harlem. Grenald had spiky black hair held down by a plastic band and was wearing a pretty blue dress and gold earrings. She suffered from schizoaffective disorder and spoke haltingly and deliberately, as if each word were an effort at control. She was trying to make a go of it in this rarity of a job-training program. That much was evident. But because she had been to prison twice—on nonviolent drug-related offenses—she didn't qualify for housing subsidies and couldn't even live with her mother because of a ban on felons in public housing. Deborah had nowhere else to live. Homeless, and just out of prison, she faced huge obstacles to building a life for herself.

People with mental illness need hospital care, outpatient care, crisis services, case management, housing, and job training. To avoid tragic encounters like the ones Peter Nadir and Alan Houseman experienced in Florida, they need police who are trained to recognize the symptoms of psychosis and respond to psychiatric emergencies. If they are arrested, they need mental health courts to divert them from jail and prison. They need to be prevented from suicide during passing moments of despair. They need drug treatment that allows them many opportunities to fail. They need to be counseled, supported, and sheltered. They need a system that in a decade will no longer be called one that is "in shambles."

Mental health care in America has long been a grandly imperfect, sometimes scandalous, exercise in trial and error. Breakthroughs in treatment in one generation have been discredited as quackery or cruelty in the next. In the early 1900s, in an effort to relieve what was called "cerebral congestion," mental patients were suspended on hammocks for hours and even days in bathtubs, sometimes with ice packs on their heads. Others were swaddled in wet sheets in which they soiled themselves and became overheated. In the 1940s, patients with schizophrenia were treated with injections of enough insulin to induce near-death coma, and after they'd been revived with glucose, they would be debilitated for weeks. They were also given multiple injections of Metrazol, a drug used as a circulatory and respiratory stimulant that caused convulsions so violent that many suffered spinal fractures. Some were subjected to electroshock treatments, a brutal, if sometimes effective, therapy that was also often used in hospitals as a form of punishment and control. Perhaps the most notorious of these outmoded treatments was the transorbital lobotomy, in which a thin, sharp stake was inserted into the tear ducts and driven through the eye socket into the frontal lobe. An obvious benefit of the lobotomy was that docile patients were less work for the staff.

A century ago, a mental hospital in the heartland listed the afflictions it addressed as "business anxiety, disappointments, over-exertion, excessive study, epilepsy, masturbation, intemperance, and religious excitement." Today, the diagnoses have changed, and more effective therapies have been developed (though, given the history of treating mental illness, researchers are encouraged to remain humble). Still, mental illness remains a uniquely troubling disease without objective diagnostic tests, with strange and exotic symptoms, and with reluctant patients. That may explain why it is a stepchild in the health care system, why change is so slow in coming. People with mental illness are difficult to understand, to reach, and to treat. They have been stigmatized. They have been easy to ignore.

In the 1980s, when I was a reporter for the *Poughkeepsie Journal* in Dutchess County, New York, I wrote a story on and later became friends with a mentally ill homeless woman named Elizabeth. Over the years I would see Elizabeth shuffling along Market Street, with her combat boots, her shaggy graying hair, her ski parka in the middle of June, her wizened, toothless mouth. Her eccentric dress and manner, along with the scent that lingered in her wake, identified her as the homeless former mental patient that she was. Afterward, Elizabeth would drop in to the newsroom every now and then to say hello, perhaps collect a couple of dollars, then camp out in the bathroom for an hour or more until someone chased her out. She was used to that. A tall, thin woman who might once have been striking, Elizabeth suffered from schizophrenia. In the decades after her release from a locked ward at the Hudson River Psychiatric Center, she occasionally lived in rundown "family care" houses in Poughkeepsie with little support, roommates of questionable pedigree, and poor security. The houses were the best the system had to offer, and she invariably left them to live on the streets.

I lived in Ulster County, on the other side of the Hudson River and about twenty miles from Poughkeepsie. One Saturday, I was driving through the county seat, Kingston, with my son and daughter, about nine and twelve, in the backseat, when I spotted Elizabeth's familiar plodding hunch. I pulled over and asked her if she needed a ride. It was a chilly day and getting late, and I was worried that she would have nowhere to stay for the night. My children had already heard about Elizabeth, part of a long line of Mama's work stories, and they were fascinated by this smelly, askew individual that I had let into the car. Elizabeth had no money. She was talking about people who were after her, about bombs going off. I calmed her, got her something to eat, and decided to drive to a homeless shelter in the basement of a lovely stone church in an old Kingston neighborhood. It seemed the solution. When we walked in, the attendant on duty took one look at Elizabeth, pointed at her, and announced, "She doesn't belong here. She's from Dutchess County."

I don't know where Elizabeth stayed that night. I briefly considered bringing her home but the kids were young and her behavior was unpredictable. I could rescue her for one night, I reasoned, but there would be a thousand more. I gave her bus money back to Dutchess County, and she was thankful. A few years later, Elizabeth disappeared from the street. I do not know what happened to her. One study found that homeless people with schizophrenia die on average twenty years earlier, and she had already outlived expectations.

Elizabeth is one of those many people I wrote this book for. Her life of mental illness was a catalogue of sorrows. When she lost her mind as a young woman, she also lost her family. It was a story she had related to me one day in disjointed pieces, in schizophrenic fits and starts that made her anxious in the telling of it. She nodded a lot, looked down at the pavement of the parking lot we were standing in, repeated phrases, and gestured. One night, she just had to leave the house, was driven to go out, she said, though her reasons weren't clear. Her husband had taken an older son out to the horseraces. Elizabeth had taken her baby boy with her and gone walking on a dark highway. They were both run down by a car. The baby was killed. That was why she shuffled in that labored gait of hers—there was a pin in her leg.

After the Hudson River Psychiatric Center released her and six thousand other residents, the system tried, but it had little to offer.

Elizabeth never found a place. She wandered, like so many others, a woman who wore rags and slept on sidewalks in the richest country in the world, the country where, in the last decade of the twentieth century, four hundred prisons were built and forty mental hospitals were closed.

In Shayne and Luke, Alan and Peter, Jessica and Joseph, America has shown itself capable of the use of force on people with mental illness, capable of the exercise of control over them, of locking them up. Elizabeth's generation was the one that was to have been set free. Instead, one straitjacket, one locked ward door, one set of restraints, was substituted for another.

When the Hudson River Psychiatric Center opened in 1869, on a thousand acres of land formerly owned by the family of Franklin D. Roosevelt of nearby Hyde Park, its Victorian halls and tree-lined walkways, its quarter-mile-long main building, its two churches and cabinet shops and farm fields all declared that its mission was important, that this attempt to heal was real. These old hospitals, many of them historic monuments, exist all across the nation, testaments not to their failure, but to the effort to heal they once represented. America needs to try again to heal its ill and to help them heal themselves, with the wisdom of history and the knowledge that the people we will help, the people we will heal, will be ourselves.

APPENDIX

My Top Ten List to Keep People with Mental Illness Out of the Criminal Justice System

1. Stop building prisons—it's throwing good money after bad—and pare them down considerably.

2. Invest in special prison units for people with mental illness—for the few mentally ill people who belong in prison.

3. Train prison officers to work with and respect mentally ill inmates. It's a role that can change both officers and inmates, prison-wide.

4. Invest in prison rehabilitation programs, which curb recidivism.

5. Stop putting mentally ill people into solitary confinement, and close supermax prisons, units that are psychologically devastating for the sane as well as the sick.

6. Roll back punitive drug laws and invest in drug treatment, giving people many chances to fail.

7. Train designated police officers to respond to mentally ill people in crisis.

8. Invest in a system of mental health care that includes inpatient and outpatient services to support vulnerable people and keep them out of the criminal justice system.

9. Provide insurance parity for mental health care, and extend federal Medicaid coverage to include stays in state psychiatric hospitals—essential steps toward normalizing the treatment of mental illness and removing its stigma.

10. Invest in housing—probably the single biggest hole in our social safety net—and eliminate rules that keep nonviolent and reformed felons out of public housing.

INDEX